GRE Analytical Writing：

Answers to the Official Pool of

Issue Topics

Chuanwei Li
Drew Chovanec

Contents

Acknowledgements

It has been twenty years since I supervised the project of China's first book of GRE test questions—*20 Simulated GRE Tests* as Head of R&D of New Oriental, the largest provider of English language training in the country. Over the years, I have been crafting test-prep books as well as teaching students who want to achieve high scores in standardized tests such as GRE and GMAT. Everyone involved in the process, including my collaborator Drew Chovanec, did their best to make *GRE Analytical Writing: Answers to the Official Pool of Issue Topics* an outstanding student study guide. For more than three years, we have analyzed and written what potential graduate students really need: The practical, specific, and efficacious GRE Analytical Writing strategies and sample essays.

I thank all the students that have provided feedback on my GRE teaching and their application of the strategies for GRE writing. A special thank you goes to the late Barbara Pan, my advisor at Harvard who commented on some of the GRE essays. Sincere thanks go to Drew Chovanec, co-author of this book, who wrote prolifically and made timely changes. Finally, I would make special mention of my family that has been supporting me, as always.

Chuanwei Li
Editor-in-Chief
Lead Author —*GRE Analytical Writing*

How to Use This Book

This book offers crucial information about the issue task of GRE Analytical Writing, including the types of prompts together with the knowledge and skills they require. The book will help you:

- Acquaint yourself with the test format and prompt types
- Acquire practical test-taking strategies for each prompt type
- Achieve progress by studying responses to the pool of issue topics

The following four-step program has been created to help you make the most use of this book.

STEP 1 Learn About the Measure of the Issue Task of GRE Analytical Writing

Chapter 1 of this book offers an overview of the issue task of GRE Analytical Writing. Read this chapter to find information about the rubric, time limit, and types of instructions. You will also learn about proven test-taking strategies for how to craft a high-scoring GRE issue essay.

STEP 2 Study Organization of Essays with Different Instructions

Chapter 2 of this book presents sample essays for each type of writing instruction. You will also find what the prompts aim to test, and you will learn organizations and language that you can use in your own essay.

STEP 3 Practice Answering the Official Pool of Issue Topics

Chapter 3 contains the official pool of issue topics and sample essays for each of them. The topics appear in the order they appear on the official website of ETS where you can find the most recent version before you take the test. Read the prompts, make outlines, and practice writing a few essays for each type of instruction until you feel comfortable crafting a good essay within the 30-minute time limit. Then, you may study the sample essays, either to determine whether yours is up to standard, or to glean some ideas, examples, and language from them. Caveat: do not use the sample essays verbatim in your future answer!

STEP 4 Learn About Most-tested Topics

Chapter 4 shows you that some topics appear more than once in the official pool, each time with a different instruction. Such topics are more likely to appear in the test. While familiarizing yourself with the pool, you can review as a group these topics and their respective sample essays, some of which are almost the same.

1 Overview of GRE Analytical Writing:

The Issue Task

Introduction to the Issue Task

In this section, we will look at the "Analyze an Issue" writing task. In this task, the examiners will evaluate your ability to engage critically with a topic of common interest and give your opinion about it in your response. You must make a convincing case for your position on the issue by discussing your reasoning based on the instructions in the prompt. According to the official rubric, your essay will be scored in terms of how well you do the following:

• Presenting a clear and discerning position on the issue (i.e., Expressing your opinion of the topic claim after critical examination of the issue)

• Organizing a focused analysis logically (i.e., Ordering paragraphs logically and with proper signal words; focusing on the topic claim and the specific analysis required by the topic)

• Developing the position adequately with persuasive evidence (i.e., explaining the reasoning for your position by discussing your evidence and how it shapes your position)

• Commanding the aspects of standard written English (i.e., using effective vocabulary and varied sentences and following good grammar, usage, and mechanics)

During the test, you will have 30 minutes to write an Issue essay of about 400 words or more. You should familiarize yourself with the computerized test format by writing the essay using the PowerPrep software that accompanies the GRE official guide. Normally, one screen will give you the essay prompt with instructions on what you should do and how you can do it. The other screen will provide the space on which you will write, with icons like time count, word count, cut, paste, and cancel.

The prompt that you will be given is from the published official Pool of Issue Topics, which usually consists of about 150 prompts. The pool is sometimes updated, with a few additions or substitutions at the end of the pool every one or two years. For the most recent pool of issue topics, please find them at

Instructions of the Issue Task

Each task includes a claim (or a claim and a reason, or two claims) followed by a type of instruction.

It is vital that you follow the specific instruction of the topic that you are given in the test. Some topics have similar claims but different instructions. You will lose points if you write the same essay for all such topics. Listed below are the six types of instructions that will appear on this task, each one asking you to address the key issue in a specific way.

1. • "Write a response in which you discuss the extent to which you agree or disagree with the statement and explain your reasoning for the position you take. In developing and supporting your position, you should consider ways in which the statement might or might not hold true and explain how these considerations shape your position."

This type of instruction asks you to write an essay to discuss whether you agree with the claim while analyzing situations where the statement would or would not be valid. In the official pool of issue topics, 53 use this instruction. For each topic with this instruction, you will see it simplified as "Discuss how the statement could or could not be true".

2. • "Write a response in which you discuss the extent to which you agree or disagree with the claim. In developing and supporting your position, be sure to address the most compelling reasons and/or examples that could be used to challenge your position."

This type of instruction asks you to write an essay to discuss whether you agree with the claim while analyzing the most convincing evidence that may be used to argue against your position. In the official pool of issue topics, 25 use this instruction. For each topic with this instruction, you will see it simplified as "Address challenges to your position".

3. • "Write a response in which you discuss the extent to which you agree or disagree with the recommendation and explain your reasoning for the position you take. In developing and supporting your position, describe specific circumstances in which adopting the recommendation would or would not be advantageous and explain how these examples shape your position."

This type of instruction asks you to write an essay to discuss whether you agree with the claim while analyzing ways in which following the recommendation might or might not be beneficial. In the official pool of issue topics, 23 use this instruction. For each topic with this instruction, you will see it simplified as "Describe advantageous and disadvantageous circumstances of the recommendation".

4 • "Write a response in which you discuss your views on the policy and explain your reasoning for the position you take. In developing and supporting your position, you should consider the possible consequences of implementing the policy and explain how these consequences shape your position."

This type of instruction asks you to write an essay to discuss whether you agree with the claim while analyzing the potential outcomes of adopting the policy. In the official pool of issue topics, 11 use this instruction. For each topic with this instruction, you will see it simplified as "Discuss positive and negative consequences of the policy".

5 • "Write a response in which you discuss which view more closely aligns with your own position and explain your reasoning for the position you take. In developing and supporting your position, you should address both of the views presented."

This type of instruction asks you to write an essay to discuss which of the two claims presented is more consistent with your own position while analyzing both. In the official pool of issue topics, 18 use this instruction. For each topic with this instruction, you will see it simplified as "Address both views".

6 • "Write a response in which you discuss the extent to which you agree or disagree with the claim and the reason on which that claim is based."

This type of instruction asks you to write an essay to discuss whether you agree with the claim and its reason presented. In the official pool of issue topics, 23 use this instruction. For each topic with this instruction, you will see it simplified as "Claim-Reason".

Steps to a Top-notch Issue Essay

A wise way to prepare for the issue task is to practice writing on some of the official issue topics, particularly those that have similar claims but different instructions. Previous experience has shown that your practice may become more productive if you follow some or all of the following steps:

Step 1 Read the issue and the specific instructions

In this step, you are advised to do the following:

• Identify the issue's claim and try to understand the specific instructions

• Identify the issue's key terms, concepts and assumptions

• Brainstorm ideas, experiences, events, and people associated with the claim and instructions

• Decide whether you agree with the claim and to what extent

• Decide what convincing reasons and examples to use to support your position

• Brainstorm what reasons and examples that someone could use to challenge or weaken your position and decide how you would acknowledge and counter them.

Aside from identifying the claim and reasoning, you do not always need to do all the other work noted above. As you analyze the issue, take notes about your position on the claim. When you have enough ideas (together with reasons and examples) you could use to support your position, think about them and number them for putting them in a logical order. Now you are ready for the next big step: writing the response itself.

Step 2 Craft the first paragraph

The difficulty of writing the first paragraph depends largely on your own writing style. It can be difficult when you sweat over small stuff and want to have a perfect intro. If you are one of this cohort, it is advisable that you skip the first paragraph until you have finished the body paragraphs. On the other hand, the intro paragraph can be easy if you adhere to the following guidelines.

The introductory paragraph usually consists of two or three parts: general topic of the prompt (optional); restatement of the claim and reasoning of the prompt; your position on the issue. You may even preview the points to be covered in the body paragraphs. For example,

> *Every year, new systems, ideas, and inventions are developed by human minds that ease the lives of people around the world* (general topic). *Because of the abundance of inventions that currently grace the globe, it is necessary that, as the author says, experts research what has already been developed before they disseminate an idea* (restatement of the prompt). *While there are exceptions to the statement, it is generally true* (author's position). *A thorough research of past failures and successes prevents ignorant duplication of another's work, which means time that could be spent elsewhere* (preview of the 1st point). *Also, such study of past work provides a knowledge base upon which to build the work further* (preview of the 2nd point).

You may paraphrase the prompt first and then present your position. For example,

> *This statement claims that one should analyze the major cities of a country if one is to understand the most significant traits of its society* (paraphrase of the prompt). *It is certainly true that the major cities of a nation provide insights into various cultural aspects, especially concerning contemporary music and art*

(acknowledgment of the counterargument). *However, I disagree with the claim as a blanket statement, as cities are themselves individual microcosms that are not necessarily similar to one another, much less representative of society as a whole* (author's position).

You may also present your position first and then preview the points to be covered in the body paragraphs. For example,

> *In pursuing a university education, students should, aside from their major-related courses, be required to attend a diverse range of other classes, such as history, economics, and other courses* (author's position). *Not only do such classes provide the student with a wide range of knowledge to draw on when he or she enters a chosen profession, but they also contribute to the creation of a more informed society* (preview of points).

You need to be careful when crafting the first paragraph for a Claim-Reason prompt where you are asked to discuss whether you agree with the claim and the reason on which it is based. Whether in your paraphrase of the prompt or in your position, you often need to address both the claim and the reason. For example,

> *The speaker <u>claims</u> that anything called a fact should not be trusted <u>because</u> much of what is considered factual proves to be inaccurate* (paraphrase of the prompt). *While <u>the reason</u> has some merit, <u>the claim</u> must be denied, as it would only lead to chaos* (author's position).

Step 3   Develop the Body Paragraphs

The body usually has about three paragraphs devoted to supporting your own argument. A typical supporting paragraph has a topic sentence and supporting details such as reasons, examples, statistics, study findings, and others. For instance, in the following paragraph, two examples are used to substantiate and support the argument about benefits of government funding for the arts.

> *Let us start by looking at the benefits that government funding can bring to the arts. <u>One example</u> can be seen in government's financial support of ethnic arts. For instance, numerous grants are given to university art departments which foster the creation and preservation of traditional handicrafts. This has led to the styles and motifs of countless cultures, from native American tribal art to Scandinavian patterns, to diffuse into the mainstream cultural consciousness through their inspiration of fashion designers, product designers, and furniture craftsmen. <u>Another example</u> can be seen in the post-WWII USA, where numerous government grants were offered in order to encourage the creation of statues, stage plays, and other great works. Such funding was provided on the grounds that whatever was created would be made free for the public, and as a result, the American arts flourished. However, there was a dark side to this movement led by the government, as artistic expression, while encouraged, was not completely free. Art that was deemed obscene or in opposition to "American ideals" was met with censure, and what later became known as McCarthyism was a death knell for many artists whose work was deemed subversive.*

When addressing the counterargument, consider the perspectives of others who might disagree with your position. One of the acceptable forms of this kind of body paragraph is to acknowledge the reasons someone might give to challenge your position, and then rebut them. For example, in the following paragraph, the author first concedes one way in which the topic statement might not be valid and then refutes such a view.

> *The statement might not hold true when it comes to students' right to choose their career path. Ultimately, they choose to enter college as a voluntary action to improve their own future. They devote their time and their money to their education for their own reasons. To this end, the school functions much like any other service provider in our society, and in this sense the institution has no right, beyond a slight suggestion, to attempt to change students' mind on which subject they wish to study. Yet, even in the context of a service provider, there are instances where the party delivering the service should attempt to discourage a customer from choosing a potentially detrimental product. Just as a waiter at a restaurant, if aware that a diner has a food allergy, would be expected to recommend that the customer not choose a dish which contains allergens, so schools should attempt to dissuade students from choosing areas of study that, based on test scores or past performance, would likely end in failure.*

Step 4   Conclude the passage

The concluding paragraph usually recapitulates the author's position on the issue, summarizes the points discussed in the body paragraphs and makes a prediction, recommendation, or just generalizes to related real-world situations. For example, in the following concluding paragraph, the author restates his or her position on the topic issue and summarizes the points of the body paragraphs.

> *While major cities can provide some useful data of certain demographics, and by no means should be ignored, they are not perfect examples to study if one attempts to gain an understanding of all the essential characteristics of a society* (author's position). *When it comes to countries that have primarily rural-dwelling populations, this is especially true, but the same also goes for more developed countries* (points).

In the following paragraph, the author reiterates his or her position on the topic issue and then broadens its application to general life situations.

> *While one's beliefs may be compromised in a few cases, without constancy in belief and character people are doomed to mediocrity* (author's position). *It takes well placed beliefs and strong character to withstand the burgeoning tide of doubt, but those who emerge on the other side are forged with the strength of transcendence* (generalization).

Putting Everything Together

To understand the most important characteristics of a society, one must study its major cities.

Write a response in which you discuss the extent to which you agree or disagree with the statement and explain your reasoning for the position you take. In developing and supporting your position, you should consider ways in which the statement might or might not hold true and explain how these considerations shape your position.

The following is a possible response to the prompt:

This statement claims that one should analyze the major cities of a country if one is to understand the most significant traits of its society. It is certainly true that the major cities of a nation provide insights into various cultural aspects, especially concerning contemporary music and art. However, I disagree with the claim as a blanket statement, as cities are themselves individual microcosms that are not necessarily similar to one another, much less representative of society as a whole.

To begin with, we can look at the counter-culture revolution in the USA during the 1960's. This period is ensconced as a significant contributor to modern music, art, literature, and social ideologies. The focal points of the movement were of course in major cities such as New York and San Francisco, places where young people of the era flocked in order to be a part of the new wave of ideas. Yet if one were to look at these cities during this time and assume that the cultural aspects that were dominant there were indicative of the nation's society as a whole, one would be greatly mistaken. Much of the USA, especially the rural areas, during the 1960's was very conservative and stood in stark contrast to the values and ideas that gained popularity in the cities.

Another example of how major cities fail to provide enough details about a society as a whole is the fact that not all countries are fully urbanized, and thus the major cities in such a nation would not represent a large enough proportion of the population to be informative. This is especially true in certain African nations in which various tribal groups live in relative isolation from one another. Said groups have their own unique cultures and lifestyles; therefore, the dynamics of the cities in these countries, whether social, political, economic, or otherwise, are not faithful representations of the nations as a whole.

One way in which the statement might hold true involves the situation where a country has been populated by a single ethnic group for a significant portion of its history. For instance, in Scandinavian countries, such as Sweden or Norway, the ethnic demographic has been homogeneous for hundreds of years. As a result, there is virtually no difference between the society of one city and that of another within these countries. If visitors were to travel to any major city in Sweden, they would experience nearly all of the important characteristics of that society, such as customs, religion, food, that the rest of the nation had to offer. However, even in this case, there are still numerous regional differences, especially in cities that lie near a neighboring nation's border. In these places, there is a unique mix of cultures whose interplay has a significant effect on the overall sociocultural picture of the country. It would, therefore, be unfair to assume one fully understands any society simply by analyzing one or two of its major cities.

While major cities can provide some useful data of certain demographics, and by no means should be ignored, they are not perfect examples to study if one attempts to gain an understanding of all the essential characteristics of a society as a whole. When it comes to countries that have primarily rural-dwelling populations, this is especially true, but the same also goes for more developed countries.

2 Organization of Essays with Different Instructions

Readers of your essays will often skim the first sentence of each body paragraph to verify whether your writing follows the instruction specific to each prompt. This is an effective way to spot responses which sound general, vague, or appear to be memorized beforehand. The issue tasks are often seeded with absolute terms like "best," "most," and "only," so that they read like an overgeneralization or oversimplification. This means that you must examine the issue closely and then use the instruction as a roadmap to think about alternative points of view and the complexity of the issue. This entails addressing reasons and examples that someone might use to refute or challenge your position as well as discussion of those that you use to support your position. Except essays with the "Address both views" instruction and the "Claim-Reason" instruction, essays with the other four sets of instructions may follow roughly the same organization, either first supporting your own position with about two paragraphs and then addressing the counterargument with one paragraph, or first conceding the counterargument with one paragraph and then supporting your own position with about two paragraphs. The following are examples of organization of essays with different instructions. After examples of each instruction, you will find additional organizations and scaffolding language that you may incorporate in your own writing.

Organization for "Discuss how the statement could or could not be true"

To understand the most important characteristics of a society, one must study its major cities. (Topic 140)

1. Write a response in which you discuss the extent to which you agree or disagree with the statement and explain your reasoning for the position you take. In developing and supporting your position, you should consider ways in which the statement might or might not hold true and explain how these considerations shape your position. (instruction)

Sample Response and Organization

This statement claims that one should analyze the major cities of a country if one is to understand the most significant traits of its society. It is certainly true that the major cities of a nation provide insights into various cultural aspects, especially concerning contemporary music and art. However, I disagree with the claim as a blanket statement, as cities are themselves individual microcosms that are not necessarily similar to one another, much less representative of society as a whole.

To begin with, we can look at the counter-culture revolution in the USA during the 1960's. This period is ensconced as a significant contributor to modern music, art, literature, and social ideologies. The focal points of the movement were of course in major cities such as New York and San Francisco, places where young people of the era flocked in order to be a part of the new wave of ideas. Yet if one were to look at these cities during this time and assume that the cultural aspects that were dominant there were indicative of the nation's society as a whole, one would be greatly mistaken. Much of the USA, especially the rural areas, during the 1960's was very conservative and stood in stark contrast to the values and ideas that gained popularity in the cities.

Another example of how major cities fail to provide enough details about a society as a whole is the fact that not all countries are fully urbanized, and thus the major cities in such a nation would not represent a large enough proportion of the population to be informative. This is especially true in certain African nations in which various tribal groups live in relative isolation from one another. Said groups have their own unique cultures and lifestyles; therefore, the dynamics of the cities in these countries, whether social, political, economic, or otherwise, are not faithful representations of the nations as a whole.

One way in which the statement might hold true involves the situation where a country has been populated by a single ethnic group for a significant portion of its history. For instance, in Scandinavian countries, such as Sweden or Norway, the ethnic demographic has been homogeneous for hundreds of years. As a result, there is virtually no

Introduction

2nd paragraph: the 1st example illustrating the author's position – counter-culture revolution in the USA during the 1960's

3rd paragraph: the 2nd example illustrating the author's position– situation in countries not fully urbanized (i.e. some African countries)

4th paragraph: concession & rebuttal – acknowledging the counterargument and refuting it

difference between the society of one city and that of another within these countries. If visitors were to travel to any major city in Sweden, they would experience nearly all of the important characteristics of that society, such as customs, religion, food, that the rest of the nation had to offer. However, even in this case, there are still numerous regional differences, especially in cities that lie near a neighboring nation's border. In these places, there is a unique mix of cultures whose interplay has a significant effect on the overall sociocultural picture of the country. It would, therefore, be unfair to assume one fully understands any society simply by analyzing one or two of its major cities.*

While major cities can provide some useful data of certain demographics, and by no means should be ignored, they are not perfect examples to study if one attempts to gain an understanding of all the essential characteristics of a society as a whole. When it comes to countries that have primarily rural-dwelling populations, this is especially true, but the same also goes for more developed countries.   Conclusion

The following example shows organization of another essay with the instruction "Discuss how the statement could or could not be true".

In any field of endeavor, it is impossible to make a significant contribution without first being strongly influenced by past achievements within that field. (Topic 146)

1 Write a response in which you discuss the extent to which you agree or disagree with the statement and explain your reasoning for the position you take. In developing and supporting your position, you should consider ways in which the statement might or might not hold true and explain how these considerations shape your position. (instruction)

Sample Response and Organization

Every year, new systems, ideas, and inventions are developed   Introduction
by human minds that ease the lives of people around the world. Because of the abundance of inventions that currently grace the globe, it is necessary that, as the author says, experts research what has already been developed before they disseminate an idea. While there are exceptions to the statement, it is generally true. A thorough research of past failures and successes prevents ignorant duplication of another's work, which means time that could be spent elsewhere. Also, such study of past work provides a

knowledge base upon which to build the work further.

It is true that there are exceptions to the statement. One way in which it might not be valid involves the serendipitous stroke of genius that has been known to occur in certain points of history. For example, Heraclitus was a pre-Socratic philosopher who was the first in his era to assert that there were predictable patterns of weather and other natural events that were not the result of the whims of deities. This was groundbreaking and controversial in his time and he stood alone for a while as a pioneer in philosophy in regard to the physical and metaphysical world. Yet this example and others like it most often took place in ancient history when humanity was just beginning to develop civilization and record-keeping. Once humanity had established a reliable system of information storage and transport, ideas diffused and were built upon one another incessantly.

2nd paragraph: anticipating objection (i.e. no need for past achievements) & addressing it

History contains some examples of ideas being cultivated in different places at different times, which has led to repetition of conclusions and unnecessary investment of time. For example, in the mid 1800's, two famous biologists, Charles Darwin and Alfred Russel Wallace, developed theories on evolution and natural selection. Charles Darwin had spent many years in the Galapagos Islands studying both the native finches as well as the marine iguanas. As he built his research, he began to see trends that led to the development of the theory of evolution as well as the theory of natural selection. Likewise, Alfred Russel Wallace spent numerous years in South America and Asia accumulating evidence for theories similar to Darwin's. Even though their research contained very similar ideas, Darwin received most of the credit, because his ideas were more substantiated by research and he published his theory first. Even though Wallace developed similar ideas without influence from Darwin, he will never be known as the originator. This situation exemplified by Darwin and Wallace is more avoidable in today's world where communication is instantaneous and widespread, but it illustrates the importance of remaining current in one's field in order to avoid near-duplication of another's work and the associated investment of time that could be spent on other research.

3rd paragraph: the 1st example supporting the author's position (i.e. past achievements are important) – Darwin & Wallace

Furthermore, a study of past work is critical because it provides a solid knowledge base concerning the question at hand and gives the scholar or scientist the ability to build on what has come before. Wilbur and Orville Wright, who receive the credit for inventing and building the first successful airplane, are an excellent example of the need to

4th paragraph: the 2nd example supporting the author's position – Wright Brothers build on prior research and learning. They studied previously developed theories on flying, such as the Bernoulli's principle and the mechanics of designing a light, yet sturdy, contraption. As a result, they were able to develop the first flying apparatus with any sustained flight time. Another example of this can be seen among the most decorated scientists of modern days: the Nobel Prize winners in Physics, Chemistry and Medicine. In recent decades, it has become the norm for multiple recipients to share the Nobel Prize in a field for working on the same problem, often collaboratively. This collaboration may be the ultimate method of studying the successful work of others; by teaming up with other scholars who are exploring similar ideas, a scholar will constantly be moving forward and building on the work of colleagues to arrive at a more substantial conclusion, and perhaps in less time. These examples illustrate how a study of past work can provide a knowledge base that is critical for generating new conclusions that rely on previous work.

In conclusion, many can claim to be inventors, scholars and scientists, but in order to be the true originator of a concept, theory, or mechanism, a person must have knowledge of previous contributions to the relevant area of study. Not only will this research prevent embarrassing and time-wasting duplications, but it will also enable the inventor to identify the areas that still require exploration and provide a knowledge base upon which to further develop his or her work.

Conclusion

For the prompt that asks you to discuss how the statement could or could not be true, you may use the following organization:

2nd paragraph: To begin with, ….

3rd paragraph: Another reason why…is….

4th paragraph: One way in which the statement might (or might not) hold true involves the situation where ….

You may also use the following organization:

2nd paragraph: The statement might not hold true in the following ways.

3rd paragraph: However, normally the statement might be valid. One way in which it might hold true involves….

4th paragraph: Another way in which the statement might be valid concerns….

Organization for "Address challenges to your position"

Universities should require every student to take a variety of courses outside the student's field of study. (Topic 1)

2. Write a response in which you discuss the extent to which you agree or disagree with the claim. In developing and supporting your position, be sure to address the most compelling reasons and/or examples that could be used to challenge your position. (instruction)

Sample Response and Organization

In pursuing a university education, students should, aside from their major-related courses, be required to attend a diverse range of other classes, such as history, economics, and other courses. Not only do such classes provide the student with a wide range of knowledge to draw on when he or she enters a chosen profession, but they also contribute to the creation of a more informed society.

Introduction

If one analyzes the greatest innovators, regardless of field or era, one finds that they all, without exception, strive to educate themselves in a variety of areas of expertise. This polymath-like behavior is regarded by these great minds as one of the key factors in aiding them when they attempt to develop creative ideas. One of the better-known examples was the late Steve Jobs, who in his famous Stanford commencement speech credited the unique font style that made his early Macintosh computers so popular to the calligraphy classes he attended. A similar message was conveyed during an interview by the great animator Chuck Jones, creator of beloved characters such as Bugs Bunny and Daffy Duck as well as some of the most well-known animated shorts in history. He stated that inspiration could come from anywhere, and that creative people should open their minds to more than one discipline, including literature, art, and other aspects of the world when brainstorming.

2nd paragraph: evidence for the author's position – taking a variety of courses outside the student's field is beneficial for individual creativity

14

The benefits of such courses are enjoyed not only by the individual, but also by a society and nation. Having a citizenry that possesses a broad understanding of a variety of subjects is vital for a nation to develop efficiently. For one thing, people that stay informed about various topics are more likely to be receptive to new technology and ideas, thus allowing technological advances and social policies to diffuse throughout society more effectively. For another thing, in societies that have representative governments, students, i.e. future voters, that study a variety of topics are able to make better decisions. A perfect example of how a lack of this negatively impacts society can be seen in the USA, where the education regarding medicine and health has deteriorated to the point where some parents are unwilling to vaccinate their children for unscientific reasons, leading to outbreaks of previously eradicated illnesses such as the measles.

3rd paragraph: more evidence for the author's position –the benefits of such courses are also enjoyed by a society and nation

There is, however, an argument to be made against forcing students to take courses beyond what is necessary for their degree. First and foremost are the financial and time costs associated with extra college courses. With ever-increasing tuition rates per credit-hour, the added financial strain would make a college education for many lower-income students prohibitively expensive. It could also be argued that our students are already distracted by social media and other forms of entertainment that take away from much needed study time for mastering their respective fields. Yet these concerns are responsibilities for the individual students to manage, and universities have a more pressing obligation to benefit society than to meet the particular financial needs of every student.

4th paragraph: concession & rebuttal – the author acknowledges the counterargument and refutes it

To conclude, I believe that a mandate requiring students to take a number of classes without a direct relationship with their major is ultimately an advantageous decision for both the students' future careers and the development of society as a whole.

Conclusion

The following example shows organization of another essay with the instruction "Address challenges to your position".

Educational institutions have a responsibility to dissuade students from pursuing fields of study in which they are unlikely to succeed. (Topic 141)

Write a response in which you discuss the extent to which you agree or disagree with the claim. In developing and supporting your position, be sure to address the most compelling reasons and/or examples that could be used to challenge your position. (instruction)

Sample Response and Organization

In the endeavor to provide a nation with citizens that are both highly skilled and well educated, I believe it is most definitely the obligation of educational institutions to discourage students from studying fields in which they are unlikely to succeed. While it is a popular belief that, as individuals, students should have the right to choose whatever path in life they wish to follow, the far-reaching consequences cannot be ignored of having too many people in a country without proper employment, a situation compounded by the significant financial burden that education places upon students and their families.

Introduction

First of all, consider the current situation in the USA, where throughout the 1990's and early 2000's there was an explosion in the number of university attendees due to the relaxation of regulations on student loans. This, combined with the perception that a college degree would allow students to obtain higher positions and salaries after graduation, meant that many students decided to choose majors in difficult fields, such as engineering, finance, and law. However, these majors require a specific mindset and much dedication, which many students were unable to live up to, resulting in quite high dropout rates. These dropouts then found themselves in a position where they had already invested a considerable amount of time and money into a fruitless education and were at a disadvantage when entering the workplace since they had no

2nd paragraph: evidence supporting the author's position —too many USA university graduates are unable to find proper employment

16

other viable skills. This problem continues even today, leading to a significant proportion of the US population fit only for service jobs, and thus remaining in a position of financial limbo that disallows their contributing to the economy through spending or investment. Colleges and Universities have the ostensible purpose of preparing people for professional careers, and if they are to continue to be viewed as such, they should put more effort into ensuring their students pursue majors in which they can succeed. This has already been accomplished to some extent through placement exams for certain levels of mathematics and sciences, but more stringency should be applied in order to eliminate cram students or those who prepare only for the tests.

Pursuing less than appropriate majors has another potentially disastrous consequence in the form of bad debt. As previously mentioned, the relatively lax lending laws in the USA in regard to student loans mean that many students have tens of thousands of dollars in student debt. Add this fact to the aforementioned difficulty in finding gainful employment and one can understand the current debt bubble that exists in the USA. It has been regarded by economists as a situation that is potentially as severe as the 2008 economic crisis, especially since most student loans are given out at the same time and will thus likely default all at once. Had these students received the proper guidance from academic advisors or professors while choosing a major, then this situation could have been avoided. For instance, every college has a "drop-add" period during the first week or two of each semester. In this period if students are closely monitored for performance or levels of stress, then those who seem incapable of grasping the concepts of the

3rd paragraph: more evidence supporting the author's position —financial burden occurs in the form of bad debt for USA university graduates

courses or unsuitable to the workload could be advised to move to majors in which they would perform better.

The most compelling reason that may be used to challenge my position is that students have the right to choose their career path. Ultimately, they choose to enter college as a voluntary action to improve their own future. They devote their time and their money to their education for their own reasons. To this end, the school functions much like any other service provider in our society, and in this sense the institution has no right, beyond a slight suggestion, to attempt to change students' mind on which subject they wish to study. Yet, even in the context of a service provider, there are instances where the party delivering the service should attempt to discourage a customer from choosing a potentially detrimental product. Just as a waiter at a restaurant, if aware that a diner has a food allergy, would be expected to recommend that the customer not choose a dish which contains allergens, so schools should attempt to dissuade students from choosing areas of study that, based on test scores or past performance, would likely end in failure.

4th paragraph: concession & rebuttal –the author acknowledges the counterargument and refutes it

In sum, I think that schools and other educational institutions have an inherent responsibility to guide students away from career paths that do not suit them. The national benefits such a responsibility would garner, along with the disasters it would aid in avoiding, trump the individual freedom of the students.

Conclusion

For the prompt that asks you to address challenges to your position, you may use the following organization:

2nd paragraph: To begin with, ….

3rd paragraph: Another reason why…is…

4th paragraph: The most compelling reason that may be used to challenge my position is that ….

Organization for "Describe advantageous and disadvantageous circumstances of the recommendation"

Governments should focus on solving the immediate problems of today rather than on trying to solve the anticipated problems of the future. (Topic 7)

3. Write a response in which you discuss the extent to which you agree or disagree with the recommendation and explain your reasoning for the position you take. In developing and supporting your position, describe specific circumstances in which adopting the recommendation would or would not be advantageous and explain how these examples shape your position. (instruction)

Sample Response and Organization

The assertion that governments should focus on immediate problems rather than proactively deal with future issues is not without its merits. However, due to several disadvantageous factors, it is not a recommendation which should be used as a primary strategy. The long-term risks far outweigh the short-term gains when governments try to simply deal with the here-and-now.	Introduction
A severe weakness of having a governing system which focuses the majority of its resources on solving immediate problems is that it takes a reactionary approach to problems. When it comes to issues of a nation-wide scale, this can be disastrous, as using resources required to deal with a problem that has already begun to gain momentum is far more difficult than maintaining preventative measures. Take for example the actions of the United States Forest Service. For many years in the states of Colorado and California, the budget for clearing forest debris was slashed and neglected; little thought was given to the need to remove fallen trees and dead branches. As a result, there have been	2nd paragraph: evidence for the author's position —focusing on solving immediate problems is a reactionary approach

19

a record number of forest fires in recent years because of the buildup of dry tinder and despite the best efforts of the combined forces of the Forest Department and the entirety of the region's fire departments, thousands of acres of conservation land and millions of dollars' worth of property have been destroyed. Evidently, relying on reactionary measures was a failed gamble and now large swaths of land have been reduced to burnt-out wastelands. Had more attention been diverted to preparing for forest fires, i.e. spending more money and manpower on forest maintenance, this tragedy would not have occurred.

Overemphasizing the present can also be harmful to a nation's economy. Whenever short-sighted greed ensnares fiscal and foreign policies, domestic economies suffer. This has been a hotly debated topic in the USA, where it has been argued by many that the thirst for wider profit margins by US corporations led to the out-sourcing of labor to foreign countries. It certainly had the desired effect of generating massive profits for the companies which were able to establish manufacturing overseas. Yet it has become painfully apparent that after decades of exporting labor markets, the domestic economy has become incredibly fragile, with many US citizens unable to find jobs which pay livable wages. This has in turn led to less disposable income and the very companies which had sought to gain massive profits by decreasing production costs are discovering that sales are decreasing as their home market contracts. Had the government utilized a modicum of foresight, it could have enacted policies which encouraged the development of domestic industry, which could have provided more jobs to the population, and led to a much more resilient domestic market of consumers over the long term.

Naturally, certain situations call for immediate attention rather than long-term planning. A contemporary example is that of the COVID-19 pandemic. When news first reached the US government of the impending wave of infections, more attention was paid to the potential long-term political consequences of implementing mandatory shutdowns and mask-mandates. The political parties, more absorbed by their desire to maintain public popularity by espousing American Exceptionalism and civil liberties, did not

3rd paragraph: more evidence for the author's position– this does harm to a nation's economy

4th paragraph: concession & rebuttal– the author acknowledges the counterargument and refutes it

20

immediately address the potential for the virus to spread quickly and uncontrollably. Spread it did, and only after it had infected tens of thousands of citizens did the government finally attempt a ramshackle series of shutdowns, social distancing, and mask-mandates. By that point, though, it was too late, and the virus had gained too strong a foothold to be effectively eliminated with haste. Had the government focused on immediately dealing with the virus, as in countries like China and New Zealand, a short period of nation-wide lockdown could have saved thousands of lives and billions of dollars of lost business revenue. However, it should be noted that this is a unique case. *Even in this case, had the government done a better job of long-term planning according to WHO and CDC infectious disease guidelines, the national healthcare system and the general public would have been able to deal with the outbreak far more quickly and effectively than they did.*

To conclude, being proactive is better than being reactive in virtually all situations. Effective governing requires careful long-term planning – history is riddled with failed states that were overwhelmed by unexpected upheavals. Focusing on the present can prove beneficial in certain situations, but doing so as a habit instead of preparing for the future is a recipe for disaster.

Conclusion

For the prompt that asks you to describe advantageous or disadvantageous circumstances in which to adopt a recommendation, you may use the following organization:

2nd paragraph: To begin with, ….

3rd paragraph: Another reason why…is…

4th paragraph: One circumstance in which adopting the recommendation would be advantageous/disadvantageous has to do with the likelihood that…

Organization for "Discuss positive and negative consequences of the policy"

Nations should pass laws to preserve any remaining wilderness areas in their natural state, even if these areas could be developed for economic gain. (Topic 147)

4 Write a response in which you discuss your views on the policy and explain your reasoning for the position you take. In developing and supporting your position, you should consider the possible consequences of implementing the policy and explain how these consequences shape your position. (instruction)

Sample Response and Organization

One of the more pressing environmental issues currently facing the world is the loss of forests and other wilderness areas to development. Therefore, I believe it is necessary for governments to take drastic measures and pass legislation to protect whatever wildlands that remain, even at the cost of losing out on the economic gains that could be garnered by development of such areas. It is my firm belief that such policies are the only way to effectively halt the destruction of habitats and return some semblance of homeostasis to the environment.

Introduction

An important part of this argument that must be considered is the current rate of habitat loss that is occurring even at this very moment and the harm it poses to human life. Most of the breathable oxygen on our planet is generated by rainforests such as the Amazon. Yet, every year nearly 80 million acres of the Amazon is burned to make way for development. It is therefore no surprise that the air quality of Brazil's major cities has declined over time. Passing laws to conserve the Amazon and other rainforests would not only serve to protect the many endangered species that call these habitats home but would also aid in improving the air quality of nearby cities. Naturally, it would prove to be an inconvenience to farmers and other developers hoping to turn rainforest land into valuable real-estate, but the long-term benefits of conservation far outweigh the short-term greed.

2nd paragraph: evidence for the author's position —habitat loss and its harm to human life make laws necessary

If it is monetary gain that drives much of the destruction of natural habitats, then instituting laws which promote conservation for the purposes of eco-tourism would be a win-win for both sides. Many wilderness areas are places of astounding beauty, such as the icy northern reaches of Alaska and the arid desert regions of the Midwest USA, which also boast unique indigenous cultures. Certainly, if these regions were legally protected, then they would prove to be valuable sources of revenue for the local people, who can

3rd paragraph: more evidence for the author's position —eco-tourism makes laws necessary

22

*sell their native crafts, and the tax coffers by proxy. There
are already similar programs in place, the famous
Yellowstone National Parks being the most famous. Every
year, thousands of people pay for hunting licenses, tour trips,
and other tourist activities to the parks, which in turn
finances their continued conservation. This not only
incentivizes their continued upkeep but also makes it
difficult for developers to match the financial gains that they
could offer in lieu of the annual tourist revenue. Thus,
legislation to conserve wilderness habitats not only preserves
the wealth of natural beauty these places offer, but also
contributes real wealth to the government through tourism.*

*Of course, many industrialists argue that it is a waste to
leave the untapped resources of the wilderness undeveloped.
A contemporary example is the desire of large oil companies
to drill in the Arctic regions of North America. The oil
companies argue that the regions are mostly uninhabited and
thus their drilling would pose little threat to ecosystems.
However, their arguments are misleading, as the Arctic
regions are an important part of seasonal migration for
caribou and other forms of wildlife, the destruction of which
would cause a negative chain reaction throughout several
distant ecosystems. Additionally, the amount of oil that
would be extracted from these regions would be an
insignificant percentage of the nation's oil consumption.
Laws protecting these regions would ensure that the
ecosystems which rely on the animals that migrate through
the Arctic would remain intact and prevent the often-
irreparable damage that follows industrial development.*

4th paragraph: concession & rebuttal –
the author acknowledges the
counterargument and refutes it

*In conclusion, I think that policies that preserve forests and
other wilderness areas in their natural states are both
necessary and beneficial. Not only do they protect ecosystems
from annihilation, but the natural havens which are
preserved through these laws can still benefit humanity
health-wise, and even economically in some cases.*

Conclusion

The following example shows organization of another essay with the instruction "Discuss
positive and negative consequences of the policy":

Governments should offer a free university education to any student who has been admitted to a university but who cannot afford the tuition. (Topic 149)

Write a response in which you discuss your views on the policy and explain your reasoning for the position you take. In developing and supporting your position, you should consider the possible consequences of implementing the policy and explain how these consequences shape your position. (instruction)

Sample Response and Organization

It is often said that education is the key to success, and in the endeavor to bring opportunity to the citizens of a nation there has, therefore, been a large movement in support of subsidized education for all university students who are unable to afford the increasing costs of tuition. I, for one, do not support the policy of socialized university education in this form, for it brings far more damaging consequences than benefits.

Introduction

At first glance, it does seem like a lofty ideal to provide government funding to university students who cannot afford the tuition. After all, children have no choice of the economic status of their parents, and many young people of high intellect and academic achievement are forced to forgo higher education due to the financial limitations of their families. It is hardly fair to doom such promising individuals to a life of unfulfilled potential for circumstances beyond their control. In fact, it can be beneficial to offer free tuition to students from poorer backgrounds. Studies have shown that such individuals are exceptionally hardworking, as they feel a psychological need to "earn" their place among the ranks of professionals they work with. Additionally, it would incentivize more young people who are financially challenged to pursue college education rather than fall into delinquent behavior as a result of feelings of disenfranchisement when faced with prohibitive tuition fees.

2nd paragraph: anticipating objection (benefit to a free university education)

However, it should be remembered that universities, even so-called state universities, are businesses first and foremost. They operate with a view to financial incomes regardless of whether they are for-profit or not, and as such this policy leaves the tax dollars of a nation open for exploitation by these institutions. Once universities realize that the government subsidizes low-income students, what is stopping

3rd paragraph: the 1st reason for arguing against the policy —exploitation of the policy

them from lowering their attendance standards to allow as many students as possible into their schools in order to make a quick profit? This has already been seen in the USA, where colleges took advantage of relaxed student loan regulations and began accepting more and more students every year. While these institutions can suffer significant financial damage if loans are not repaid, they would have nothing to lose by taking the money the government provided for low-income students. This would drive up government spending and would not necessarily benefit the country as a whole.

But why would it not benefit the country to have more educated people? Many argue that a country always benefits from having skilled professionals. The answer is simple: because the number of graduates is not evenly distributed across all majors, meaning that certain fields, particularly those promising high salaries, receive far more applicants than others. Not only are these majors often the most expensive to pursue, leading to the aforementioned drain of government funds, but the huge influx of students that would occur due to the subsidy would lead to an oversaturation in the job market for those fields. Such a situation has already happened in some Asian countries, where partially subsidized college education and the value placed on education have led to so many students gaining business and STEM field degrees that many graduates have a hard time finding jobs that pay a decent wage.

4th paragraph: the 2nd reason for arguing against the policy – oversaturation in the job market

Another issue with having subsidized university education is that the quality of education may decrease drastically. As stated before, colleges would have little to lose by accepting more students in order to gain the government money that came with them. In addition, there would be little motivation for colleges to improve or maintain their staff and facilities. All they would need to do is to keep them at acceptable levels to continue to attract students. Looking again at the situation in some Asian countries, one can see the truth in this. Public university campuses there are often run down, with obsolete or non-functioning equipment and teachers that care little about the success of their students. On the other hand, some private universities are on par with Ivy League schools in the West in terms of education and

5th paragraph: 3rd reason for arguing against the policy –lower quality of education

facilities.

While it at first seems like a noble cause to provide government assistance to students that cannot afford to attend universities, a blanket policy would be far too vulnerable to exploitation, and ultimately lead to a destruction of job markets and overall decrease in the quality of education.	Conclusion

For the prompt that asks you to describe positive and negative consequences of implementing a policy, you may use the following organization:

2nd paragraph: To begin with, ….

3rd paragraph: Another reason why…is…

4th paragraph: One likely negative/positive consequence of implementing the policy is that …

Organization for "Address both views"

Some people believe that government funding of the arts is necessary to ensure that the arts can flourish and be available to all people. Others believe that government funding of the arts threatens the integrity of the arts. (Topic 144)

5 Write a response in which you discuss which view more closely aligns with your own position and explain your reasoning for the position you take. In developing and supporting your position, you should address both of the views presented. (instruction)

Sample Response and Organization

Art, especially what is generally referred to as "high art" is not free. Great works, whether sculptures, paintings, or performances, all require a significant amount of funding to create. For this reason, I can understand why some people believe that government funding of the arts is vital for the proliferation and accessibility of the arts. Yet I think that government involvement inevitably damages the integrity of art and should therefore be kept to a minimum.	Introduction
Let us start by looking at the benefits that government	2nd paragraph: addressing one view

funding can bring to the arts. One example can be seen in government's financial support of ethnic arts. For instance, numerous grants are given to university art departments which foster the creation and preservation of traditional handicrafts. This has led to the styles and motifs of countless cultures, from native American tribal art to Scandinavian patterns, to diffuse into the mainstream cultural consciousness through their inspiration of fashion designers, product designers, and furniture craftsmen. Another example can be seen in the post-WWII USA, where numerous government grants were offered in order to encourage the creation of statues, stage plays, and other great works. Such funding was provided on the grounds that whatever was created would be made free for the public, and as a result, the American arts flourished. However, there was a dark side to this movement led by the government, as artistic expression, while encouraged, was not completely free. Art that was deemed obscene or in opposition to "American ideals" was met with censure, and what later became known as McCarthyism was a death knell for many artists whose work was deemed subversive.*

(i.e. need for government funding of the arts) & introducing the other view (i.e. threat that government funding poses to arts)

This kind of government oversight is the ultimate enemy of the free expression which is necessary for art to progress and develop. Looking at the art from each dynasty of some Asian countries, one notices significant periods of time in which there was no variation between styles or motifs during the centuries-long reign of each dynasty. This is largely a result of either the extremely strict limitations placed upon artists by the government patrons of the time, or worse, the wholesale destruction of works as mandated by new rulers to make way for the works they wished to fund. Moreover, while we can view many pieces of ancient fine art now, these works were by no means accessible to their average contemporary citizens, as they were treasured possessions of the nobility alone.

3rd paragraph: addressing the other view (the author's position)

It is also worthy to note that the financial support of art by a government inevitably leads to the weaponization of artistic works in the form of propaganda. One need not look any further than Nazi Germany to see the multitudes of paintings and films propagating messages of vile animosity towards minority groups such as the Jews, culminating in the

4th paragraph: addressing the other view further

27

tragic genocide we now know of as the Holocaust. On the flip side, artistic freedom and integrity was perhaps the deciding factor in ending the United States' war in Vietnam in the 1970's. Were it not for the deluge of songs, poems, paintings, and other such works, which all derided the war as unjust and destructive, who knows how many more lives would have been lost to the conflict!

In a nutshell, it is my firm belief that the financial contribution to the arts made by governments is appreciated but decidedly harmful, for it acts as a chain with which the government enslaves art for its own devices. Art can be created and made accessible without the aid of the government, and all the better for it, since free expression is what allows great art to be made.

Conclusion

For the prompt that asks you to address both views, you may use the following organization:

2nd paragraph: One camp contends that….

3rd paragraph: Another camp maintains that….

4th paragraph: I agree with the first/second camp. …

Organization for "Claim-Reason"

Claim: We can usually learn much more from people whose views we share than from those whose views contradict our own.

Reason: Disagreement can cause stress and inhibit learning. (Topic 37)

Write a response in which you discuss the extent to which you agree or disagree with the claim and the reason on which that claim is based. (instruction)

Sample Response and Organization

While disagreement certainly can cause stress and inhibit learning, it is not the case that we usually learn much more from people whose views we share. This reasoning, suggesting that interacting with people who have differing

Introduction

views from our own will always cause stress and disagreement, asserts several implied truths that are not necessarily factual.

First, let us establish the obstacles that prevent people from learning. The reason identifies disagreement as a possible inhibitor to the learning process. "Disagreement" in this context is a loosely defined term that could be interpreted several ways. Certainly, if disagreement is permitted to become contentious, angry, or malicious, then it certainly will prevent learning. In general terms, learning will be inhibited any time an individual permits strong negative emotion to cloud his or her thoughts. Consider a typical interaction between sports fans of opposing teams. Each fan, being loyal to his or her team, will not be inclined to change positions to match the view of the opposing fan. Additionally, because sporting events are naturally competitive, arguments and contentions are usually near the surface, so it is easy to imagine two individuals becoming angry or even malicious in a debate of which team is superior. Disagreement, if allowed to reach the point of malice, contention, or anger, will create strong emotions in both parties involved that prevent clear, rational thought or learning.

2nd paragraph: agreeing with part of the reason— disagreement may involve negative emotions

Before we move on to other obstacles that keep people from learning, it should be noted that healthy disagreement, in which individuals act with respect and tolerance, can be extremely beneficial to learning. In the seventeenth century, Czar Peter I of Russia recognized that his nation trailed significantly behind his European neighbors in the arts and sciences. Peter himself took a tour of Europe, meeting with kings and government leaders in several different countries. Certainly, these people were nothing like Peter, but he visited them with the intent to learn from them how to govern his own country more effectively. Because he approached their differences without competitive or malicious attitudes, he learned from them and changed his nation to be more modern and effective.

3rd paragraph: disagreeing with part of the reason –disagreement may be healthy

Another significant obstacle to learning can easily occur when individuals think too much alike. This obstacle is complacency in thought and feeling, a phenomenon that

4th paragraph: disagreeing with the claim –thinking too much alike is an obstacle to learning

occurs when someone decides that they are "good enough."
Without differing ideas and opinions to challenge what an
individual considers to be "right" or "good," it is easy for
that individual to believe that his or her personal perspective
is correct without question. The individual's learning and
thoughts then become stagnant, and no progress is made.
This effect can sometimes be seen in large corporations that
attain some high level of success. The individuals charged
with leading the organization, seeing the great success of the
corporation, may begin to believe that everything in the
corporation is perfect. They will gradually stop challenging
the status quo and allow policies and procedures to go
unchanged. The corporate leaders' aversion to change will
ultimately handicap their potential to learn and take their
company further. The negative emotion of complacency can
be just as inhibitive to learning as anger or contention.

The types of emotion that can adversely affect learning   Conclusion
potential are numerous. One is the anger that can arise
from disagreement. Another is the complacency that can
arise from similar views. While the second part of the
reasoning, that disagreement can indeed lead to stress and
inhibit learning, is true, this does not necessarily imply that
we should surround ourselves with like-minded people if we
intend to learn. Each individual must gauge, for himself or
herself, which emotions that inhibit learning he or she is
susceptible to in a given situation. Having determined that,
the individual can make the best decisions to maximize
personal learning.

For the prompt that asks you to examine the claim and its reason, you may use the following organization:

2nd paragraph: The claim is valid/invalid. ….

3rd paragraph: Also, ….

4th paragraph: However, the reasoning is (not) sound. ….

30

3 Answers to the Official Pool of Issue Topics

1. **Universities should require every student to take a variety of courses outside the student's field of study. (Address challenges to your position)**

In pursuing a university education, students should, aside from their major-related courses, be required to attend a diverse range of other classes, such as history, economics, and other courses. Not only do such classes provide the student with a wide range of knowledge to draw on when he or she enters a chosen profession, but they also contribute to the creation of a more informed society.

If one analyzes the greatest innovators, regardless of field or era, one finds that they all, without exception, strive to educate themselves in a variety of areas of expertise. This polymath-like behavior is regarded by these great minds as one of the key factors in aiding them when they attempt to develop creative ideas. One of the better-known examples was the late Steve Jobs, who in his famous Stanford commencement speech credited the unique font style that made his early Macintosh computers so popular to the calligraphy classes he attended. A similar message was conveyed during an interview by the great animator Chuck Jones, creator of beloved characters such as Bugs Bunny and Daffy Duck as well as some of the most well-known animated shorts in history. He stated that inspiration could come from anywhere, and that creative people should open their minds to more than one discipline, including literature, art, and other aspects of the world when brainstorming.

The benefits of such courses are enjoyed not only by the individual, but also by a society and nation. Having a citizenry that possesses a broad understanding of a variety of subjects is vital for a nation to develop efficiently. For one thing, people that stay informed about various topics are more likely to be receptive to new technology and ideas, thus allowing technological advances and social policies to diffuse throughout society more effectively. For another thing, in societies that have representative governments, students, i.e. future voters, that study a variety of topics are able to make better decisions. A perfect example of how a lack of this negatively impacts society can be seen in the USA, where the education regarding medicine and health has deteriorated to the point where some parents are unwilling to vaccinate their children for unscientific reasons, leading to outbreaks of previously eradicated illnesses such as the measles.

There is, however, an argument to be made against forcing students to take courses beyond what is necessary for their degree. First and foremost are the financial and time costs associated with extra college courses. With ever-increasing tuition rates per credit-hour, the added financial strain would make a college education for many lower-income students prohibitively expensive. It could also be argued that our students are already distracted by social media and other forms of entertainment that take away from much needed study time for mastering their respective fields. Yet these concerns are responsibilities for the individual students to manage, and universities have a more pressing obligation to benefit society than to meet the particular financial needs of every student.

To conclude, I believe that a mandate requiring students to take a number of classes without a direct relationship with their major is ultimately an advantageous decision for both the students' future careers and the development of society as a whole.

2. **A nation should require all of its students to study the same national curriculum until they enter college. (Discuss positive and negative consequences of the policy)**

Decision is not to be made lightly on whether all students of a country should be required to study the same national curriculum preceding entry to college; there are valid points to be made on either side of the argument. Supporters of such a policy would posit that it would provide equitable access to quality education and ensure a more robust curriculum created by academic experts on each subject. These points are noble in their own right, yet equally valid is the fact that disregarding a required uniform national curriculum provides a wider range of educational techniques and theories to be applied, which is a superior recipe for a nation's growth and success. Therefore, I do not agree with the statement that a nation should require all of its students to study the same pre-college national curriculum.

A primary source of evidence which contradicts the statement is that the implementation of a mandated national curriculum would stifle the development of a country's talent. Indeed, it is well established that there is not just a single kind of students; every pupil has their own unique hobbies, affinities, and born talents. In this vein, it is very improbable that a uniform curriculum would be effective at fostering the growth of individual strengths, because an academic regimen of this type appeals to the abilities of the lowest common denominator. Those who have specialized interests would be left to fend for themselves. Thus, a variety of curriculums must be made available to suit the needs of individual students.

Additionally, with uniformity comes conformity and the elimination of regional knowledge and culture. As a nation focuses on a singular academic dialogue, little to no room is made for the important cultural traditions that peoples of different areas pass down to future generations. This presents a clear danger of many cultures being pushed to the brink of extinction, which has negative effects on a nation. On the other hand, preserving regional cultures in a curriculum can have a tremendous benefit to a country. For instance, the Harlem neighborhood of New York City in the USA was a traditionally African American neighborhood. There had been attempts for many years in the early to mid 1900's to diversify the area and bring it into the fold of the standard "American Way", which was a euphemism for "White, Anglo-Saxon, Protestantism". Yet the perseverance of the African American community in Harlem led to the Harlem Renaissance, a cultural revolution of art, literature, and music that has had lasting influences in the USA even to the present day. A uniform national curriculum that imparts mainstream culture at the expense of such dynamic culture would be unfair and insipid. Therefore, policies which encourage a rigidly uniform academic curriculum should not be allowed to take the place of the vibrant cultural education that can be found in a country.

Supporters of the statement can, of course, create a level playing field for all students. Yet, an issue with this line of thinking is that, more often than not, the opposite is true. Forcing all students into the same box suffocates those with unique abilities. Their exceptional talents are overshadowed by their apparent lack of aptitude in other areas, and they are left feeling inadequate in the face of a system that rewards mediocrity. This is not fair by any standard, and ultimately leads to self-esteem and confidence issues in students, hardly the desired crop of graduates for any country.

Furthermore, it could be argued that implementing a similar national curriculum would create a more efficient process of designing courses for students. This is undoubtedly true, at least in the context of creating a cookie-cutter model in which topics may be copy-pasted to suit the basic educational requirements for a particular course or semester. Nonetheless, this would render courses completely devoid of meaningful content with which students could prove themselves to be exceptional. The very concept of competitive scores would be made meaningless as everyone would know the same content as everyone else; how then could the cream of the crop be selected? A nation is grown by its leaders, regardless of the field, not the blasé drones.

While implementing a uniform pre-college national curriculum is on its face a beneficial policy, after deeper consideration a less advantageous picture forms. Such a curriculum would exclude academic excellence and effectively eradicate the rich regional knowledge and culture upon which a nation thrives. Therefore, a more diverse range of curricula may be far more beneficial to the students of a nation, and by proxy, the nation itself.

3. **Educational institutions should actively encourage their students to choose fields of study that will prepare them for lucrative careers. (Address challenges to your position)**

The singular purpose of education is to prepare students for their future careers. To this end, it is in the best interest of students if their schools make an effort to encourage them to pursue fields of study that will guarantee high-paying jobs. To do anything less would be a disservice to the incredible investment made by students and their parents when choosing an institution to attend.

It is important to remember that in the highly competitive economic environment in which we live today there is little leeway for mistakes when students choose a field of study and, by proxy, a future career. Since students are usually not as knowledgeable as their adult counterparts in the education administration, it is not always a good idea to allow them to choose whatever field they wish to study. Take liberal arts majors as an example; some of them lead to the lowest paying careers after graduation since few real jobs are available to degree-holders in these areas other than teaching the same subjects which they have studied. There are certainly large sums of money to be made in these fields for those savvy enough to apply their knowledge and skills in the right way, but such skillsets are not often taught in school, but rather learned through experience.

There is no doubt that most students will be initially unhappy with adults advising them to give up what they believe to be their dream jobs in favor of other means of employment, but this preliminary dissatisfaction will often give way to greater overall contentedness once they find that the career path suggested to them will provide a salary which supports a lavish lifestyle. In addition, what most people presume is their passion, as with many aspiring musicians and other artists, is often downgraded to a hobby or minor interest when faced with the titanic amount of practice needed to hone their ability, as well as the compromises they must make in order to turn such skills into a profitable means of employment.

Some may counter by saying that encouraging students to take a major that promises high-paying jobs will sacrifice one's passion. They argue that students become locked into career paths that require them to dedicate the majority of their time and slowly but surely take over their lives, leaving little to no time to pursue hobbies or passion projects. This is evident in the great amount of dissatisfaction many adults face nowadays, when they work for hours on end and succumb to mid-life crisis after realizing they no longer take any enjoyment from anything they do. Given the choice to relive their lives, many older adults today would likely choose instead to follow their dream careers, knowing they would feel more fulfilled in the long run. It is even said that "if you do the job you love, you will never work a day in your life." However, the world would likely be a better place if this were true for everyone. The unfortunate reality that we must all face as we enter adulthood is that not everyone can turn their passion into a career, whether due to the overabundance of people with similar skills, or an inferior level of ability compared to that of others. It is for this reason that students are better off listening to those who understand the job market and can offer guidance into a job that would adequately suit their abilities and provide enough money so as to allow them to live a comfortable adult life.

In summary, while it may not be exactly what students want, it is in their best interest to be advised by educational institutions to find a major that would be ideal for finding a well-paying job. The financial stability brought about by a better career would, in time, compensate them for the short-term sacrifice of giving up a hobby-oriented major.

4. **Some people believe that in order to be effective, political leaders must yield to public opinion and abandon principle for the sake of compromise. Others believe that the most essential quality of an effective leader is the ability to remain consistently committed to particular principles and objectives. (Address both views)**

Effective political leaders differ from scholars and artists in that they must represent and even make choices for an entire group. This responsibility should shift the focus of political leaders from a singular view on voting and progress to a more holistic one. While their outlook should be holistic and choices should be made with their constituents in mind, this does not mean that politicians should abandon their own principles for their people. Instead, politicians must carefully determine what is best for their constituents while remaining true to themselves.

There are certainly situations where politicians must give way to public opinion. Even the greatest leaders, when faced with the total dissolution of the people whom they are dedicated to caring for, must bend their principles to the whims of the masses. A famous historical account of Alexander the Great encapsulates this notion. After a long campaign in Eurasia, crossing the Indus River and reaching the Hyphasis River, Alexander's troops were exhausted, and their morale was nearly broken. Alexander wished to push on to secure his victory in the region and his legacy. Yet his men would be pushed no longer, and Alexander realized that in order to maintain control over his armies, he would need to submit to their demands for rest and return home. Nonetheless, Alexander was forever disappointed with this concession, and his recounting of this fact at the famous mutiny of his troops at Opis was enough to rally his mutinous generals to his side once more. Thus, leaders' strictest adherence to their principles can be their most noble trait.

Indeed, in most cases politicians must abide by principle. The decision to act on principle might defame the people and country represented and be grueling for any political leader; yet, following principle and truth will always serve the people better than ignorance. In 1942, the French police, under Nazi orders, rounded up 10,000 Jews, placed them in the Vélodrome d'Hiver under horrible conditions, and then sent them to a French work camp and on to Auschwitz. Though the orders came from the Nazi regime, it was French policemen and the French government who carried them out. For decades, the role that the French played in this horrific event was covered up, until President Jacques Chirac officially apologized for the complicit role the French had played in the extermination of the French Jews, many of whom had been born in France. His acknowledgement of and public apology for these horrors could have tainted the reputation of his country; yet, Chirac acted on principle, attempting to do right for all who were involved in this tragedy. Chirac was not betraying his constituents with his candor; instead, he was demonstrating the integrity of his people through his own words.

Gandhi was another powerful political leader who was unwilling to abandon his principles despite pressure from his constituents. Gandhi's practice of non-violence was not popular among many Indian politicians. India had often been treated as a commodity under British rule and a more aggressive and forceful approach was supported by many of Gandhi's counterparts. While compromise could play a role in resolving this disagreement, Gandhi did not waiver from his stance not to use violence, even after enduring long fasts that weakened his body. In the end, it was Gandhi's method of non-violence that was given credit for the emancipation of India. His dedication to his own principles changed the fate of his country and set an example for the world of the power of peace and self-sacrifice.

Politicians must lead through their examples and the greatest example they can impart is one of integrity and truth. This might not win an election, but the decisions made on the basis of these principles will at least be done in honesty and ultimately serve politicians and their constituents better.

5. **Formal education tends to restrain our minds and spirits rather than set them free. (Discuss how the statement could or could not be true)**

Compulsory education has often been hailed as one of the greatest contributors to the development of nations both socially and economically. However, as beneficial as it may be to society, I contend that formal education is far more likely to crush individuality and innovation more than any other system.

One of the greatest minds of the modern era, Albert Einstein once said, "The only thing that interferes with my learning is my education." A common fact given about Einstein is that he failed primary school. While that is not exactly true, he actually had excellent scores but struggled with some subjects unrelated to math and science, which were his passion. Nonetheless, this quote is insightful, as it implies that he found that the requirements to study subjects he had no interest in limited his ability to focus on what he was good at and enjoyed doing. There is no doubt that numerous other young minds have potentially gone undiscovered in the formal education system due to the limitations placed upon them as a result of their low scores in classes they despise. Nowadays, the strict standardized testing systems in place act as barriers to those seeking higher education in a specialized field they excel in, due to arbitrary course requirements that they wish to ignore.

Another drawback that comes with a formal education is the rigid curriculum, which, with a set of questions with limited acceptable answers, forces students to think one way or be shamed for being rebellious or even stupid. There is little room for free thought when teachers are established to be authoritative sources of knowledge to rely on and not contested under any circumstance. One need only look at the school systems in some countries, where disagreeing with a teacher in class, even if the student is in the right, can lead to punishment and social stigmatism. It is, therefore, no surprise why these countries are criticized time and again for their students' lack of creative thought.

Yet, there is still an argument to be made for the necessity of formal education. As mentioned before, it does provide a minimum educational standard for a country and offers access to learning and knowledge that would otherwise be hard to come by for many people in developing countries. In fact, formal schooling for girls and women in "third-world nations" is listed as one of the greatest contributing factors in lifting the majority of citizens out of poverty. As a result, individuals are set free through their ability to draw on knowledge and skills acquired through formal education, including general skills such as critical thinking and specific skills such as disciplinary thinking. For example, having received a formal education, a person from a poor farming family may apply the mathematics and critical thinking skills to their agricultural process, calculating basic rates of return for certain crops and choosing to plant in such a way that maximizes the return on their harvest.

Aside from this caveat, though, formal schooling does little else beyond providing a minimum standard of education. Students in developed nations, especially in the modern era, are able to access the entirety of human knowledge instantly on the internet, and by all accounts have proven perfectly capable of doing so. One can only imagine how well these young people could pursue their own avenues of innovation and personal development if they could use as they please the time wasted on going to school six or more hours a day. In fact, many have already done so; the number of small businesses started by young adults has exploded since the proliferation of the internet access, and the trend seems only to be more evident as smart devices become cheaper and more powerful.

While certainly beneficial to some groups where ignorance is endemic, formal schooling is ultimately detrimental to our minds and aspirations. It teaches us only to meet arbitrary course requirements and discourages debate, a practice that is not conducive to the development of individual learning and passion.

6. The well-being of a society is enhanced when many of its people question authority. (Discuss how the statement could or could not be true)

In the preamble to the United States' *Declaration of Independence*, arguably one of the most significant and influential political documents ever written, it is stated that "Governments are instituted among Men, deriving their just powers from the consent of the governed, that whenever any Form of Government becomes destructive of these ends, it is the Right of the People to alter or to abolish it, and to institute new Government…." While I do not condone the outright rebellion of a people against their government, the wisdom imparted by these words is undeniable: the ability to question their government's authority is essential to the health of a nation.

The root of totalitarianism can always be found in the establishment's insistence that it be beyond criticism. Once an authority presents itself as infallible, it essentially erects a wall between the government and those who are governed. This makes productive change practically impossible, at least when it concerns legislation that benefits society, as those in power are no longer able to be held accountable for their actions. This lack of oversight is the very same cause of regimes such as Hitler's Germany, where dissent was violently oppressed, and the common people suffered needlessly.

Outside the political spectrum, the destruction wrought by unchallenged authority can be seen in societal ills such as sexism and de facto discrimination. In older western societies, such as Victorian England, women were treated as second-class citizens, excluded from the voting process and bereft of equal treatment. Often labeled as being hysterical, which at that time was considered a legitimate mental illness that could condemn a woman to a sanitarium, female activists took to the streets to protest in support of women's suffrage. The inequality experienced by women of that era, and the activism with which they met it, severely destabilized English society, and it was only after their complaints were met with reform that a semblance of harmony was again reached.

This is not to say that there are no situations in which authority should be trusted and left to its own devices. There are times when, in order to protect a nation, those in power must conduct cloak and dagger practices that are better left outside of the realm of public opinion. No example illustrates this better than times of war. A consensus has always existed among military commanders that, following the adage that the right hand should not see what the left hand does, civilians should not have a say in the actions of the military. War is indeed hell, and in such a situation the emotions and philosophies of civilians may not be conducive to victory. Yet, can any society's moral well-being benefit when its government abandons principles simply to achieve victory and goes unchallenged? If one looks at the actions in the prison known as Guantanamo Bay, the answer is a definite "No." The treatment of prisoners at this place, once revealed to the public, sent shockwaves throughout society, and led to the ongoing moral crisis the nation has been dealing with until this very day.

In summary, I believe that no authority should be viewed as infallible if the well-being of a society is to be guaranteed. While there may be some benefits to giving up free agency to dissent in the short term, such freedoms, once deferred, are often never returned.

7. **Governments should focus on solving the immediate problems of today rather than on trying to solve the anticipated problems of the future. (Describe advantageous and disadvantageous circumstances of the recommendation)**

The assertion that governments should focus on immediate problems rather than proactively deal with future issues is not without its merits. However, due to several disadvantageous factors, it is not a recommendation which should be used as a primary strategy. The long-term risks far outweigh the short-term gains when governments try to simply deal with the here-and-now.

A severe weakness of having a governing system which focuses the majority of its resources on solving immediate problems is that it takes a reactionary approach to problems. When it comes to issues of a nation-wide scale, this can be disastrous, as using resources required to deal with a problem that has already begun to gain momentum is far more difficult than maintaining preventative measures. Take for example the actions of the United States Forest Service. For many years in the states of Colorado and California, the budget for clearing forest debris was slashed and neglected; little thought was given to the need to remove fallen trees and dead branches. As a result, there have been a record number of forest fires in recent years because of the buildup of dry tinder and despite the best efforts of the combined forces of the Forest Department and the entirety of the region's fire departments, thousands of acres of conservation land and millions of dollars' worth of property have been destroyed. Evidently, relying on reactionary measures was a failed gamble and now large swaths of land have been reduced to burnt-out wastelands. Had more attention been diverted to preparing for forest fires, i.e. spending more money and manpower on forest maintenance, this tragedy would not have occurred.

Overemphasizing the present can also be harmful to a nation's economy. Whenever short-sighted greed ensnares fiscal and foreign policies, domestic economies suffer. This has been a hotly debated topic in the USA, where it has been argued by many that the thirst for wider profit margins by US corporations led to the out-sourcing of labor to foreign countries. It certainly had the desired effect of generating massive profits for the companies which were able to establish manufacturing overseas. Yet it has become painfully apparent that after decades of exporting labor markets, the domestic economy has become incredibly fragile, with many US citizens unable to find jobs which pay livable wages. This has in turn led to less disposable income and the very companies which had sought to gain massive profits by decreasing production costs are discovering that sales are decreasing as their home market contracts. Had the government utilized a modicum of foresight, it could have enacted policies which encouraged the development of domestic industry, which could have provided more jobs to the population, and led to a much more resilient domestic market of consumers over the long term.

Naturally, certain situations call for immediate attention rather than long-term planning. A contemporary example is that of the COVID-19 pandemic. When news first reached the US government of the impending wave of infections, more attention was paid to the potential long-term political consequences of implementing mandatory shutdowns and mask-mandates. The political parties, more absorbed by their desire to maintain public popularity by espousing American Exceptionalism and civil liberties, did not immediately address the potential for the virus to spread quickly and uncontrollably. Spread it did, and only after it had infected tens of thousands of citizens did the government finally attempt a ramshackle series of shutdowns, social distancing, and mask-mandates. By that point, though, it was too late, and the virus had gained too strong a foothold to be effectively eliminated with haste. Had the government focused on immediately dealing with the virus, as in countries like China and New Zealand, a short period of nation-wide lockdown could have saved thousands of lives and billions of dollars of lost business revenue. However, it should be noted that this is a unique case. Even in this case, had the government done a better job of long-term planning according to WHO and CDC infectious disease guidelines, the national healthcare system and the general public would have been able to deal with the outbreak far more quickly and effectively than they did.

To conclude, being proactive is better than being reactive in virtually all situations. Effective governing requires careful long-term planning – history is riddled with failed states that were overwhelmed by unexpected upheavals. Focusing on the present can prove beneficial in certain situations, but doing so as a habit instead of preparing for the future is a recipe for disaster.

8. **Some people believe that college students should consider only their own talents and interests when choosing a field of study. Others believe that college students should base their choice of a field of study on the availability of jobs in that field. (Address both views)**

The question of which major should be chosen when one enters college is never an easy one. Should one seek a field that would provide the greatest opportunity for gainful employment after graduation, or instead pursue one that aligns with what one is passionate about and talented in? For me, I would have to agree with the former of the two positions.

A central point that is often forgotten in the debate over educational choices is that the primary purpose of attending school is to develop the skills needed to acquire a job. In the modern era, this fact is obscured by the accessibility and low cost of going to university, relative to previous centuries, when only the extremely wealthy elites could attend higher education institutions. Nevertheless, the simple truth of the matter is that the only real purpose for going to school is to get a degree that qualifies one for a position at a company. After all, if companies did not have education requirements, one could be reasonably certain that few people, if any at all, would bother to attend colleges or universities.

It should also be noted that the talents or interests that one possesses may not be particularly useful or sufficient for any job. For example, one may be decently adept at playing guitar, but may lack the talent to catch the interest of the public to the extent that one could support oneself as a musician. Or perhaps this person is a prodigy of the musical arts but lives in a time and place where the market is inundated with talented musicians. In this scenario it would be disastrous for this student to waste time and money on a music education; instead, the student could pursue a degree in a career that paid for his or her necessities and gave him or her time to focus on creative efforts that might become appreciated in later years.

However, I do not want anyone to think that they should immediately give up on their dreams to settle for a major that is in high demand. After all, job markets can shift radically with new developments in technology. A good example can be seen in the dot-com bubble in USA in the early 2000's. In this period, with the advent of the Internet, speculation around the potential economic benefits of tech companies led to a glut of those pursuing degrees in IT and other fields related to internet technology after the bubble burst. Anyone who had wanted to cash in on the bubble by sacrificing their passions was sorely disappointed. Yet this is a rather isolated incident, and in general, a person who stays well informed on employment trends and the state of the world economy should be able to avoid such mistakes.

To sum up, while it is a nice idea to follow one's dream when one chooses a major, to do so is a luxury that most cannot afford, and a risk not worth taking in a job market that is increasingly competitive. Students are often better off choosing a major that may guarantee a job after graduation and then following their passion in their free time.

9.   **Laws should be flexible enough to take account of various circumstances, times, and places. (Consider ways how the statement could or could not be true)**

As aviation became increasingly important for military strategists during World War I, the United States found itself confronted by a paralyzing legal hiccup: *The Constitution* clearly said that US tax dollars could be used to support the armed forces, but no consensus yet existed as to whether that included an air force.

Law, established within the norms of one era, becomes a stumbling block in later eras. Furthermore, because law cannot consider every scenario, unwavering adherence to the written rules may lead to individual injustices. However, law, and especially US Constitutional law, exists primarily to check the unrestrained power of government, not the vice of citizens. Therefore, law must remain fixed until ratified despite the above listed objections.

According to Locke and the Framers of *the US Constitution*, law must operate within the bounds of the higher laws of nature, which grant to all people the right to exist, choose, and control property. In this view, law does not maintain order or cynically oppress the masses but rather saves them from the most oppressive agglomeration of force imaginable: government. Law, then, cannot simply be called the institutions and rules whereby collective units maintain security among individuals but must also be viewed as the restraints against the institution itself becoming a threat to liberty. Law protects rights. These rights exist prior to law; indeed, law must only attempt to codify those preexistent prerogatives. For a proposed law to do this effectively, it must first be ratified by the people.

In other words, for law to be a legitimate protector of rights, it must be contractual. It requires not only the stamp of approval from technocracies but also from the public at large. And a law once codified by the will of the people cannot be simply danced around because it is inconvenient in some other time or place. For justice to remain relevant in society only the people can take away what the people first gave. Amendment can only be struck down by amendment, just as civil law can only be repealed by another.

This line of argument becomes especially relevant when considering constitutional law in the United States. Here *the Constitution* exists as the first contract and final authority. Its structure and various amendments ensure that the people cannot be overwhelmed by the institutions in which they place both their trust and their power.

Alarmingly, *the Constitution* has with increasing frequency become not a shield against tyranny but rather a tool for fixing individual injustices. In this paradigm, *the Constitution* is only convenient insofar as it can serve as an effective means to an end, not as the end in itself. This dangerous view ignores the necessity of immutability to guarantee law's continued effectiveness as a refuge from injustice.

One controversial example involves the Supreme Court ruling striking down the McCain-Feingold campaign finance reform law. The majority opinion claimed that, although inconvenient, corporations as collections of individuals must be allowed to speak. They further argued that no law could pretend to protect the rights of the people if it in fact made political discussion infeasible. Opponents claim that corporations will warp the workings of democracy, and that may well be true. But the right of individuals against the coercive force of government must take precedence over the inconveniences corporate cash might have on a specific political agenda.

Law must be rigid to be legitimate. Flexibility can too easily become oppression. The people are and must remain the final approvers of law, and they must be willing to accept the consequences of individual injustices for the sake of a life free from tyranny.

10. **Claim: The best way to understand the character of a society is to examine the character of the men and women that the society chooses as its heroes or its role models.**
    Reason: Heroes and role models reveal a society's highest ideals. (Claim-Reason)

The speaker declares that analyzing the character of the people chosen by a society as its "heroes" or "role models" is the best way of appreciating the society, because its heroes or role models represent its grandest ideals. I disagree with the claim but agree with the reason. Indeed, the nature of heroism is about celebrating the finer attributes of certain people and ignoring their weaknesses and failings, rather than acknowledging the full spectrum of attributes composing any person or society.

The great classical God-heroes of Greece and Rome had strengths and weaknesses, although it is most often their strengths that are celebrated and emulated. These Greek and Roman gods and demi-gods are reputed to have saved mankind and even helped form modern society. The etymological Greek and Latin roots of the word "hero" refer to people of divine descent. This evokes thoughts of perfection and true nobility; while there are those who perform amazing feats and act in noble ways, all heroes have faults. These faults, which are depicted in mythology as "tragic," set up the hero to fail despite his or her wonderful attributes. For example, the great warrior, Achilles, was invincible aside from a small spot on his heel. Despite his valor, he died when he was shot in the heel. Achilles becomes a type for heroes; all heroes have flaws which would be expected and looked over in normal people, but for a hero, any minor flaw can lead to social, spiritual, or physical downfall. Thus, the pressure of being labeled as a "hero" seems too great a weight for anyone—even a demi-god—to bear, and we should be wary of trying to analyze the realities of ancient Greece or Rome through the prism of such figures who represent a society's ideals.

Mythology aside, history is rife with examples of people who are extolled as heroes or role models by their society and subsequent generations, yet whose character flaws should not be imputed to an entire society. Some people consider the conqueror, Genghis Khan, to be a hero; he had an amazing ability to assemble many tribes into one empire, yet he was ruthless in warfare and had no mercy for his enemies. One cannot assume that because Genghis Khan acted in this manner all of Mongolian society followed suit. A more modern example of the dual nature of most heroes is Thomas Jefferson, the author of the American *Declaration of Independence*. Jefferson had a legendary mind and was a scholar of many disciplines: he was a farmer, a lawyer, and later the President of the United States. However, he held slaves and is believed to have fathered children with at least one of his slaves. It has only been in recent years that the less attractive components of Jefferson's life have been widely acknowledged, and that Jefferson has been viewed as a man rather than as a reflection of early Americans.

Finally, the true pulse of a society's character is found in the masses of commoners, rather than in the heroes or role models who belong to the small elite. Christopher Dyer, in his research on the population of medieval England, has revealed that the vast majority of people in England were involved in the wool trade: spinning, carding, and weaving. But it was the knights in armor that were lauded as the heroes of the time. Thus, to truly understand the character of medieval English society it is more important to study those involved with sheep than those involved in war. That is, the character of any society is found in its body rather than its head.

In summary, understanding of the character of a particular society should not be attempted through an examination of that society's heroes or role models. Such heroes or role models reflect merely the narrowest ideals of any society. Moreover, every hero has flaws, and these flaws cannot fairly be imputed to every member of that society. From a statistical standpoint, the character of a society is more likely to be found through an analysis of the myriad common people, rather than a select few.

11. **Governments should place few, if any, restrictions on scientific research and development. (Describe advantageous and disadvantageous circumstances of the recommendation)**

Do the ends justify the means? This question, fundamental to many areas of philosophy, is a focal point of heated debate in the realm of scientific research. Some would simply state the adage "If you want to make an omelet, you've got to break some eggs," dismissing negative consequences as inevitable collateral damage that occurs during the march of progress. Those who side with that notion are often against government restrictions on research, while their opponents, whom I agree with, argue that the ends do not justify the means and that certain things should be off-limits in regard to research.

A prime example that is brought up when we discuss research restrictions is human experimentation. Whether it is testing a new weapon, or medicine, or psychological studies, the desire to get results often tempts less scrupulous scientists to inflict horrendous suffering on people. With respect to medical experimentation one need look no further for justification for limits on research than the abhorrent experiments of the Nazi doctor, Josef Mengele. His monstrous excursions into human experimentation are too horrific to list here but it may suffice to say that his study resulted in the unimaginable suffering of those subjected to his tests. Perhaps the saddest part of this story is that there was no established international law regarding human experimentation with which to punish him and his subordinates until he had escaped into exile.

During what could be considered the golden age of modern psychology, the time between the 1950's and the 1970's, numerous social experiments were carried out with little oversight, traumatizing hundreds of people, oftentimes for life. One such experiment, dubbed the Stanford Prison Experiment, set out to test how people reacted to being given unlimited authority over others by placing two groups in the role of prison guards and prisoners. Otherwise normal people became tyrants, and the 'prisoners' were subjected to dehumanizing treatment such that the experiment was shut down. Another experiment, called the Robber Cave experiment, divided young boys into different teams and left them in a forest for a period. Without adult supervision, the boys quickly devolved into behaviors reminiscent of the famous novel *Lord of the Flies*, resulting in violence among the groups. At that time there were no laws to protect the subjects from the psychological damage caused by those experiments, and many were scarred for life, literally and figuratively.

One caveat is in order here. We must favor the side of less limitation on scientific research when such research is shown to do little harm to the test subjects and offers a great number of benefits. The poster child for this argument was, and in some cases still is, stem cell research. The distaste with which politicians view stem cells, due to the early days of research that used fetal cell tissue, has poisoned the well in regard to current research that does not require cells from fetuses but instead uses adult muscle stem cells gained from relatively non-invasive surgeries. The research stands to change many fields of medicine radically but is hindered by restrictions on research put in place by uninformed or biased policymakers. With this exception aside, I reaffirm my statement that, for the most part, government limitations on scientific research are absolutely necessary to keep gross abuse and harm from occurring.

In sum, there may be no way to prevent completely the dedicated scientist from going rogue and conducting unethical research. However, I believe that it is in the best interest of society if the government at the very least devises a set of guidelines that provides a morally sound framework for scientific development.

12. The best way to teach is to praise positive actions and ignore negative ones. (Discuss how the statement could or could not be true)

The job of imparting new knowledge unto others is often considered an unenviable task due to the burden of managing how exactly to teach effectively. Some have argued that the best route is to commend positive behaviors while ignoring others, but I cannot completely agree with this method, for although positive reinforcement is certainly useful for teaching, an educator should not simply ignore bad behavior.

Anyone that studies education and behavioral science understands that one of the most effective tools to ensure that a behavior or piece of information is learned is through positive reinforcement. This is summed up nicely in the proverb that one can catch more flies with honey. A more tangible example is well known to students that have been in a class where their engagement and contributions are acknowledged compared to one where what they do seldom receives positive feedback. In the former class, information is remembered quickly and utilized easily, and time seems to pass quickly. Yet, in the latter class, concepts seem impossible to grasp and time moves at a snail's pace.

However, when it comes to bad behavior, especially among young people such as students, an apathetic attitude by the teacher towards such behavior can go so far as to encourage the behavior. No example is more relevant than bullying, an age-old and pervasive problem in schools. Whenever bullying is ignored by teachers and administrators, bullies become more and more audacious in the treatment of other students, and the bullies will develop extreme anti-social tendencies that can even lead to psychopathy as they do not learn to value their peers as individuals.

It is worth pointing out that while bad behaviors should be addressed rather than ignored, I do not condone harsh punishment. This can cause as many problems as it attempts to remedy. Instead, I support an approach that involves seeking out the root cause of the negative behaviors and discussing with the student and employee why the behavior is unacceptable so that they understand why they should not repeat it. This can be difficult with adult employees, who may feel patronized by such a conversation. However, if they are raised in a system that uses such corrective measures, they would be highly receptive to it.

In conclusion, I cannot fully agree with the claim presented. I absolutely agree that positive behaviors should be properly rewarded, but I strongly disapprove of the idea that negative behaviors should be ignored.

13. **Governments should offer college and university education free of charge to all students. (Describe advantageous and disadvantageous circumstances of the recommendation)**

Due to the rise in demand for highly educated workers, and the exorbitant financial cost of university education, it has been argued that college and university education should be made free to all students by the government. While such a notion is not without merit, I think that it would ultimately lead to more problems than it would solve.

Consider first the primary consequence of subsidizing the education for all students. It would entail a huge burden upon the government's budget, leading to increased taxes, especially when one takes into account the fact that tuition costs have been steadily rising and show no signs of stopping. Since this argument mentions nothing about placing price caps on tuition, there would be nothing to stop colleges from continually hiking up, or even artificially inflating, their prices to exploit the government money they would receive for the predictably large number of students that would flock to 'free' degree programs. On the other hand, if the government is to limit the budget allocated to schools in order to avoid this problem, then there stands the risk of the quality of education dropping as programs and resources are cut.

This plan would also pose a great risk to the stability of the nation's economy, in the form of employment gaps. If college education were free, students would apply, in large numbers, to programs that promise high salaries. In that four to eight-year span between graduating classes, the job market would stagnate, as fewer new workers entered the market, and the lack of experienced workers would lead to unemployment as employers become unwilling to hire graduates that have not worked in relevant fields. Alternatively, the flood of new graduates into the job market may also cause the salary of those jobs to plummet, as employers would take advantage of the surplus of applicants, repeating yet another vicious cycle wherein fewer people apply to those fields, leading to a decline in that industry.

This is not to say that there are no benefits to offering free higher education. After all, studying at a university can impart a diverse range of knowledge to students, who then become better equipped to deal with a variety of different situations in a professional job setting. This could also lead to a nation's economy developing if enough people become educated in fields such as advanced manufacturing, international business, and so on. However, these benefits are predicated on the assumption that a majority of students will choose such majors, and more importantly, pursue careers in related fields. Since this is not necessarily the case, and considering the fact that many jobs required for the running of a country do not need a college degree, offering free higher education for everyone would not guarantee a positive result.

Given these points, it should be clear that while it is a noble idea to provide free education for all students, it should be remembered that nothing is free: the cost of conferring this subsidy would have dramatic consequences on the financial stability of not only the government, but the country as a whole as the employment market is shaken by the shifts in the number of applicants in specific job fields.

14. **The luxuries and conveniences of contemporary life prevent people from developing into truly strong and independent individuals. (Discuss how the statement could or could not be true)**

Society's advent into the digital age has brought with it specialization, automation, prosperity and an exponential improvement in the quality of life for even the masses. Yet, no action in life is without reaction; this cataclysmic introduction of wealth also steals from its beneficiaries. The expansion of the leisure class to a majority of the population with its luxuries and conveniences robs the general populace of a life of independence and inner strength.

The conveniences of contemporary life allow an individual to work, live and grow with no true connection to the earth or the skills necessary to survive on it. While this can be viewed as a freedom, and indeed it does free up time and agency, in reality it creates a dependency on conveniences such as stores and machines. This can have severe ramifications. In modern times machines have taken over the jobs of rural farmers, displacing entire communities, leaving them destitute and forcing the groups to travel in search of livelihood. These groups of people exist in all societies, societies in which doing things more efficiently takes precedence over the soul of the man and the earth. Thus, the ability of individuals to make their own way in the world by living off the land has been supplanted by an overreliance on automated machinery and other modern conveniences, to ill effect.

This overreliance that results from the extra time and money of a leisure class has shifted self-worth from a place of holistic possibility into a world where pedestaled images are constantly sought after and never achieved. Plato's theory on forms describes a similar situation: in a world where only shadows of true forms are seen, the forms are representative in some way, but can never become the actual thing. When applied to people this theory is devastating, and this is what a world of luxury and commodities is doing; people can only become shallow half-selves judged on beauty or test scores, never able to become whole, and thus never able to heal the scars that this world can leave. Without the ability to grow and change, no real strength or independence is possible.

There are ways in which this statement might not hold true. For instance, the digital age has brought smart devices such as cellphones, laptops, and tablets, alongside the vast knowledge of the internet. This accessibility to an almost limitless base of knowledge has made it possible for people to move upward economically who, for most of history, were delegated to lives of poverty as a consequence of their ignorance and inability to afford an education. Now they have been able to start their own business using the resources made available to them by the internet and cheap computers. However, once the transition from impoverishment to the standard middle class occurs, the statement is largely true. A dependency on the devices that liberated them renders people incapable of existing without the support of the digital infrastructure.

The danger in lives of luxury and ease can verge on being destructive; without the ability to consciously live each day and strive towards a centered and balanced soul and mind the civilizations of the world are slowly engulfed by consumerism and information overload. This dependence on technology and readily available information handicaps modern people and limits their ability to function once they are stripped of modern conveniences.

15. **In any field of inquiry, the beginner is more likely than the expert to make important contributions. (Discuss how the statement could or could not be true)**

A famous expression in English goes, "Out of the mouths of babes comes the truth", which means the wisdom that can sometimes be pointed out by young people. As reasonable as this sounds, however, I do not think that these are words to live by; in matters of inquiry, experts rather than beginners remain the primary contributors.

In arguing against the notion that beginners can contribute more to research, one really need not look any further than history itself. When analyzing the circumstances in which new inventions have been discovered, we may find that the vast majority have been realized by professionals that have spent a lifetime working in their field. This fact is often forgotten in the modern era of movie montages showing the intrepid hero mastering a skill in a short period of time. The plain reality is that advancements in any field require long periods of painstaking work, followed by review and analysis. Beginners may be able to do the first part of that process, but experience is necessary for the latter part.

Another important fact to remember is that understanding research and drawing conclusions from it requires a deep understanding of the field of study. While beginners may have a basic understanding of the subject matter, it is probable that they lack the detailed comprehension necessary to make an adequate diagnosis. For example, in medicine, a doctor in training may observe the obvious symptoms of a patient and then assume that the patient has some illness. Yet many diseases have similar or even overlapping symptoms of which the inexperienced doctor is unaware, leading to a misdiagnosis. In situations such as this, a medical expert would be far more adept and reliable than the beginner; hence, new doctors often practice under a veteran doctor.

Of course, it can be argued that inexperienced people can offer fresh insight into a particular problem, since they have not developed informational bias. For instance, a humorous story is passed around by mechanics about an experienced repairman trying to fix a car, and after all his attempts to make the car run fail, an apprentice points out that the car has no gas in it. While it is a clever story, it functions more as a lesson to check for the most obvious problems first. It is still more often the case that even if a beginner brings a hint of inspiration to an issue, most of the legwork involved in turning that idea into a reality is done by experts.

In conclusion, if we wish to have successful contributions when conducting research or take on a venture of some kind, it is better to rely on those that possess intimate knowledge and experience of the subject than one newly acquainted with the material.

16. **The surest indicator of a great nation is represented not by the achievements of its rulers, artists, or scientists, but by the general welfare of its people. (Discuss how the statement could or could not be true)**

Throughout history, those nations that we look back upon as prime civilizations have always been admired for the singular achievements of their scientists, artists, and leaders. Yet these achievements were not necessarily what made the nations themselves great. Rather, it was the well-being of their citizens that determined whether the country flourished and was held in high esteem by its neighbors.

First of all, it should be noted that genius can come from almost anywhere. Even the least developed nations have had their own great minds arising from their populations, but this does not make the nation great. For example, the great civil rights leader Mahatma Gandhi is an icon of political thought and protest, yet India could not be considered a great nation during his lifetime. In Gandhi's time, India was still a colony of Britain, and the oppressive regime there had stifled the economic development of almost the whole country. Poverty and famine were rampant, and no matter how impactful Gandhi's words and actions may have been on the future of India, the nation itself during Gandhi's time was not considered great. Now, however, things have changed drastically; in terms of technological and economic development India's people have flourished, and the nation is now considered one of the most powerful on the world stage.

Another example can be seen in the self-proclaimed great nation of Nazi Germany. A large portion of scientific discoveries from the 1940's and 1950's was made by or with the help of German and Austrian scientists fleeing the Nazi regime. If the nation had truly been as great as it alleged itself to be, then there would not have been so many great minds that left it. At the time, persecution of a variety of categories was common; political, religious, social, and virtually all other aspects of life that may have posed a threat to the regime were ruthlessly culled by the Gestapo secret police. The country was still unsustainable from an industrial standpoint; the entire Sudetenland annexation was planned in order to seize the natural resources and utilize the labor force of nearby nations to feed the German economy. As a result, the revolutionary discoveries of Nazi Germany's scientists were almost completely overlooked in most cases since their achievements did little to improve the nation's overall well-being.

One way in which the statement may need qualification involves the fact that the general welfare of a great nation is often inextricably intertwined with the accomplishments of its rulers, artists, and scientists. In other words, the general well-being of a great nation is almost impossible without competent rulers and difficult to achieve without notable artists or scientists. This means that the achievements of such eminent people do demonstrate that the nation is great. A historical example can be seen in Tang Dynasty China, the era which is generally accepted as one of the nation's greatest premodern periods of cultural and scientific development. The people in China at the time were extremely well-cared for as compared to previous eras, and some of the most iconic Chinese poets, such as Li Bai and Du Fu, became ensconced in the annals of cultural greatness. To this day, the people of China still look back to the Tang Dynasty as a period to be emulated in regard to its artistic accomplishments as well as the welfare of the people: accessible education, cultural enrichment, available food, and other resources; the list goes on.

In conclusion, I believe the only relevant factor for a great nation is the welfare of its people, for without it, not only are great minds less likely to thrive, but the nation itself will suffer and in all likelihood cease to exist.

17. **The best way to teach — whether as an educator, employer, or parent — is to praise positive actions and ignore negative ones. (Address challenges to your position)**

Here the speaker asserts that in every avenue of life the best way to teach is to praise the positive and ignore the negative. Like the speaker I find that praising the positive is a powerful motivator and teacher in every aspect of life. However, the idea that an educator, employer and parent can all use this method of praising and ignoring equally to achieve desired results fails to understand the unique roles of these three institutions.

Education is most often a group situation where a body of students is learning from one teacher. The role of the teacher is to teach students both subject matter and how to learn so that they can go on to self-teach. While educators are often close to their pupils, they are not only paid to comment on what the students do well. The idea that an English teacher would return with only positive comment a paper that received the grade of "D" would just seem absurd. Since education is meant to push and teach there must be a means to communicate how to improve. As for misbehavior, the classroom is meant to help all the students. When one begins to disrupt them all this becomes unacceptable and it is right that that student be reprimanded or removed for a time. However, the more a teacher is able to praise a student who might be prone to ill-behavior, the less she will find herself having to remove him from the room.

Unlike educators, employers are not focused on teaching. Though this might be an aspect of many jobs, the employer hires you to work and produce some form of tangible or intangible goods. You are being paid for what you already know and are willing to do. In this situation praising can also be a powerful tool in achieving the highest level of commitment from employees and in keeping up a high morale. Nevertheless, the idea that an employer would ignore things like being late or abusive behavior towards other employees seems out of the question.

Parents are the group with which the speaker's assertion rings the truest. Parents have the key teaching role in children's life and as their main caregivers are looked to for guidance, direction, and love. Parents can focus on the individual and with their praise and attention guide a child into appropriate behavior and an understanding of moral integrity. Praising the positive is essential as children are often seeking attention, but if that attention comes more readily when they misbehave it can encourage them to continue on that path. That said, I do not feel that parents need to ignore negative behavior as much as allowing natural consequences for the problems. The natural consequence for not eating will be hunger and the child will soon learn that eating is a good idea. Over-praising for things that can be taught through natural consequences might also backfire. If you are constantly praising your child for eating their food they will learn that eating is an emotionally charged issue and makes them good or bad when this is not reality. Instead, parents need to help children navigate their way and offer them the praise that will teach them how wonderful and important they truly are.

Educators, employers, and parents must constantly work efficaciously as stewards. Though the methods might differ, all of them are working with unique individuals. Praising is a powerful way to help these individuals reach their potential in distinct ways, although over praising may render a disservice. Also, in no way should negative actions be ignored.

18. Teachers' salaries should be based on their students' academic performance. (Address challenges to your position)

In the attempt to improve the grades and learning of students in schools, the idea has been put forth that the salaries of teachers should be based upon the academic performance of their students. While this may seem reasonable on its face, after further examination of the potential ramifications I cannot agree with this claim.

Firstly, this claim makes no mention of the workload that comes with being a teacher. Perhaps in some countries, or even counties within countries the number of students in a class is small, with only ten to twenty students. However, in other countries such as African nations and East Asia, classes can be composed of over forty students. Taking into account the lesson planning, homework and test assignments, classwork, and grading of all these materials the teacher in question has almost no time to monitor the individual performance of students, meaning that their performance in class is due mostly to their own studying and the efforts of their parents to ensure they are reviewing daily. Therefore, to base the salary of teachers on the overall performance of their students is unfair, since it does not account for the actual labor they put into their job.

Secondly, students themselves may not be particularly adept at studying or willing to cooperate in class. In fact, in many countries students that tend to perform poorly are often grouped into single classes. Should teachers that are expected to teach these classes be forced to accept a lower pay? Definitely no. In addition, this system would give a coercive power to students that become aware of the pay system, as the sometimes vindictive nature of young students may lead them to perform poorly on purpose to get back at a teacher who they feel wronged them.

I would be remiss if I did not address the potentially beneficial aspect of this kind of pay system. It would certainly motivate many teachers to do their best to teach students effectively, as their livelihood would otherwise literally hang in the balance. For those teachers skilled or lucky enough to have high-performing students, they would be able to turn teaching into a lucrative career. This in turn would create an incentive for them to provide a higher quality education. Through this system, teachers who did not develop effective teaching strategies would be weeded out, leaving the best possible educators, who would in turn receive ample reward for their efforts. After all, one of the reasons for the struggling education systems of many nations is the lack of funding for teacher salaries, which stigmatizes the profession for aspiring educators. However, herein lies a major flaw with a performance-based pay system: corruption and falsification. Under this system, a teacher with a group of under-achieving students tends to be tempted to inflate their students' scores in order to save their pay, and as a result the quality of education may drop, and certainly the quality of students entering universities would fall as well.

In sum, I must disagree with any plan that proposes that we pay teachers based on the scores of their students. At its core, it is unfair for the amount of hard work that teachers must put in just to teach normally, and it offers too much temptation for abuse in the form of inflated grades.

19. **Society should make efforts to save endangered species only if the potential extinction of those species is the result of human activities. (Discuss positive and negative consequences of the policy)**

With the continued deterioration of the natural environment here on Earth, green movements have sprung up in large numbers, proposing that we attempt to save as many species from extinction as possible. Yet, I, for one, find myself agreeing more with the idea of saving only those species that humans have affected.

It does sound harsh at first. After all, no one enjoys the idea of losing an animal or plant species forever. But the sad fact of the matter is that conservation costs a considerable amount of money, manpower, and other resources to implement effectively. Most protection and conservation agencies are either charities or government bureaus with limited funding since most people tend to support conservation with happy thoughts rather than cash or volunteering. Therefore, trying to save every species that is in danger simply is not feasible. Indeed, it would be best if we accept the responsibility for those animals that are suffering from habitat loss and pollution arising from human activities.

It is also important to point out that many of the species which we affect are ones on which we rely for our own needs. For example, many of the fish we eat are being fished to extinction, and there are only so many edible species. Many of these species are connected in the food chain, so the destruction of one often leads to the loss of another. Thus, it is in our own best interest to preserve just these species, if only for our own benefit.

When it comes to every other species of plant and animal that is dying out, while many plead that we should protect them from extinction, there is no reason for us to save all of them. After all, countless species have died out over the course of our planet's history. Life on Earth is constantly growing and dying, and there is a strong argument to be made for the notion that species should die out because they are weak, which then leaves room for better-evolved species to thrive. This can be seen in extremophiles such as those curious animals that live on the ocean floor. These animals need no protection and likely outlive humans due to their survivability.

To conclude, we only have obligation to the dying species on our planet whose extinction we have contributed to. While it is more moral than practical, it is our responsibility. As for the others, the hard truth is that they are not our responsibility and have simply drawn the short straw, evolutionarily speaking.

20. College students should base their choice of a field of study on the availability of jobs in that field. (Address challenges to your position)

The question of which major should be chosen when students enter college is never an easy one. Should one seek a field that would provide the greatest opportunity for gainful employment after graduation? My answer is a resounding "Yes."

A central point that is often forgotten in the debate over educational choices is that the primary purpose of attending college is to develop the skills needed to acquire a job. In the modern era, this fact is obscured by the accessibility and low cost of going to university relative to previous centuries when only the extremely wealthy elites could attend higher education institutions. Nevertheless, the simple truth of the matter is that the only real purpose for going to school is to get a degree that qualifies one for a position at a company. After all, if companies did not have education requirements, one could be reasonably certain that few people, if any at all, would bother to attend colleges or universities.

Choosing a major that promises an abundance of jobs after graduation from college may help students save time and money. When focusing on a major with a broad scope of careers in mind, students can target courses which develop relevant skills that are applicable to certain jobs. Too often, students choose a major that does not have a direct correlation to any particular job. As a result, they fill their semesters with classes that cost significant amounts of time and money, which results in a tragic waste of energy. For instance, a degree in philosophy will lead a student to take numerous classes on literature and schools of thought, few of which may be readily useful in any workplace setting. Also, such courses are rarely transferrable as college credit to other majors if a student has second thoughts and decides to change his or her field of study. Thus, selecting a major related to specific jobs ensures that students are making the most of the considerable chunk of their lives and bank accounts in their university education.

However, I do not want anyone to think that they should immediately give up on their dreams to settle for a major that is in high demand. After all, job markets can shift radically with new developments in technology. A good example can be seen in the dot-com bubble in USA in the early 2000's. In this period, with the advent of the Internet, speculation around the potential economic benefits of tech companies led to a glut of those pursuing degrees in IT and other fields related to internet technology after the bubble burst. Anyone who had wanted to cash in on the bubble by sacrificing their passions was sorely disappointed. Yet this is a rather isolated incident, and in general, a person who stays well informed on employment trends and the state of the world economy should be able to avoid such mistakes.

To sum up, college students are often better off choosing a major that may guarantee a job after graduation because this is the purpose of a college education. While it is a nice idea to follow one's dream when one chooses a major, to do so is a risk not worth taking in a job market that is increasingly competitive.

21. **As we acquire more knowledge, things do not become more comprehensible, but more complex and mysterious. (Discuss how the statement could or could not be true)**

Of all characteristics distinguishing man from beast, perhaps the most revealing is man's innate drive for greater understanding. Every meaningful cultural activity, from religion to science, has at its roots a larger truth claim that not only asserts exclusive access to knowledge but also exclusive access to the mechanisms to discover further knowledge. However, while these activities attempt to enlighten understanding, they frequently have the opposite consequence. Knowledge, in short, often obscures rather than reveals truth. These effects are apparent both on a societal and individual level.

Increased knowledge frequently complicates rather than simplifies entire societal structures. Throughout the Middle Ages, people could not be bothered by the unknowable complexities of the universe; theirs was a life focused on continued survival in the face of famine and disease. As such, they required only a simplistic understanding of nature and God; their explanations for suffering, for example, did little more than reaffirm the inscrutability of God's will. However, with philosophical advances of the 16th Century, these old conceptions of reality soon broke down. The humanism championed by the writers and artists of Renaissance Italy questioned the assertion that man stood ultimately accountable to an overwhelmingly powerful God. These humanists asserted the transcendent beauty of the individual, emphasizing realistic art and rigorous education systems. This secularized focus on the individual had considerable ramifications on the political realm. Leaders such as Richelieu, emboldened by the notion that they were ultimately responsible not to God but to the anthropomorphized state, soon fought the Thirty Years War, which remains one of the bloodiest in European history. Simple questions of religious loyalty in international relations soon devolved into a confusing web of entangled alliances as states made bids for hegemony in a polarized system. Furthermore, this new truth claim advanced by the Humanist school, rather than simplifying the life of the peasant, complicated it by adding violent conquest on top of the scourges of famine and plague.

Individuals also recognize the muddying influence of new knowledge. For example, the layman's understanding of policy remains elementary at best, and necessarily so. As people understand more thoroughly the complexities behind social ailments such as child prostitution and drug trafficking, they also realize that bumper-sticker solutions such as "Tough on Crime" will not work. The realm of professional policy-making deals with complicated questions of value-maximization in often desperate and high-stress situations. A full understanding of these concerns, rather than empowering the average voter, would cripple their ability to differentiate between the merits of policy proposals. People as political actors need simplifying assumptions. International relations theorists explicitly accept the need for simplifying models in the face of overwhelming amounts of data. Individuals likewise cling to reductionist assumptions about reality, for without them they would be overwhelmed in a world increasingly defined not by a scarcity of information but by an overload of information.

There are ways in which the statement might not hold true. After all, as we gain knowledge throughout our lifetimes, it becomes easier to understand the world around us. It is undeniable that we are born completely ignorant of the world, but this situation changes as we age and acquire facts about our surroundings. Consider the fact that a primary school student today could comprehend far more than the great physicist Stephen Hawking himself as an infant. However, Hawking in his later years understood more about the cosmos than the majority of people who ever lived. The defining characteristic of the former and latter situations is that Hawking, throughout the course of his life, learned new information which facilitated his ability to gain a deeper understanding of the universe. Therefore, in contrast to the claim of the statement, the acquisition of knowledge does in fact allow people to comprehend more about the world around them and demystifies things rather than complicates them.

History provides evidence verifying man's innate drive for greater clarity through greater understanding. However, this knowledge frequently complicates rather than elucidates; and with these complications comes the responsibility to act more conscientiously in what seems to be an increasingly complex and ultimately unknowable reality.

22. In any situation, progress requires discussion among people who have contrasting points of view. (Discuss how the statement could or could not be true)

In attempting to make progress on an issue, whether it be scientific, political, or otherwise, one would think that the most conducive situation would involve a unanimous consensus of those involved. However, it is my opinion that discussion among those that hold differing views is preferable to unanimity if we want to make real progress.

One consequence of working in a group of people where all agree with one another is what is often called the echo chamber effect, wherein the repetition of opinions and information within a closed system becomes amplified and leads to bias. This occurs quite often in the media industry, which incidentally coined the phrase, and as a result, news organizations become extremely polarized. Take for example the rival US news stations, FOX and CNN, conservative and liberal-leaning respectively, which trumpet the party line to the point of propagandizing. Because of this, there is rarely any progress in political or social discourse on these channels, and instead independent journalism has become far more reliable when trying to disseminate current events objectively.

Opposing viewpoints are also vital to the development of law and higher philosophy through debate. In fact, addressing the counterargument is such a central component in this context that there is even a rhetorical device based on it called "playing the devil's advocate", in which people will attempt to support the side they disagree with in order to better develop their own argument. This is because a debater's argument is only as strong as their understanding of their opposition. In fact, the entire premise of a debate is that opposing viewpoints are attempting to justify themselves over others. This is clearly seen in the process of making an argument in school where we are taught that we should address the opposing evidence. In fact, this writing assignment itself is an example of this process.

However, a consensus is not without merit. Quite the contrary, a consensus is vital to the formulation of conclusions. No situation illustrates this better than that of the scientific community where new research and theories must be reviewed and agreed upon by one's peers. It would be tantamount to intellectual insanity to allow all potential theories equal footing simply to support having differing viewpoints. However, even in this system dissent is encouraged, for it is through the crucible of testing viewpoints that scientific truth is distilled. If it were not for this system, we would still be practicing pseudoscience such as phrenology and astrology, which only thrive in environments where people dogmatically follow their belief in the system and ignore opposing evidence.

To sum up, if we are to make progress in any field, we must be willing to allow our ideas to run the gauntlet of opposing opinions and scrutiny, or risk stagnating in an echo chamber of sycophantic thought.

23. Educational institutions should dissuade students from pursuing fields of study in which they are unlikely to succeed. (Discuss positive and negative consequences of the policy)

In the endeavor to provide a nation with citizens that are both highly skilled and well educated, I believe it is most definitely the obligation of educational institutions to discourage students from studying fields in which they are unlikely to succeed. While it is a popular belief that, as individuals, students should have the right to choose whatever path in life they wish to follow, the far-reaching consequences cannot be ignored of having too many people in a country without proper employment, a situation compounded by the significant financial burden that education places upon students and their families.

First of all, consider the current situation in the USA, where throughout the 1990's and early 2000's there was an explosion in the number of university attendees due to the relaxation of regulations on student loans. This, combined with the perception that a college degree would allow students to obtain higher positions and salaries after graduation, meant that many students decided to choose majors in difficult fields, such as engineering, finance, and law. However, these majors require a specific mindset and much dedication, which many students were unable to live up to, resulting in quite high dropout rates. These dropouts then found themselves in a position where they had already invested a considerable amount of time and money into a fruitless education and were at a disadvantage when entering the workplace since they had no other viable skills. This problem continues even today, leading to a significant proportion of the US population fit only for service jobs, and thus remaining in a position of financial limbo that disallows their contributing to the economy through spending or investment. Colleges and universities have the ostensible purpose of preparing people for professional careers, and if they are to continue to be viewed as such, they should put more effort into ensuring their students pursue majors in which they can succeed. This has already been accomplished to some extent through placement exams for certain levels of mathematics and sciences, but more stringency should be applied in order to eliminate cram students or those who prepare only for the tests.

Pursuing less than appropriate majors has another potentially disastrous consequence in the form of bad debt. As previously mentioned, the relatively lax lending laws in the USA in regard to student loans mean that many students have tens of thousands of dollars in student debt. Add this fact to the aforementioned difficulty in finding gainful employment and one can understand the current debt bubble that exists in the USA. It has been regarded by economists as a situation that is potentially as severe as the 2008 economic crisis, especially since most student loans are given out at the same time and will thus likely default all at once. Had these students received the proper guidance while choosing a major, then this situation could have been avoided. For instance, every college has a "drop-add" period during the first week or two of each semester. In this period if students are closely monitored for performance or levels of stress, then those who seem incapable of grasping the concepts of the courses or unsuitable to the workload could be advised to move to majors in which they would perform better.

One likely negative consequence of implementing the policy is that educational institutions may give the wrong advice: what was initially deemed the fields in which students were likely to succeed may prove the opposite when they graduate. This has been known to happen before. For instance, in the USA during the early 2000's the law field gained enormous interest as globalization picked up more steam, and as a result there was a projected need for new corporate lawyers and a boom in the legal field in general as the standard of living increased. Thus, academic institutions advertised heavily to encourage students to get legal degrees: not only was the profession highly respected, but it was also very lucrative. Predictably, this boosted law major admissions substantially, but the result was that it became difficult to find a job in the legal field due to the overabundance of law graduates. However, this boom-bust cycle in education and employment opportunities has been heavily researched in recent years, and many colleges and universities now use up-to-date job market analysis to recommend majors to students. In this way, schools can still be reasonably relied upon to dissuade students from choosing majors that will not fully benefit them in the future.

In sum, I think that schools and other educational institutions have an inherent responsibility to guide students away from career paths that do not suit them. In my mind, the national benefits such a responsibility would garner, along with the disasters it would aid in avoiding, trump the individual freedom of the students.

24. **Governments should not fund any scientific research whose consequences are unclear. (Describe advantageous and disadvantageous circumstances of the recommendation)**

Since one of the primary functions of governments is to ameliorate quality of life for its citizens, it stands to reason that scientific research should be a top priority when they spend budgets. However, since government spending relies on the tax dollars of its people, there is a limit to how much money can be devoted to research, and thus only those projects with clear goals and results and lacking ethical ambiguity should be approved for funding.

One of the foremost concerns that comes up whenever scientific research is conducted is the moral implications of the discoveries. In fields such as medicine, the results of certain tests may have far reaching effects on the human dignity of patients. For example, one highly controversial research topic has been the development of stem cell therapy. This treatment was and still is considered morally abhorrent in the minds of many people that view the harvesting of stem cells from fetal tissue as desecrating life. They argue that this process effectively commodifies human life, and they are entitled to their civil right to urge their representatives in the government to either make such research illegal, or in terms of this argument, prohibit spending on research into this field that conflicts with their beliefs and has many more repercussions than originally identified.

Also, some kinds of research may reveal knowledge that is too dangerous for anyone to possess. Such knowledge may be unclear before the research, but given the potential dire consequences, governments are not supposed to fund it. Take nuclear weapons as an example. It is undoubtable that numerous ills have been caused by the development of nuclear technology, not only in the cost of human life in the two detonations during WWII, but also in the political tensions between nations in the dispute over who should be allowed to have such weapons. It could therefore be argued that governments should abstain from financially supporting any kind of technology research that could lead to the development of more powerful weapons with unknown consequences so as to avoid further death and conflict.

Some may argue that one cannot predict the ramifications of developments that come from research, and therefore the consequences are never clear. One such piece of evidence for this was the development of the first airplanes thanks to the Wright brothers. They envisioned their creation as something that would promote the quick and convenient transportation of man and goods around the globe, yet they lived to see the descendants of their invention being used as a conveyance for the Hiroshima and Nagasaki nuclear bombings. According to this camp, the government would either have to cease funding of research altogether, or fund all projects equally, which simply is not feasible. In addition, there are certainly areas of research where the potential negative impacts of an experiment are far more numerous than the proposed benefit, as in weapon development or social experiments. This does not mean governments need to stop funding scientific research completely; they need to fund research with well-defined goals and free of ethical risks.

In sum, I believe that when one considers the extensive financial burden imposed by scientific research as well as the ethical responsibility a government has towards its people, it is certainly reasonable for a government to deny funding to scientific research that does not provide a clear benefit, or has morally problematic consequences.

25. Society should identify those children who have special talents and provide training for them at an early age to develop their talents. (Describe advantageous and disadvantageous circumstances of the recommendation)

What would be the inevitable result if children who demonstrate prowess and exceptional talents were supported by society, enabling them to train and perfect those things at which they naturally excelled? The speaker declares that the downside to not implementing this sort of system simply would be a resource of natural talents and abilities left dormant. I agree that a system designed to develop and enhance the natural abilities of children at an early age contains many benefits such as more opportunities, better work ethics, and increased confidence; however, these benefits could only be realized if society still allowed for individual choice in the training of children.

The gifted program or advanced learning service for children at an early age provides opportunities for them to nurture their talents. In many societies, there are young children who long to develop certain skills or talents but lack the opportunity due to poverty or other constraints. Fortunately, some countries now provide integrated or independent advanced learning programs to students at a young age who have passed tests for such programs, and this offers the opportunity to develop talents in subjects such as math and science. For example, some school districts in the United States have offered advanced programs for children from elementary school up through high school. Those who do well in the screening tests can study math and science for a higher grade in separate classes in their own school or in an independent program in a different school of the same school district, whereas those who are not so academically inclined can pursue their studies in the assigned grade. As a result, those who have the motivation and talent for advanced learning are admitted by relevant programs tailored to their needs. Otherwise, they would feel bored if they could only take classes that teach materials too easy for them. Systems like this enable young children to choose the path that best suits their inclinations and talents.

As children are given the opportunity to develop at an early age a skill or ability at which they naturally excel, they can better learn the importance of hard work and develop increased confidence, because such traits take time to nurture. For example, many children are trained to play sports or musical instruments even before school, and the process of repeated failure and noticeable progress teaches the rewards of hard work and the necessity of trying again and again. These lessons will persist throughout a child's life. Additionally, their confidence in themselves and their capabilities would grow as they begin to realize the extent of their potential. Learning how to make an effort, even in the face of defeat, and experiencing an increase in confidence are critical lessons for young children and will enable them to succeed as adults. Therefore, training children to develop certain talents and abilities early on can be incredibly important.

However, if a system of training exceptional children at an early age does not include individual choice, the results can be tragic. A system that forces children to cooperate, denying them liberty in their own life, will ultimately dehumanize these children and teach them that they are only valuable because of their talents. In the former Soviet Union, there were many programs in place for training exceptional children. Most legendary, perhaps, are those that prepared children to compete at Olympic levels in gymnastics. Children were tested for aptitude and certain physical characteristics, and, if identified as promising, they were generally taken away from their families to devote their childhoods to training. Although the former Soviet Union produced many champion gymnasts, it is unclear whether these children or their families had much choice in this matter. Requiring involvement without consent sends a message of worthlessness and could instill in these children a hatred for the society that only values them for a specific talent.

In conclusion, a system designed to develop and enhance the natural abilities of young children can have many positive outcomes: increased opportunity, confidence and understanding of the importance of hard work. However, such systems need to include the element of individual choice, or else the benefits will be negated.

26. **It is primarily through our identification with social groups that we define ourselves. (Discuss how the statement could or could not be true)**

Is one's identity the result of personal development, or a form molded by the influences of those with whom we spend the most time? This question dates to the earliest days of psychological inquiry and has stirred much debate. Personally speaking, I think that both the individual decisions that we make and the expectations of the groups we choose to associate with define who we are.

As people age, they often encounter difficult life choices that determine the future path that their life will take. These choices usually require a great amount of introspective thought and thus become a foundation for the individual's personality. Situations such as deciding which field to study, which person to marry, and the like, while having some social expectations, are largely determined by a person's own views on life and happiness.

People's identity may also stem from how impressionable they are. Those who are easily influenced by the actions and opinions of those around them would owe far more of their own personality to the social groups they associate with. On the other hand, those with highly individualistic personalities tend to ignore the status quo and pursue their interests regardless of society's expectations. A perfect example is noted in shock-rocker Marilyn Manson who often employed graphic words and imagery in his music that stunned and revolted parents throughout his career. Despite his eccentric career, Manson remained soft spoken and intelligent in his interviews, which confused those in the media that wished to represent him as abhorrent. He was and still is a man defined not by the expectations of others, but by his own drive to create his art.

There is something to be said for the influence of social groups. The impact of taboos on a person's identity is a case in point. Taboos often ensconce the feelings of disgust, embarrassment, or other negative emotions that society expects a person to feel and are taught both consciously and subconsciously to individuals from a very young age. As a result, even the most staunchly independent person will acquiesce to the norms of society when in public. For example, nudism is highly frowned upon in many cultures, and those with such predilections will feel a sense of shame for desiring to perform actions that society views as distasteful. It is for this reason that nudists and others with similar tendencies will often form their own enclaves or colonies away from mainstream society. Here we can find a clear example of how societies shape individual opinion and how determined individuals associate with groups to define themselves in spite of it.

Another important instance of the effects of social influences on a person's identity can be seen in childhood development. Parents are constantly concerned about the negative impacts of celebrity role models in the media. There is the notion of "monkey see, monkey do", meaning that children will often imitate the actions and fashion styles of their idols and this is quite true in many cases. However, it is questionable as to whether they imitate these styles out of a sense of social pressure or because of genuine interest.

In conclusion, I feel that one's identity owes itself to both the rumination upon the decisions one has made in one's life, as well as the influence of social groups with which one identifies. Regardless of how independent a person may be, humans do not develop in a vacuum and there is bound to be something that they take away from their social groups.

27. **College students should be encouraged to pursue subjects that interest them rather than the courses that seem most likely to lead to jobs. (Describe advantageous and disadvantageous circumstances of the recommendation)**

Is it better to be rich, or to be happy? Many would answer "to be rich." After all, the major one chooses in university ultimately determines the career opportunities available once a person graduates. However, if one were to ask my opinion on the matter, I would say that college students should be guided towards fields that interest them over ones that may lead to jobs. Doing so will not only increase the chances of the students being satisfied with their lives in the future, but also prevent oversaturated job markets and inflated tuition costs.

One of the biggest issues that plague many developed countries around the world is a trend of low job satisfaction. One would think that higher education rates would lead to better employment opportunities, higher salaries, and thus greater happiness overall, but it seems that the opposite is the case. According to job surveys in the USA over the past few years, around 40% of workers are unhappy with their jobs. Now, it could be argued that this has more to do with stagnating wages and other economic factors. However, this is all the more reason for college students to choose a field they enjoy, for even if a job is guaranteed, it does not mean that the salary will be great or that conditions at that job will remain constant. At least, if students are fulfilled in their positions, they will be able to weather hard economic conditions with less stress than an overworked office drone.

Even if students will be guaranteed high-paying positions at good companies if they are encouraged towards such majors, the problem of over-saturation in the job market needs to be considered. Anyone with even the most perfunctory knowledge of economics understands the law of supply and demand, which means that if the number of available employees in a field increases, the value of their labor will decrease. As a result, if colleges encourage students to pursue degrees only in fields that promise good positions and salaries, those fields will quickly become flooded with workers, leading to a steep decline in salaries as employees are forced to underbid one another for jobs. If, on the other hand, students are allowed to choose whatever fields that interest them, there will be a more balanced distribution of employees entering various sectors of the job market, thus reducing the chances of employment market bubbles.

Similarly, problems such as spike in tuition costs may arise when too many students enter some majors in a university or college. It is an all too familiar issue for those who have entered higher education institutions in the past ten years that the cost of classes has increased significantly, especially for fields which promise high salaries, such as engineering, finance, and so on. This has largely been the result of the very argument being opposed in this piece – universities should encourage students to study majors that promise good jobs after graduation. If there were less persuasion on the part of colleges to get students to pursue such fields, educational institutions would not be able to charge such a high premium for classes that are in high demand, simply because that demand would not be so extreme. This would put far less financial pressure on students, which is a leading cause of college drop-out rates, leading to higher graduation rates and less student debt.

One circumstance in which adopting the recommendation would not be advantageous has to do with the likelihood that college students have no idea of their interest or that their interest may change. This has become more common nowadays, as students are presented with a vast array of potential majors, many of which have no clearly specified career avenues. Thus, many new college students end up picking majors that sound interesting or align with a particular interest but lack any practical job applications. Some universities even allow students to declare their major as "undecided" and take a variety of unrelated courses in order to spark some notion of the direction in their future career path. Yet, as irresponsible as this may seem, it is nonetheless the right of the students to choose as they wish. In fact, it can even be beneficial to students later on to allow them to explore various academic avenues. The co-founder of Apple,

Steve Jobs, did this himself, and the inspiration he gained from the eclectic mix of classes he sat in on led to his creation of what is arguably the most famous computer of all time.

In sum, I believe that students must be free to follow their own passion when choosing their major. Encouraging them to choose a field that may guarantee employment, while seemingly well-meaning, is ultimately harmful not only to the students themselves, but to the economy as a whole.

28. **Claim: When planning courses, educators should take into account the interests and suggestions of their students.**
    Reason: Students are more motivated to learn when they are interested in what they are studying. (Claim-Reason)

The speaker claims that teachers should consider the interests and advice of their students when developing their curriculum. The claim is strongly supported by the argument that students are more motivated to learn when they demonstrate interest in the subject they are learning.

Concerning the interests of the students, it is obvious to anyone that has ever gone to school, i.e. the majority of the developed world, that attending a class that one finds boring offers little potential in the way of actual learning. Students that are bored in class will find themselves drifting off to sleep, doodling on their notepads, or becoming otherwise distracted with unproductive activities. In the case of younger students, they cannot be faulted for this, as they already are prone to short attention spans. As for older students, they should not be subjected to this because they are often paying for their education, making it a service which should be tailored to their wants and needs as customers. Thus, teachers that try to make their material more interesting will better guarantee that their students are paying attention and getting their money's worth out of the service they are paying for.

Another way in which this reason supports the claim involves the idea that whether a certain subject, such as math, history, or some other subject, is interesting is based upon the overall perception held by the majority of students. For example, in many western nations, such as the USA and Canada, math is culturally viewed as a difficult and boring subject. As a result, students go into class with a preconceived notion that the material will be hard to learn and wholly unfun. However, in East Asian countries, such as China and Japan, there is less of a stigma associated with math, thanks largely in part to teachers learning how to effectively teach their students. This may be attributed to differing work ethics, but at the very least, teachers of math in these countries do not encourage their students' dislike of the course material, whereas in the West many will say "OK, I know this is boring, but you have to learn it," a practice that poisons the well, so to speak.

Lastly, in regard to lesson planning, it is always a good thing when teachers involve their students in the development process, particularly when the latter's interests and suggestions are incorporated. The traditional method of having the teacher act as an unapproachable bastion of knowledge, one who tells students what is right and wrong and cannot be questioned, is not conducive to learning in a modern world where facts can be accessed instantly on a smartphone. Rather, allowing the students to feel that they have some control over their learning can be very empowering, and can lead to a greater interest in the subject matter, or a development of certainty in what their interests are at the very least. This is a concern that is growing ever more important in modern society, where facts are not as important as competence, which derives from true interest in one's field of study. Therefore, the provided reason is valid because a teacher who allows students to participate, or even to a minor extent, includes their interests and advice in the creation of lessons is contributing to individuals that can think for themselves and make better decisions regarding their future education.

In conclusion, the reason given fully supports the claim being made. To be specific, teachers who listen to the advice of their students and take into account their interests when developing their teaching material are more likely to have students that remain engaged during class and develop lasting interest in otherwise boring subjects. All this is more likely to create students that thirst for learning and are better able to focus on the fields in which they can excel.

29. **The greatness of individuals can be decided only by those who live after them, not by their contemporaries. (Discuss how the statement could or could not be true)**

Vyacheslav Molotov, an unheralded and obscure foreign minister for the USSR during Stalin's reign, does not even enter the greatness arena. Stalin is the one whose name remains famous in the history book; yet, just after the Nazis breached their non-aggression pact, invading Soviet borders with over three million troops, it was Molotov who stepped in for the missing Stalin to bolster morale and raise a call to arms for the Soviet people. Stalin may be the one people of forthcoming generations recollect, but on that summer day it was Molotov that was the herald of hope. Greatness cannot always be determined more objectively in a future where the ability to remember is limited and warped by time.

Obscure but significant events surface daily, forcing people to choose, and with the power to choose comes the power to be great. Dick Hoyt was an average father and a hard worker; he had a loving family, "beer gut" and all. When his son Rick was born with the umbilical wrapped around his neck he was devastated. His son was left with severe brain damage and the inability to communicate. Dick and his family were told there was nothing going on in his son's brain and encouraged to put Rick in an institution. Dick and his wife did not believe the experts. Eventually, they were able to get Rick a computer he could control by moving his head. At this point the world burst open for Rick, and he was even able to go to school. A charity run was being held for a classmate and Rick told his father that he wanted to help. Instead of taking Rick to cheer on the sidelines his father trained and was able to push Rick for the entire run. Rick loved the movement, freedom, and the feeling of not being disabled anymore. Since then Dick and Rick have finished 85 marathons, Dick running, and Rick feeling the wind in his hair. One hundred years from now nations may never read Dick's words or see his silhouette in their history books, but Dick made a choice, and that choice qualifies him for greatness.

The goggles of time, though replete with insight, often obscure the true nature of those being lauded for their greatness. John F. Kennedy is characterized in an almost saint like fashion. To the hyperopic eye he was young, beautiful, had decent international politics and was able to bring a country together in his martyrdom; however, on closer inspection his imprudence comes raging forth. He won elections by bribing the mob, he was consistently found cheating on his wife, among other indiscretions, and his leadership in the Bay of Pigs invasion was disastrous. While he should not be expelled from the halls of prominence, the passage of time has not added to the objectivity in regard to his eminence; if anything, it has masked his true nature in lieu of an iconic one.

The one truly objective thing which future generations can provide is the ramifications which time has had on the ideals and thoughts of those being judged. President Roosevelt's "New Deal" was popular among the electorate of the time but was not the long-term economic fix that it was touted to be. Likewise, the longevity and value of works of art or scholarship changes over time and can grow into a classic or clandestinely find its way into oblivion. Monet, Van Gogh, and Seurat have withstood the test of time and their greatness solidified by its purging fires while most of their contemporaries remain nameless.

Given the above analysis, it is clear why greatness of individuals is not determined only by future generations. While those who live after them can be objective about the repercussions of time on the ideals and thoughts of those being rated, the posterity tends to be forgetful and misled by misrepresentations. Hence, the search for this greatness should never cease until we have a more accurate picture of greatness of the individuals that we lionize.

30. Students should always question what they are taught instead of accepting it passively. (Discuss how the statement could or could not be true)

When students are learning, it is easy to think that having the students absorb the knowledge presented by the teacher should be the status quo, and this currently happens to be the case – for the most part. However, there is some benefit to encouraging the questioning of ideas that are not logically consistent. The key to this dynamic is, in my opinion, a balance between the two.

On the one hand, if students are never taught to question the information they receive from authority figures, even if that information is wrong or immoral, there is a much greater likelihood that negative consequences may result. For example, children who live in societies that emphasize extremism do not generally receive any sort of education about questioning information from leaders, and thus fall prey to indoctrination into terrorist cells. For a more specific example, look at areas of the Middle East, where there have been numerous extremist coups or civil wars, with jihad named as a reason for many of them. If the people in those parts had been educated on questioning morally or logically reprehensible ideas while those ideas were still in their infancy, who knows how much blood would have been spared!

On the other hand, in a classroom environment, there must be a certain flow to the lesson, guided by the teacher, with the intention of meeting certain educational goals. It is, therefore, somewhat unproductive for students to constantly question every statement made by the teacher, as it cuts time away from the activities that the teacher planned. Thus, it should be remembered that when students are taught to question ideas or information they receive, instruction regarding the appropriate time to ask questions is also important in order to avoid wasting time. Additionally, the teacher may plan some time during or after each activity to allow for questions, so that each lesson is not unnecessarily interrupted.

The benefits of a balance between accepting and questioning what instructors teach are evident in that when teachers promote the information that they give students, they gain the ability to use it as a gauge for student comprehension. For example, the teacher can purposefully insert some mistakes into something they are reviewing with their students and then wait to see if any of them notices it and points it out. Or similarly, they can play the devil's advocate during a classroom discussion to see if any students will agree or disagree. In this way, the questioning of the teacher serves a specific classroom function, and students are taught to raise contentions intelligently and effectively.

In summary, it is important to manage a balance between students' productive questioning of teachers during class and rampant, non-stop interrogation. It can thus be concluded that teachers should educate their pupils on the importance of questioning what they are taught and of understanding that during class questioning should be polite and proper in order to facilitate the learning process.

31. The increasingly rapid pace of life today causes more problems than it solves. (Discuss how the statement could or could not be true)

While it is true that contemporary life runs at a much faster pace than before, I disagree with the statement's inference that the haste with which life moves creates more problems than it solves. Human life has benefited dramatically from the rapid rate of development that has occurred in the past two centuries. Just look at the decline of disease world-wide, and the vast numbers of people that have been brought out of poverty.

In the digital age of today, with daily life moving at such blinding speed, the medical industry has been able to make great strides to benefit mankind. New diseases are researched by hundreds of scientists in several countries at once who can communicate instantaneously thanks to the Internet. As a result, new medicines are developed within months or even a year or two, rather than decades. For example, most recently the COVID-19 pandemic has ravaged the world's population. However, less than a year after its discovery, the scientific community has already developed four vaccines to combat the virus. This is an unprecedented rate of research, overshadowing the speed at which medical professionals of the past could ever hope to accomplish the same amount of work. Were it not for the advanced technologies at researchers' disposal and the rapid speed at which information is gathered, processed, and transferred, this virus would likely plague humanity for many years to come.

It is also important to consider the implications of society's obsession with speed in the context of national development. Nowadays, the Internet has allowed for such a rapid diffusion of knowledge that people from even the poorest areas of the globe not only have access to previously inaccessible information, but can cross the line from poverty to being wealthy within a single generation! In the past, it took at least two to three generations for a family to cross social or economic boundaries due to the cost of education and the deeply ingrained notions of caste or level in society. But now, most societies are more meritocratic than in the past, valuing the contributions individuals can make to the world rather than the station of their birth. Those armed with a smart device, an internet connection, and a dream are now exponentially more capable of starting a business, or self-educating themselves in a scientific field than their forefathers. The blinding speed at which nations such as China and India have become economic powerhouses is a testament to this, with many of the wealthiest families having been poor farmers only fifty years before. The incredible speed at which modern life moves has even enabled great enterprises to be created that benefit millions of lives.

Of course, this does not mean that there are no serious issues with living in today's fast-paced society. One of them is the stress from always having to work, combined with a growing sentiment that one's job makes no real difference in the world around them, or worse, that it harms the world around them. Such stress can lead to depression, anxiety, and combined with other forms of civil unrest, can lead to widespread social or political tensions, as have been seen in the USA and parts of Europe recently. However, none of these negate the positive changes that have occurred due to the current speed at which life goes; we are far better off than we would be if the current medical, civil, and scientific infrastructure that has been put in place did not exist.

To summarize, I do not agree with the statement that the rapid pace of modern life causes more problems than it solves. As facets of society speed up, developments such as those in the medical or industrial fields, arise and alleviate various stressors in our lives. We may not notice how far we have come, since the developments have all but erased the evidence of a more primitive way of life; what minor inconveniences that we may experience as a result of the speed of modern life are almost inconsequential when pitted against the benefits such a rate can bring.

32. Claim: It is no longer possible for a society to regard any living man or woman as a hero.

Reason: The reputation of anyone who is subjected to media scrutiny will eventually be diminished. (Claim-Reason)

I do not agree with the notion that it is not possible for society to regard any living person as a hero anymore based solely on the reasoning that media scrutiny will eventually eat away at the person's reputation. Not only are there a number of examples of famous individuals with a clean record, but also the public is not unanimous in its opinion of media reporting about beloved heroes; even respected people that do get dragged through the mud are still able to make a comeback.

Warren Buffett is a good example of someone who is successful and philanthropic; although the media has spent years covering his life, his company, and his charitable works, he has stayed clean. In fact, it is largely the media coverage itself that led to Warren Buffett being idolized. The publication of his life and achievements was and still is a great motivator for young investors and entrepreneurs. Another celebrity that has avoided scandal is the actor George Clooney. He has been hounded by paparazzi for years, yet he maintains a stellar image. Having no relationship scandals, drunken rants, or other Hollywood drama, Clooney keeps mostly to himself and his family. Malala Yousafzai, the young girl who won a Nobel Peace Prize for her activism in the areas of female education and human rights, has upheld a similarly untarnished reputation despite concentrated coverage and is a role model for young people around the world. Some celebrities have made fools of themselves in the news, but there are still plenty of talented people worthy of being role models.

Also, this claim forgets the resilience of people's opinions. If a public figure is panned or heavily criticized by the media for something they have done, there remains the chance that most people will simply look past it or forgive it, depending on its severity and the following actions of the person. Take American actor Robert Downey Jr. for example. He burned many bridges in the film industry, alienated many fans, and nearly killed his career thanks to his drug addiction. After a stint in rehab and coming to terms with the possibility of never appearing in a film again, Downey Jr. cleaned up and regained his place in audience's hearts, such that he is now one of the highest paid actors in Hollywood. In the case of other famous stars, numerous rappers have been accused and convicted of crimes and their fans cheer for them in spite of that fact. Therefore, I do not think people will stop considering their heroes as such for anything but the most heinous revelations about their character or behavior.

This is not to say that no person considered to be a hero for people has never been torn asunder in the eyes of their followers by the media. Look at American comedian Bill Cosby. He was once considered to be "America's Dad" for his performance on the acclaimed sitcom *The Cosby Show*, where he as the titular character managed a raucous family to humorous and dramatic effect. Unfortunately, after a number of allegations and court hearings Bill Cosby was found guilty of sexual assault against a number of women over the years, and the backlash against Cosby has forever marred his legacy. Now when people look back on his shows, they see a monster parading as a man; he is no longer an icon to be looked up to. But this is luckily an isolated incident, not a common occurrence among those in the spotlight. There remain a large majority of role models with nigh-pristine records, and thus it would be improper to assume that such is the norm and that there are no heroes anymore.

In conclusion, I do not agree with the statement that media scrutiny reveals the faults of all famous people, and that there are no heroes anymore as a result. There are still numerous examples of famous people who are not morally or otherwise corrupt and there are those that have recovered. Even if some are abhorrent, this is not evidence of an all-encompassing trend.

33. Competition for high grades seriously limits the quality of learning at all levels of education. (Discuss how the statement could or could not be true)

As the number of students entering the education system has increased exponentially since the turn of the century, and continues to rise at a staggering rate, the value of competition for high marks has diminished significantly. Where once the desire to be head of the class was both a productive and obtainable goal, the sheer number of students in any given class, combined with the standardization of course materials, eliminates any meaningful differences between students that strive to achieve. Additionally, the labor market needs that the grade-based system was designed to meet no longer exist. Therefore, while there was once some semblance of an argument for having students compete against one another for high grades, I find myself agreeing with the statement that such a system serves only to inhibit true learning – regardless of the level of schooling.

If one is to walk into the classroom of any developed nation at the moment, one of the first things that becomes apparent is the number of students in the classroom. In most European and American schools, the average class size is about thirty students, whereas in parts of East Asia, class sizes reach upwards of seventy students per class. Take into account the total number of students in a single school and then extrapolate for all the students in the county, province and nation, and it becomes obvious that the academic performance of a single student, or even a group of students is not very impressive. This becomes clearer still considering the increasingly test-based education system, where a standard curriculum must be taught in preparation for level-determining exams. Since a human being can only effectively study a limited amount of material each day, whenever one finds a group of high-performing students in a single class, the notion of competing for the highest grade is more counterproductive than not, as the minute differences in scores do not accurately represent differences in the retained knowledge between students. Indeed, the students become so focused on getting the top score that they forget the reason why they need to learn the class material in the first place.

This brings us to the next point, that the purpose of the education system as it currently exists is not conducive to real education. Schools are in the form that we generally think of, classrooms have rows of seats, and ringing bells signal beginning and ending of class time and lunch time. All of this was designed during the Industrial Revolution to create a society that provided a minimum level of education that would prepare people for work in factories. One sees the parallels in the orderliness, the scheduling, and even the authoritarian hierarchy of teacher and student, quite different from the equally rigid but far more intimate and personal apprentice system of the pre-industrial eras. Simply put, technology and society have developed past the necessity of the current school system design. Competing for grades is analogous to the factory line in that it trains students to compete to see who can perform the most menial tasks in the most efficient way possible. It does not encourage critical thinking; it rewards only those that can exactly meet the criteria on the curriculum, nothing more and nothing less. Thus, when students from this system enter the modern workforce, they are ill-equipped to meet the needs of a tech-based society that requires innovators.

One way in which the statement might not be valid has to do with the fact that grades are one way to measure students' performance. Whenever it comes time to evaluate the progress of students' learning, the most efficient way that has been developed thus far has been the grading systems which are currently in place. The competition for higher grades is, therefore, a competition to see who has had the best performance overall, so how the performance is recorded matters little to the overall issue. Whether with grades, gold stars, or other awards, there will be some competition over who is best, if only because there are not enough spots at prestigious institutions to go around. Still, the competition over a letter grade or score distracts the purpose of learning away from its ultimate goal: to improve the skill being learned, not the score itself. Thus, a focus on grades and scores can still be harmful to a student's progress.

All in all, competing for high grades is a method of preparing students for a life in the factory, not for a life of learning and development. It may have been effective in its time and may even aid some people in getting some education, but it does not contribute to knowledge and skills required in contemporary society, and the system is, therefore, obsolete.

34. Universities should require every student to take a variety of courses outside the student's field of study. (Describe advantageous and disadvantageous circumstances of the recommendation)

As romantic as the notion of pursuing higher education for education's sake may be, the hard truth of the modern job market is that a university education in a career-related major is a prerequisite for even entry-level jobs. Therefore, I disagree with the statement, because it is unjustifiable for universities to mandate that students must shoulder ever-increasing tuition costs to take a range of courses that do not directly relate to their major.

A common argument in favor of requiring students to take a wide variety of courses is that it creates "well-rounded" people. Not only is this redundant, as most universities are looking for "well-rounded" candidates from high school, but it is also extremely vague. Sure, someone entering the professional world should have a dynamic skillset so as to be adaptable to unexpected challenges that may arise. However, the very fact that such challenges are unexpected and thus unpredictable in nature means that one cannot fully prepare for them; then, why waste time learning about superfluous subjects when one could put more focus on the actual field of study? Furthermore, when students apply for jobs, most companies ask for a CV rather than a full résumé, because they are only interested in the skills that specifically apply to the job one is looking for. This is all a part of the specialization of jobs, a system that is designed to address any aforementioned problems by having people with skillsets that are specifically suited for such issues. Therefore, to reiterate, the "well-rounded" argument is a moot point.

On a more practical note, consider the fact that over the past thirty years or so, tuition prices at universities have skyrocketed by over a thousand percent, whereas median incomes have almost stagnated. Add this to the extremely competitive job market as well as the immense time constraints that most high school graduates have to choose their life paths, and one comes to understand that going to university is a substantial investment. As with any investment, a cost-benefit analysis must be conducted, and in the context that has already been established, there simply is no tangible benefit of paying for classes that fall outside the curriculum of one's major. The best example would be from people in STEM fields. Students in these majors are already overburdened with a staggering amount of work for their required classes, which cost more than usual due to the price of each credit and the expensive textbooks that they require; therefore, it is ludicrous to demand that they pay more money for and spend more time on irrelevant courses. This gets worse when one considers that these frivolous classes can keep an otherwise stellar student from graduating if they do not pass them. Thus, not only do mandated courses that fall outside one's major hurt the student, but they also have the potential to hurt a nation's economy as a whole, since they may limit the number of qualified candidates who can enter the job market based on performance in classes that have no relation to the job.

Adopting the recommendation would be beneficial when students need to switch to jobs that relate to courses that fall outside their major. This is an important consideration, as it is quite common for students to pursue careers which do not relate to their major of study. For instance, taking at least a basic course in business management would be beneficial to students of any major, since entrepreneurship is not unique to any field. If students, at any point in their career, wished to start their own company, having at least an introductory level of knowledge of the process of opening a business would significantly aid in their success. Furthermore, several courses are tragically underemphasized, such as computer literacy, but are essential to functioning in any profession. The number of students who enter the workforce without an understanding of how to use spreadsheets or other basic office software is staggering, a situation that is ultimately detrimental to them in the long run. However, the benefit of such classes is not a suitable justification for mandating a series of filler courses to students seeking to study advanced majors, and therefore the recommendation remains ill-advised.

In conclusion, I cannot agree with the statement that universities should require students to take classes other than those required by their field of study. Such classes are a great waste of time and money, do not contribute to their ability to perform their job in any measurable way, and in fact damage their ability to enter their chosen careers.

35. **Educators should find out what students want included in the curriculum and then offer it to them. (Describe advantageous and disadvantageous circumstances of the recommendation)**

No one can argue that balancing student interest and required teaching material is an easy job. While it is tempting for a teacher to want to always ensure that students are engaged in the lesson, I would be wary of putting too much stock in the actual desires of students when it comes to designing a curriculum. On the one hand, not all students may agree on what they want to learn, or even understand what they need to learn, depending on their level of education. On the other hand, students entering university are paying for a service and thus are entitled to all the rights over their product like any customer.

One of the biggest problems with modern schooling is the class size and time constraints. A standard class size in most high schools and middle schools is around thirty students per class, and each teacher may have five separate classes to teach. That means each teacher can have at least three-hundred students each semester! Imagine trying to figure out what each individual student wants to learn in each of those five classes and then having to develop a separate curriculum for each class. Sure, the teacher could theoretically simplify it, and have a survey that allows students to choose from a list of topics to include in the curriculum, but that means a portion of students are going to have to learn things that they are not interested in, dooming them to a school year in which they will be bored and therefore more likely to perform poorly on assignments and exams. Even if student opinion is fairly uniform, there is still the issue that students do not exactly know what they need to be learning, that is, why they are in school in the first place. Thus, the unjust workload and unreliable metric of student opinion constitute a damning argument against allowing student input in curriculum development.

Once one reaches college or university, however, the previous argument no longer applies. Students in university are akin to clients. Sure, they go to class and do homework, but they are, for all intents and purposes, paying for a service. It is also important to note that the age at which most students enter college is the same at which they become legal adults. This incurs a certain level of responsibility on top of the rights afforded to customers that makes it reasonable to offer a choice regarding their curriculum material. Just as a person may ask that a craftsman add certain features to a commissioned piece of work, so a university student may have a particular educational goal in mind. Since the tuition at most major universities can cost savings of an entire life, there is an obligation on the part of the institution to consider their students' demands.

To summarize, I agree with the statement as it applies to universities due to the transactional nature of the school-student relationship in this case. However, when it comes to levels of schooling such as primary school, middle school, and to a certain extent, high school, I do not think that class sizes allow for student input, nor are students developmentally capable of making educational choices.

36. Educators should teach facts only after their students have studied the ideas, trends, and concepts that help explain those facts. (Describe advantageous and disadvantageous circumstances of the recommendation)

A widely accepted notion among experts that study education is the importance of memorization to the learning process. Yet, in the endeavor to teach in the most effective manner there has been some debate over whether the acquisition of facts should precede or follow a student's mastery of conceptual knowledge and critical thinking skills; it may be argued that the two are corequisites for effective learning.

Having a natural proclivity for remembering pieces of information is a neat skill that can be used to entertain classmates but is not necessarily evidence of true understanding of the core concepts. After all, not every person who is gifted with rapid mental arithmetic becomes a famous mathematician by virtue of that ability alone. This is due to the fact that mathematics, or any scholastic field for that matter, requires an in-depth understanding of a variety of complex concepts and theories rather than simple rote memorization of multiplication tables. In this vein, when it comes to taking tests, those students who use their ability to quickly memorize bits of information are unable to effectively apply them to questions that are not imitative of the recalled information, nor can such students solve problems in a creative capacity. Therefore, it could be argued that students who rely on memorizing facts alone are hardly educated at all.

Nonetheless, a significant issue with receiving a true education is that concepts, theories, and trends are difficult to teach straight from the outset. When young children begin their education, their learning abilities are far more attuned to memorizing the date that Christopher Columbus arrived in the Americas than grasping the consequences of European expansion for indigenous tribes. It takes an accumulation of pure facts, which can then be pieced together to form a more cohesive whole, before an understanding of complex theories and relationships can occur in a student's mind. This is analogous to a person's ability to fully comprehend a Rembrandt painting's beauty, which can only take place after the person learns the meaning of terms such as "chiaroscuro" and the baroque movement.

Perhaps the most important job of teachers is to encourage their students to memorize and analyze facts throughout their continuing education. A child's biological advantage to memorizing slices of information is beneficial to acquiring foundational pieces of knowledge and is evident in the reliance on education by rote in the ancient world. However, the law of diminishing returns begins to take effect on using memorization as a crutch with more complex problems that require higher-order thinking skills. Augmenting memorization with analytical skills pays enormous dividends as a student progresses up the academic ladder.

Therefore, while there are some notable benefits to teaching through pure fact acquisition, it does not exist in a state of mutual exclusion with studying higher-order skills. A highly effective student will be able to incorporate large amounts of facts into their knowledge base as well as analyze the overall context and application of those facts within an academic setting.

37. **Claim: We can usually learn much more from people whose views we share than from those whose views contradict our own.**
Reason: Disagreement can cause stress and inhibit learning. (Claim-Reason)

While disagreement certainly can cause stress and inhibit learning, it is not the case that we usually learn much more from people whose views we share. This reasoning, suggesting that interacting with people who have differing views from our own will always cause stress and disagreement, asserts several implied truths that are not necessarily factual.

First, let us establish the obstacles that prevent people from learning. The reason identifies disagreement as a possible inhibitor to the learning process. "Disagreement" in this context is a loosely defined term that could be interpreted several ways. Certainly, if disagreement is permitted to become contentious, angry, or malicious, then it certainly will prevent learning. In general terms, learning will be inhibited any time an individual permits strong negative emotion to cloud his or her thoughts. Consider a typical interaction between sports fans of opposing teams. Each fan, being loyal to his or her team, will not be inclined to change positions to match the view of the opposing fan. Additionally, because sporting events are naturally competitive, arguments and contentions are usually near the surface, so it is easy to imagine two individuals becoming angry or even malicious in a debate of which team is superior. Disagreement, if allowed to reach the point of malice, contention, or anger, will create strong emotions in both parties involved that prevent clear, rational thought or learning.

Before we move on to other obstacles that keep people from learning, it should be noted that healthy disagreement, in which individuals act with respect and tolerance, can be extremely beneficial to learning. In the seventeenth century, Czar Peter I of Russia recognized that his nation trailed significantly behind his European neighbors in the arts and sciences. Peter himself took a tour of Europe, meeting with kings and government leaders in several different countries. Certainly, these people were nothing like Peter, but he visited them with the intent to learn from them how to govern his own country more effectively. Because he approached their differences without competitive or malicious attitudes, he learned from them and changed his nation to be more modern and effective.

Another significant obstacle to learning can easily occur when individuals think too much alike. This obstacle is complacency in thought and feeling, a phenomenon that occurs when someone decides that they are "good enough." Without differing ideas and opinions to challenge what an individual considers to be "right" or "good," it is easy for that individual to believe that his or her personal perspective is correct without question. The individual's learning and thoughts then become stagnant, and no progress is made. This effect can sometimes be seen in large corporations that attain some high level of success. The individuals charged with leading the organization, seeing the great success of the corporation, may begin to believe that everything in the corporation is perfect. They will gradually stop challenging the status quo and allow policies and procedures to go unchanged. The corporate leaders' aversion to change will ultimately handicap their potential to learn and take their company further. The negative emotion of complacency can be just as inhibitive to learning as anger or contention.

The types of emotion that can adversely affect learning potential are numerous. One is the anger that can arise from disagreement. Another is the complacency that can arise from similar views. While the second part of the reasoning, that disagreement can indeed lead to stress and inhibit learning, is true, this does not necessarily imply that we should surround ourselves with like-minded people if we intend to learn. Each individual must gauge, for himself or herself, which emotions that inhibit learning he or she is susceptible to in a given situation. Having determined that, the individual can make the best decisions to maximize personal learning.

38. Government officials should rely on their own judgment rather than unquestioningly carry out the will of the people they serve. (Describe advantageous and disadvantageous circumstances of the recommendation)

The role of government workers as public officials is fraught with difficult decisions. Should they execute their duty according to their own interpretation of the law, or should they follow the commands of public opinion? If one were to ask my opinion, I would have to say that government officials should use their own discretion rather than march in lockstep to the drumbeat of the common people.

Across the span of human history, one of the most vivid lessons is that people in groups commit some of the most horrific crimes against their fellow men, with unquestioning officials acting as the instrument of such abuses. A most visceral example can be witnessed during the French Revolution when Maximilien Robespierre was in power. It was during this period that thousands of people were officially sentenced to death by guillotine at the demands of the revolutionary masses who opposed the privileged classes. Dissent by public officials was nearly nonexistent throughout this morbid affair, as any opposition was seen as an attack on the government founded on the general good. With men of conscience in such short supply in positions of power, the Reign of Terror, as it became known, stained the streets of Paris red.

For a less macabre example of the specious nature of public influence on politics, one must fast forward to the present-day USA. Here one sees a polarized society, where the parties in power cater to the demands of their voter base, for better or for worse. On the conservative front, blue collar workers and WASPs from America's heartland cry out for deportations of illegal immigrants, and President Trump, who rose to power by riding a wave of populism pushed forth by these people, happily obliges. Officers of U.S. Immigration and Customs Enforcement separate and detain immigrant children, many of whom have been kept in camps while their parents are processed and sent back to their home countries without them. Even those in office that know such actions are immoral stand idly by while families are torn apart in the land of the free.

There are certainly situations in which the proper course for civil servants is to put aside their own opinions and bend to the will of the public at large. If we put contemporary America in the spotlight once more, the area of police brutality is a prime example of when those in office should lend an ear to their constituents. Too often occurs blue fraternity, the colloquial term for the protectionism practiced by officers in cases where unjustified use of force is suspected, used to allow aggressive officers to escape punishment. The uncomfortably high numbers of videos released online of young men of color being shot by police with itchy trigger fingers, followed by a lukewarm internal investigation that results in mere wrist-slapping, more than earn the public outcry that has come as response. As the demands of the public in this regard are ignored, society splits in twain even more than before, and public trust in government evaporates. Yet even this is not itself justification for mob rule. Public officials must engage in reasonable analysis on a case-by-case basis, lest the rule of law be undermined completely.

In conclusion, officials in government must tend to their duties first according to their own judgement and then according to the demands of the public. Otherwise, government descends into little more than mob rule, and anybody who disagrees may be at the mercy of unrestrained retribution.

39. Young people should be encouraged to pursue long-term, realistic goals rather than seek immediate fame and recognition. (Describe advantageous and disadvantageous circumstances of the recommendation)

People today live in an insanely fast-paced world. The rapid consumption of media, fueled by globalization and the internet, has bombarded the youth of all nations with countless celebrities, all of whom rise and fall with apparent ease. As a result, young people develop a desire to follow in these celebrities' footsteps and make a name for themselves as soon as possible. However, I see danger in this way of thinking, which is why I strongly agree with the statement that young people should instead be encouraged to pursue long-term goals over short-term fame.

A perfect example of the dangers of this attention-seeking behavior can be seen in the rise and fall of various online vloggers, most notably those on the popular website YouTube. It is here that many young people have found fame, even fortune to some extent, by posting their content on the site. A particularly pernicious genre of these videos is prank videos. In such videos various acts, ranging from harmless gags to actions that could be considered assault or harassment were performed for the amusement of viewers. The popularity of these videos and the potential for internet stardom led many young imitators to attempt their own prank videos, with ever more daring pranks. Numerous young people ended up being arrested or prosecuted with criminal charges after acts of vandalism or disturbing the peace occurred. Had these youths been directed to more productive enterprises, they would have avoided receiving permanent criminal marks on their records.

An even more convincing argument for impressing the need for long-term goals on young people exists in the inner-city areas of the USA. Here, some young people are entranced with visions of getting rich and infamous quick by becoming notable rappers, gang members, drug dealers, or some combination of the three. Because of this, these communities have consistently ranked among the poorest and most crime-ridden areas of the country. Notable civil rights activist Malcom X even addressed this issue, stating that young men and women in the areas should educate themselves and invest in their communities if they were ever to truly lift themselves out of poverty.

Yet for young people today, it is understandable to seek only short-term fame. After all, the social and economic stratum of most developed countries has solidified, and the unpredictable shifts in the political and economic climates have left little room for any long-term plan to remain viable for more than a few years. All is not lost, however, at least for those enterprising enough to remain constantly adaptable. Numerous new successful startups, especially in the tech sector, are evidence of the merit of goal setting, and the relatively young age of many of these entrepreneurs shows that such goals are achievable. Thus, if people stick to their passions throughout their teens and into their young adult life, there is still a good chance that they too can become the next Mark Zuckerberg or Elon Musk.

To conclude, it would be irresponsible to suggest to young people that seeking immediate fame and recognition is a superior alternative to long-term planning. Unless they plan to die young, they will have to keep on living, and despite the cycle of upheavals that have wracked the world of late, there is still much room for the well-motivated among the planet's youth to create a lasting legacy for themselves.

40. The best way to teach is to praise positive actions and ignore negative ones. (Describe advantageous and disadvantageous circumstances of the recommendation)

Teaching is often underappreciated despite the amount of thought required to impart lessons effectively to pupils. To teach most effectively, it is suggested by the given statement that positive actions be met with praise, and negative actions intentionally overlooked. I can agree with the former half of the statement, but not the latter.

From a psychological perspective, it is important to remember that all humans actively seek validation. This is especially true among children, who vie for the attention of their parents, authority figures, and idols. Compliments, words of praise, and other forms of positive encouragement have profound effects on students, and there is a noticeable difference when such reinforcement is absent. Students that receive no recognition for their accomplishments often lose the will to develop their abilities any further unless they are already highly intrinsically motivated. Since it would be unfair to expect every student to be inherently self-motivated, praise for positive behavior is advisable.

As for ignoring negative behaviors, it is difficult to see how a reasonable argument could be made in favor of this action. Take bullying for example. Children that cause physical or emotional harm to their peers rarely stop on their own, and such actions greatly hinder other students' ability to complete assignments or focus in class. Even if bullies get tired of tormenting one child, they will often simply seek out another victim, so ignoring them is ineffective. It is only through the intervention of teachers and administrators that such negative behaviors can be prevented or rectified so that learning can occur unhindered.

One may argue that not all negative actions in a learning environment are as serious as bullying and thus do not warrant attention from educators. Passing notes in class, for example, has existed since classrooms existed, much to the ire of instructors. Full supporters of the statement may assert that while sending a clandestine message to a friend or crush may be distracting, it is ultimately benign in the grand scheme of things and will not significantly affect a student's academic performance. Yet there is a fatal flaw with this argument in that the classroom dynamic is made up of a chain of interacting rules and systems, i.e. the teacher as an imparter of knowledge and the student as a receiver. Any actions that interrupt this process erode the links in the chain, and from there it is a slippery slope. A line must be drawn, and by that it is meant that any negative actions should be addressed rather than intentionally overlooked.

In sum, while I agree with praising students for their positive actions, I do not agree that negative behaviors should be ignored. Commendations act as further motivation, especially for younger students, while apathy towards negative actions simply acts as silent assent to such behaviors.

41. If a goal is worthy, then any means taken to attain it are justifiable. (Discuss how the statement could or could not be true)

Are any means taken to achieve a worthy goal defensible? The speaker asserts that any actions are appropriate when done in pursuit of a worthy goal. I thoroughly disagree for two reasons. First, determination of whether a goal is "worthy" is subjective, so merely pointing to a specific goal as justification for one's harmful actions is not sufficient. Second, actions that harm other people cannot be condoned regardless of their purpose.

There are many examples in the twentieth century of individuals who set a certain goal, which they deemed to be "worthy", and caused a great amount of harm to others in the process of pursuing that goal. Perhaps the ultimate example of this behavior is Adolf Hitler. He had several goals, which he and his followers determined to be commendable, such as his leadership of a new empire and racial purity of the German population. He was willing to undertake any actions required in pursuit of these goals, including the invasion of other countries to extend his empire, and systematic killing of millions of people who—for various reasons—did not fit into Hitler's vision of a "pure race". Historians estimate that World War II caused 50 million to 70 million deaths. Additionally, cities were destroyed, families were torn apart, and livelihoods were lost. And yet Hitler deemed his goals to be worthy. Few people would support any claim that his actions were justifiable because they were in pursuit of a goal that he considered to be admirable.

A somewhat less controversial example of using any means required to accomplish a goal is that of Prime Minister Indira Gandhi's national beautification program in India in the 1970s. The Prime Minister ordered that the gigantic slums on the outskirts of cities such as Mumbai be entirely destroyed, in order to beautify the cities and drive the poverty-stricken masses away. She thought that this was a worthy goal; perhaps she anticipated that it would reduce crime rates as well as improve the appearance of the cities. However, this goal was attained with little thought of the implications, and many people were injured in the process. Many residents of the slums had paid corrupt city officials in order to construct a dwelling on that property. Yet, with no forewarning, bulldozers arrived and razed the hastily-constructed dwellings in the slums, destroying personal property and causing personal harm. Although less dramatic than the example of World War II, this also illustrates the idea that a goal that may be deemed "worthy" by some still does not validate actions that cause harm to others.

Even a goal that might be universally considered as "worthy" does not justify any means of accomplishing that goal. Consider the noble goal of supporting one's family and keeping them out of poverty. Even this goal does not merit actions that cause harm; a person who provides for a family by engaging in harmful but lucrative activities—such as drug-dealing or theft—is not justified in those actions. Clearly, there are other ways to support a family, although they may not be as financially rewarding. And such a person should not be exempt from legal punishment associated with those unlawful behaviors, even though the person is in pursuit of a noble goal.

In sum, it is wrong to claim that any actions performed in pursuit of a worthy goal are justified. Such a claim ignores the fact that the merit of goals is subjective; what is worthy to one person is not necessarily worthy to another. And any actions that cause harm to others or limit their choices should not be forgiven, regardless of their purpose.

42. **In order to become well-rounded individuals, all college students should be required to take courses in which they read poetry, novels, mythology, and other types of imaginative literature. (Describe advantageous and disadvantageous circumstances of the recommendation)**

From Greek mythology to the existential musings of Dostoevsky, imaginative literature has transformed the world and provided a vital outlet for fun, explanation, and external processing. Indeed, it is a nourishing and key aspect of modern life. Although imaginative literature is not necessary for college students who want to become well-rounded individuals, imagination is essential for them.

College students need imagination for survival, regardless of whether they try to grow in a more balanced way. Imagination is not a gift everyone is born with, but it is imperative to piecing together the world; the ability to imagine allows the mind to see images, hear sounds, touch surfaces and then combine all those senses into one memory or thought. Imagination is also the ability to think of something which is not there or not yet reality. Children are known for this type of imagination: having imaginary friends and making imaginary food. In adults, including college students, imagination often shifts to innovation. Sir Richard Branson is a well-known industrialist, i.e. a person with ambition, business sense and a vivid imagination. His projects include newspapers, record stores, airlines and most recently a spaceship where normal citizens can enter space. Branson's imagination and belief in ideas which no one else would have thought feasible has changed the entire world and the realms of possibility. College students who are imaginative may turn out to be as versatile as Branson.

However, college students do not need imaginative literature to help them become well-rounded individuals. Imaginative literature may enable them to nurture imagination and creativity, but they also have access to other avenues of developing imagination. It may be detrimental to require all college students to take courses in imaginative literature in order that they may balance their subjects. Some students do not want to be well-rounded for various reasons. Even if they hope to become well-rounded individuals, taking courses in imaginative literature may not be the ideal way, since such a requirement is costly and time-consuming, undermining their ability to take courses related to their major that promise plentiful jobs. Students may read poetry and novels that they relish by themselves, without incurring costs in time and money.

Another imaginative outlet that is separate from literature, but equally fulfilling, is art. By studying art, college students may acquire imagination and creativity. One new and progressive form of art today is called tagging or graffiti. It is a wonderful example of imaginative outlets because the world is the canvas. Artists paint on a gamut of surfaces and for innumerable reasons. One of the best-known artists is named Banksy and is believed to reside in England. Banksy remains anonymous and does not sell his work. His art has shown up in numerous places including Los Angeles and Palestine and is often connected with street music. This new and inclusive form of art shows the imaginative process outside the bounds of literature and even the bounds of language. It is clear that art such as graffiti affords college students another avenue of enhancing their imagination.

In summary, the ability to imagine is one of the built-in survival instincts in humankind. Outlets for imagination have shifted throughout the generations. In this time of wide-spread literacy the written word is not the only outlet. Thus, asking all college students to take courses in imaginative literature is not feasible in terms of time and cost.

43. **In order for any work of art — for example, a film, a novel, a poem, or a song — to have merit, it must be understandable to most people. (Discuss how the statement could or could not be true)**

Must any work of art be understandable to most people in order to have merit? The speaker claims that this is the case, but I heartily disagree, because this discounts the value of the creative process, the resonance that a work of art may have with a minority group, and the fact that comprehension of art is often contextual.

The statement that the merit of a work of art depends on whether it is accessible to the majority ignores the worth of the creative process. Most artists are choosing to produce art because they have a strong desire to experience the creative process repeatedly and generate a unique, original product. Although some artists gain fame and fortune as a result of their work, the vast majority do not. And yet, they continue to create, because they are passionate about their art and the means it provides for self-expression. If an artist creates a work that is understood by no one, she has still been engaged in the creative process during that time, and this should not be discounted. Therefore, a work of art does not have merit only if the majority understand it; a work of art allows an artist to create, and this process in and of itself contains merit.

Furthermore, the speaker states that merit comes from "most people" understanding a work of art. However, this ignores the fact that a piece of art might resonate with just a small group, to whom that piece has incredible merit. Many works of art have a strong impact on a small number of people, even though they may not have a mainstream appeal and be understandable to the majority of people. This is often seen in the music world, where there are many bands whose music is off-putting to mainstream audiences yet has incredible appeal to some members of society. There is a wide range of artistic preferences in this world, which results in very different artists being able to find audiences for their work, even if it is not widely understood. These works of art that appeal to only a select few do not lack merit; to the people who do understand and appreciate the art, they have tremendous merit. For example, novelist James Joyce's *Ulysses* that was structurally modeled on Greek mythology and crafted with stream of consciousness was daunting to most readers who must know its relation to Greek mythology and his brand-new writing technique. The book was inaccessible to many readers at the outset, but it has immense merit in terms of technique, theme, and language, as evidenced by its growing popularity until it becomes one classic of the world literature canon.

Finally, the understanding of art is largely contextual; its reception is likely to vary by culture, time period, or other circumstances. In many instances an artist has been uncelebrated during his or her lifetime, only to receive acclaim posthumously. One such example is Vincent van Gogh, a Dutch post-Impressionist painter who used vivid colors to portray landscapes, flowers, café scenes and people. He received little recognition in his life and was basically broke when he died. However, in subsequent decades, his fame grew, and his works of art are now celebrated by the majority. His paintings command vast sums, and most of them now hang in the world's foremost museums and private collections. Today, his work is judged to have "merit", but this was certainly not the case during his lifetime. Therefore, a work of art does not have merit merely from being understood by the masses, because appreciation is often subject to culture and timing.

In sum, I disagree with the claim that a work of art only has merit if it is understandable to most people. This statement ignores the worth of the creative process experienced by the artist, does not acknowledge the passion that a select few may feel for a piece of art, and overlooks the fact that the ability to understand art is often contextual.

44. Many important discoveries or creations are accidental: it is usually while seeking the answer to one question that we come across the answer to another. (Discuss how the statement could or could not be true)

The speaker declares that people tend to make great discoveries when they are searching for the answer to another question. I agree with this statement; there are many examples in history—spanning multiple fields of study—that support this idea. However, even in these cases of accidental discovery, "seeking" is involved; important discoveries are not just discovered by chance. They require a prepared, inquisitive mind that is actively seeking to answer questions, and is thus able to notice the sometimes-obvious answer to a long-standing question.

The history of medicine contains many relevant examples of "accidental" discoveries made by inquiring people who were investigating certain issues. For example, a scientist by the name of Edward Jenner, who lived in the 18th century, stumbled upon an unlikely cure for one of the most virulent diseases of all time: smallpox. As he studied the disease and searched for a vaccine, he observed that milk maids never succumbed to smallpox. They had pits and scars on their hands from the cow pox they caught while milking cows, but they never died from this, or from smallpox. Edward Jenner extracted some of the pus from infected cow pox and set to test it. He eventually developed a vaccine, and inoculated a child who had smallpox, resulting in the quick recovery of the boy. Thus, Edward Jenner put an end to one of the world's most feared diseases by chance, but also through preparation and hard work; in the process of looking for a vaccine, he was able to notice an unlikely solution, and was willing to put in the effort to develop that solution into a vaccine.

Another example of a product developed through a chance discovery—but by the possessor of a prepared, curious mind— is Velcro. In the 1940's, when George de Mestral, a Swiss engineer, was hunting with his dog in the Alps, he noticed the annoying burs that clung to his clothing and his dog's fur. Upon further inspection under a microscope, he observed the hooks on the tips of the burs that caused them to stick to other surfaces with any sort of small loops, such as many fabrics. After years of development, he perfected this process, and now Velcro is sold around the world as a critical component in clothing and household products. Although this was a somewhat accidental discovery, de Mestral had a mind that was trained in engineering and the curiosity to follow up on an observation. He was also willing to work hard over many years to develop the product.

Perhaps the most famous example of an "accidental discovery" is Alexander Fleming's discovery of penicillin. Fleming was a well-known bacteriologist, and had spent years investigating whether anti-bacterial agents could be developed to fight infection like what he had seen kill his fellow soldiers in World War I. One day in 1928, he returned to his laboratory after a vacation and noticed that a fungus had grown in one of his bacterial cultures, killing the bacteria. He named the substance released by the fungus "penicillin", and spent years testing penicillin and figuring out how to grow the fungus. Thus, even though he stumbled upon this important medical discovery, he was already very knowledgeable about that area of work and was committed to exploring and developing the discovery through much hard work.

In conclusion, technologies and innovations have entered the world as prepared individuals stumbled upon answers to burning questions, and then put in years of effort to develop those answers further. From the medical innovations of Edward Jenner or Alexander Fleming to George de Mestral's development of Velcro, it is apparent that many important discoveries have an element of chance, but also require a prepared mind and strong work ethic.

45. The main benefit of the study of history is to dispel the illusion that people living now are significantly different from people who lived in earlier times. (Discuss how the statement could or could not be true)

The speaker claims that the primary benefit of studying history is to break down the illusion that people in one time period are significantly different from those in former eras. I agree with this statement, for several reasons: history allows people to understand that they are not different from others who came before, and this leads to the ability to learn from prior mistakes, build on previous advances, and connect oneself to past generations.

Understanding that people of one's own era are analogous to those of the past, which is the chief benefit of the study of history, allows one society to learn from the mistakes of past societies, rather than discard them as irrelevant to current challenges and situations. One example of learning from past mistakes occurred in the financial crisis of 2008-2009 in the United States. The Chairman of the United States Federal Reserve, Ben Bernanke, is an economist who has extensively studied the Great Depression of the 1930s. Bernanke agreed with other economists that a key contributor to the severity of the Great Depression was the fact that the Federal Reserve had reduced the money supply at the time. As a result of this learning from the past, Bernanke did the opposite, and lowered interest rates instead. Thus far, a repeat of the Great Depression has been averted, although the United States has still suffered a severe recession. Bernanke recognized that people of his time period were similar to those from the past and was thus able to learn from past mistakes.

Similarly, a society that understands that people living in past eras are not different from them can build on the advances and learning that have come before. This is evident in agriculture, where one advance built on the next, because successive societies further developed ideas from previous times: the first heavy iron plow in about 1000 A.D., the windmill that enabled quicker grinding of grain in the 12th century, and Eli Whitney's invention of the cotton gin in the 18th century, among other advances. It is clear that people of one era can provide substantive learning which can be the basis of new advancements, but only if people of a later era recognize that their predecessors were not different from them.

Another positive result of dispelling the illusion of the difference between people in various eras in history is the ability to connect oneself with one's ancestry. If through the study of history, people are able to understand that they are similar to the generations that came before, they are likely to have an increased desire to learn about their heritage. Exploring one's family history brings a greater comprehension of oneself and an appreciation for the many ancestors who lived in disparate eras and cultures. There has been an increased interest in family history in recent years with the advent of websites that enable people to conduct genealogical research and connect to others who are studying similar people and places. Arguably, this cultivation of a connection to one's heritage and ancestors brings an increased sense of belonging and link to past humanity that spans centuries. Therefore, the falling apart of the assumption that people differ dramatically across eras enables further exploration of one's ancestry, which leads to greater connection with the past and understanding of oneself.

In conclusion, the chief benefit of the study of history is to dispel the illusion that people in one time period are considerably distinct from those in other time periods. The breakdown of this illusion allows people to learn from past mistakes, build on prior advances, and connect oneself to the ages that came before.

46. Learning is primarily a matter of personal discipline; students cannot be motivated by school or college alone. (Discuss how the statement could or could not be true)

At first glance the speaker's assertion that education is primarily personal seems valid. After all, it is within our brains and bodies that learning is taking place, and primarily our own person that will reap the rewards from this education. It is also the drive of the individual which in later years can determine much of what is learned and the effort that goes into the learning. Yet, after much reflection the idea that any person could take credit for his or her own education seems self-centered and indicative of a lack of the aforementioned education.

The brain develops most rapidly during the first five years of life. It is during this time that a person goes from baby whimpers to full sentences, from reflex movements only to running and skipping, and from no social interaction to playing and making friends. Each normal body is capable of making these changes, but each ends up being unique. The popular nature versus nurture argument applies here. Children come with some natural instincts, but much of what becomes important is due to who and what surrounds them. If a family places a high value on reading, then the child will at least be exposed to books and words whereas another child might not have this exposure until school begins. Individuals are surrounded from birth by people and experiences that will teach and train them how to survive in their own reality. While individuals have to take and act upon that learning they cannot take the credit for the lessons they were dealt.

The speaker's qualifying statement about education having little to do with school seems obsolete as school has never been the sole arena for learning. That said, school can be an amazing springboard for a mind and expose students to ideas and ways of communicating that can assist them in achieving what they feel is important. This reflects back to the fallacy of education being mostly personal. In a classroom setting, as in any collaborative effort, a synergistic effect can often be achieved making the students' thoughts and abilities together far surpass what they would create alone.

The statement might hold true when it comes to self-taught students. Students that are auto-didacts do not require external motivation that comes from attending school. Indeed, there are numerous individuals that studied on their own to learn all sorts of subjects such as mathematics and even nuclear physics. To achieve such abilities without guidance from teachers or professors doubtlessly requires incredible self-discipline. Thus, there is much truth in the statement that schools and colleges are not the sole progenitors of motivation for students.

Education as a process of learning has always been fought over by gatekeepers of knowledge. The modern age has come with systems of learning that attempt to usurp the credit for the hard work of individuals that wish to seek out facts on their own terms. Nonetheless, the deeply held drive to inquire and experiment is one that cannot be instilled by institutions alone; it requires a curious mind and a will to overcome the barriers of ignorance.

47. **Scientists and other researchers should focus their research on areas that are likely to benefit the greatest number of people. (Describe advantageous and disadvantageous circumstances of the recommendation)**

"That's one small step for man, one giant leap for mankind." These were the famous words spoken by American astronaut Neil Armstrong as he exited the lunar lander and became the first human to set foot upon the Moon. This timeless quote perfectly encapsulates the reason why I agree with the notion that scientists and researchers should focus on advancements that have the potential to help the greatest number of people – that the goal of science is to push humanity forward as a group rather than on an individual basis.

Looking at research from the point of view of scientists themselves, one must consider the reason they wish to conduct research in the first place. Many avid researchers wish for glory, having their names go down in history for their endeavors to demystify the universe. Think of Richard Feynman, one of the key researchers on the Manhattan Project that developed the world's first atomic bomb. Here was a man that reveled in his intelligence, and his efforts to express complex physics mathematically led him to develop the Feynman diagrams that are now used today to describe quantum electrodynamics, which are now part of cutting-edge research into new computer processors that are smaller and more powerful than ever before, a feat that would be virtually impossible without the theories that he developed to create a weapon to put an end to one of the bloodiest wars in human history.

In the field of medical science, perhaps the most celebrated researcher in this area is Jonas Salk, the scientist that created the first mass-produced polio vaccine in the late 1950's. A disease that ravaged populations across the globe for centuries, regardless of their relative level of development, polio was a scourge upon human life and well-being. Because of Salk's research, the number of people whose lives were saved cannot be measured. Who knows how much progress in less developed countries would not have occurred, due to the deaths of innovators and leaders, had Salk chosen a more obscure area of research!

From a purely practical point of view, research that aims to benefit the greatest number of individuals is one of the surest ways to secure funding. Especially in the current economic climate, investors demand a return on the vast sums of money they put into scientific research, and such profit is incumbent on the research netting some sellable product. Whether it is a medicine for a common disease, or a technology that will make consumers' lives more convenient, like the smartphone, all of these technologies were developed with the intention of benefiting a majority of people and thus justified the expense necessary for the research each technology required.

One circumstance in which adopting the recommendation would not be advantageous involves the situation where it is hard for scientists and researchers to determine what areas will probably benefit most people. This applies to fields of science that delve into theoretical concepts. Particle physics is one such area in which little to none of the research conducted has any direct applications to the lives of people but is integral to the furthering of our understanding of physics and how it functions. Making breakthroughs in particle physics has required technologies to be invented which have been revolutionary in other fields. Touch screens are one example, developed at the CERN particle physics lab and now ubiquitous in almost every digital consumer product. However, while the findings of particle accelerators are fascinating and the tangential discoveries are useful, the research is incredibly costly. It consumes millions of dollars of research that could go to curing cancer or other discoveries. Thus, I assert that research with a clear goal to benefit the greatest number of people is more deserving of focus and funding.

All in all, whether one looks at the issue from a moral point of view, personal desire for fame, or simply the profit margin associated with research, it can be said with little hesitation that it is far better for scientists and other researchers to focus on projects that stand to benefit the largest number of people possible.

48. Politicians should pursue common ground and reasonable consensus rather than elusive ideals. (Describe advantageous and disadvantageous circumstances of the recommendation)

The world of politics is unique in its breadth and diversity. Issues that may arise in political areas can span from moral issues of what many consider to be of spiritual importance on one extreme to more commonplace and almost mundane administrative tasks of government on the other extreme. The goal of a politician may vary from occasion to occasion. In cases of strict moral issues, a politician must persist in the pursuit of an ideal. However, in instances of more commonplace administrative tasks, the goal should be to find compromise and consensus to accelerate the political process.

Political issues of a strict moral nature demand the dedication of those involved to pursue a solution they believe is right. Politics and government are one instrument of social change, and it is imperative to a well-balanced society that those entrusted as public servants are willing to pursue a difficult and complex issue to secure a right solution when the alternative is, in a moral sense, wrong. Consider, for example, William Wilberforce, a member of British Parliament in the late eighteenth century. At the time, the slave trade between Africa and other British colonies was at its peak. For religious reasons, Wilberforce believed the practice of buying and selling human beings as slaves was wrong. In his opinion, many other politicians had compromised their beliefs to cater to the desires of businessmen who profited from the slave trade. Wilberforce led a political movement to end the slave trade that nearly cost him his career. He was, in the end, successful, and his efforts ended a practice that he believed to be wrong.

Other issues, such as the practice of slavery in America, abortion, or the practice of same-sex marriage, are moral issues that have entered the political arena. In these cases, politicians have a moral obligation to pursue what they believe is best, as the political resolution is often interpreted to reflect the moral views of the society they represent.

Not all political matters are concerned with moral issues, however. Many political issues involve much more common concerns that are not cast in terms of right or wrong but are constructed in terms of determining the utilitarian "greatest good for the greatest number of people." Some examples of this type of issue are decisions on zoning, voting districts, budgeting, and other administrative tasks that are determined by a political body. In these cases, there is not necessarily a solution that is superior in a moral sense. Rather, the best solution is the one that will help the most people politically or socially, or the one that will increase efficiency in administration. On these issues, the political machine should not be viewed as a vehicle of social change, but as an incubator for brainstorming to find the best solution to a problem. The goal of a brainstorming session is to combine the best components of different people's ideas to find the best possible hybrid of ideas. This combination of different ideas is, in essence, a process of compromise. Then, on issues of only administrative or utilitarian importance, the goal of politics, or of a politician, should be to compromise to find not only a suitable solution, but the best solution to meet the diversity of needs and interests of the people.

In sum, the goal of politics must depend on the situation and on the issue at hand. Those employed as public servants have a responsibility to recognize which issues are moral issues and which are not, and then to handle each issue appropriately. Moral issues should be pursued with ideals in mind. Issues not of a moral nature should be pursued with an attitude of compromise.

49. **People should undertake risky action only after they have carefully considered its consequences. (Describe advantageous and disadvantageous circumstances of the recommendation)**

Should people stop to think of the possible consequences of what they might do, rather than take quick action? The speaker asserts that this is the case, but I disagree. Thought mediates action, but it does not necessarily lead to better or more ethical behavior. Thought of consequences more often results in more calculated and goal-driven pursuits, regardless of the rightness or wrongness of said behavior. Therefore, intense thought concerning the consequences of action can lead to either positive or negative outcomes. There are many examples in history of people who thought a great deal about their actions, and this had disastrous consequences.

Some powerful people exercised no restraint in the pursuit of power, yet, after attaining power, they exercised thoughtful consideration. One example of this is Augusto Pinochet, who led Chile through the 1970's and 1980's. Pinochet came to power through a military coup. Accompanied by his military cronies, Pinochet ruled with an iron fist that included the murder of those opposed to his politics. Pinochet ruled his people more by the military than by democracy, yet during his tenure Chile's gross domestic product (GDP) exceeded that of many other nations on the earth that were embroiled in oil and debt crises of the 1980's. Though authoritarian, Pinochet maintained a relatively stable nation where direct foreign investment thrived. Pinochet must have calculated the consequences of his outcomes; he ended up causing great pain and preserving Chile from some of the economic turbulence of the era. In this case, putting forethought into a decision resulted in mixed results.

In some situations, thoughtful consideration before taking action produces completely harrowing results. Adolf Hitler is an example of one who stopped at nothing to achieve his aims. Millions of Jews were slaughtered by the Nazi regime, which was instigated by Hitler's engaging rhetoric and brutal policy enforcement. Hitler was proud of what Germany was accomplishing; in his own eyes, he was an effective leader. Yet, from the perspective of myriad others, his leadership was simply wrong, because of the consequences resulting from his leadership: millions were killed, cities were destroyed, German citizens feared their own leaders, and the legitimacy of law enforcement embodied by the secret police was maintained through terror. Hitler's actions were carefully considered; he did not act on impulse, but instead planned and built an empire over the course of many years. Taking the time to think of the consequences only served to make Hitler's "Final Solution" to the Jewish question more calculated and extreme. In this case, unplanned action with no forethought would have resulted in far fewer lives being lost.

Adopting the recommendation would be advantageous when one needs to determine whether it is worth the risk. For instance, the casino industry thrives on individuals who are enticed into spending vast sums of money in the hopes of winning big and becoming rich overnight. Most of these people fail to thoughtfully consider the risks involved in playing games of chance, and they lose more often than they win as a consequence of their hasty decision making. In fact, from a statistical perspective, the actual returns one stands to gain from gambling are far smaller than the amount of money which must be spent in order to have a reliable chance of winning, and thus most habitual gamblers lose everything they have long before they win their sought-after jackpot. Therefore, before one undertakes activities involving high risk, the smartest course of action is to consider what one stands to lose first.

In sum, by and large, thinking about the consequences of one's actions is a positive experience and can lead to increased consideration of the effects of one's actions on others. However, in the wrong hands, premeditated thought can lead to destructive actions that become effective proportional to the thought invested.

50. Leaders are created by the demands that are placed on them. (Discuss how the statement could or could not be true)

Throughout human history, men and women have taken the reigns of nations or movements for a number of reasons. Some believe that their success in these matters depends on the demands of the moment, akin to the idea of great power requiring great responsibility. This can certainly be said for a number of well-known leaders, yet there are also many whose talents are apparent before their defining moments come.

If one wishes to find an example of a leader that owes his abilities to the responsibilities thrust upon him, one need not look any further than the ancient Hellenistic king now known as Alexander the Great. After the assassination of his father by Persian spies, Alexander succeeded to the throne of Macedonia at only twenty years old, becoming the leader and general of his country in a period when it was threatened by the formidable Persian empire. Shortly after his succession, he began a campaign that would take him across the known world, resulting in his conquest of the Persian empire itself and many other smaller nations. He was a man that rose to the occasion, taking the reins of his nation and creating an unprecedented empire.

For further examples of people that become leaders by virtue of their situation, one can look at the various leaders of civil rights movements in history. Mahatma Gandhi and Martin Luther King Jr. rose to prominence due to the outcries from their people. Both came from relatively poor families and experienced the discrimination against their respective races until they could bear it no more. As each became more important to their struggle for independence or equality, they developed their skills as leaders to fit their situations, which happened to be similar. Gandhi, realizing that violent rebellion would only hurt the Indian people more, and King, learning from Gandhi's example, chose instead to commit to a strictly non-violent form of protest. Their methods were a direct consequence of the context of their roles as civil rights activists; had they been freedom fighters, they could have chosen quite different practices to achieve their goals.

Yet, not all leaders are shaped by the context of their positions. Some, like Steve Jobs, co-founder of the tech giant Apple, are by all accounts born to lead. From a young age, Jobs was rambunctious and determined to get whatever it was that he wanted by his own efforts. He landed his first job at 13 working for the HP printer company after he personally called the owner in search of parts for his own project. Throughout his life he would demand that those working under him strive for visionary innovations rather than follow the status quo, and while that did not always work in his favor – his demeanor was often abrasive, and he was even kicked out of his own company at one time – his legacy lives on today through the products he developed.

Shakespeare once wrote something to the effect that some men are born great, while others have greatness thrust upon them. A cursory glance across human history, as has been done here, easily provides numerous examples to prove his words to be true.

51. **There is little justification for society to make extraordinary efforts — especially at a great cost in money and jobs — to save endangered animal or plant species. (Discuss how the statement could or could not be true)**

"Humankind has not woven the web of life. We are but one thread within it. Whatever we do to the web, we do to ourselves. All things are bound together. All things connect." This quote by Chief Seattle illustrates the interwoven nature of the human race and the world it lives in. There is no separation; thus, any attempt to save a bird, fern or warthog is in reality an attempt to save ourselves.

Some animals play a large part in the greater food chain and may even provide benefits to humanity if preserved. The horseshoe crab has existed for more than 350 million years. Over the past decade it has become a popular source of live bait for fishermen; it is both easy to catch and apparently very tasty. The mass extinction of the horseshoe crab has left the red knots, the animals most directly reliant on it, in a perilous situation. The horseshoe crab has also opened a new course in viral research using its blue blood. While the retrieval of the blood is still under debate, it can be obtained without killing the animal. The crab's ancient blood will clot around any foreign infection or disease. This simple but powerful immune system could reportedly transform the world of medicine.

The horseshoe crab is not isolated in its symbiotic connection to our world. All creatures fill a commission on this planet. The question then is not whether the animals or plants should be saved, but whether human crusades to save would impair the animals and plants further. First, the encroaching humans would upset the natural laws of survival, either creating a new environment or removing some basic instincts from the species. This danger can already be witnessed as animal rescue teams attempt to place species back in the wild. Second, the intervention would backfire as it would upset the creatures' natural environments to an even greater extent, exposing the animals to human contact and disease.

That said, the damage done by humans to the planet and its species is so grievous that some attempt at rectification is in order. There can be no backpedaling, but the more opportunities found for co-existence and regulation instead of invasion, the greater human redemption will be. In the case of the horseshoe crabs, there has been a ban on using their flesh as bait. This will not restore what was lost, but slowly the crab population will swell; they will lay more eggs, and the red knot will be fat enough to make its journey, hoping that enough will survive in the interim to repopulate the species. This decision has not only helped the horseshoe crab and red knot but will assist humans in their fight against immune attacking diseases.

The statement might hold true in the event that humans do not have a hand in the endangerment of a species. It is understandable to demand that humanity take responsibility for the damage it causes to the species of the world and their respective habitats. However, what justification is there, if any, for humans to sacrifice their own well-being to give obscure plants or animals a second chance at existing? For instance, in some countries there are laws that prohibit development of areas that are used as nesting grounds for certain birds. In the event that a single nest is found, an entire area may be cordoned off, even if it is already inhabited by a human homeowner. That individual will be prohibited from conducting any activity that may disturb the bird's ability to reproduce, even at significant financial loss to the human. Such an infringement of human rights is intolerable; after all, it is not the responsibility of a single person to propagate an endangered species. Nonetheless, when it comes to larger parts of the natural food chain, humans should remain cognizant of the importance of preserving certain species in order to prevent the collapse of entire ecosystems.

The attempt to study and support the planet defines human beings in the value they place on life, their ability to move beyond the self-destruction of selfishness, and the level of wisdom which dictates their actions. By showing a strong regard for the environment and attempting to preserve its assets, people show a love for themselves and the future.

52. The human mind will always be superior to machines because machines are only tools of human minds. (Discuss how the statement could or could not be true)

Ever since the notion of automata and robots existed, a debate has raged over whether human intellect will remain forever dominant over machines. Many have argued that since machines are little more than mindless tools, human hegemony is all but guaranteed. However, with the dawn of the digital age and the increasingly advanced forms of computer programs and technical advancements in robotics, this notion has been called into question.

It is true that machines are just products of human minds, and there exists a notion that nothing created by human hands can exceed the abilities of their creator. After all, humans have such a limited understanding of the universe, so it is easy to see why such theoretical limitations could be placed on the works of human creation. For example, no matter how hard we have tried, there has been little success in creating a machine learning program that could adopt new information and create coherent inferences. A human mind takes new information, then compares it and applies it to hundreds of different scenarios and contexts in a fraction of a second in order to make sense of it and then draw inferences. However, a machine must be programmed with the contexts and scenarios beforehand, and thus is dwarfed by the fact that the human mind is adding new variables constantly in real-time. Thus, the inferences drawn by a machine are often inaccurate or jumbled due to a lack of necessary information.

However, this does not mean machines will always be inferior to the human mind. One of the most common ways that the proficiency of the human mind is quantified is through its ability to play and win games of strategy. For many years, chess was the go-to standard for proving that a person could outthink a computer. Yet since the late 1960's computers have beaten humans in chess matches, and in the early 90's the supercomputer known as Deep Thought, designed specifically to play chess, was able to best a grandmaster. Since then, numerous other computers have been able to compete against and win grandmasters in chess, and as such the bar for human superiority was raised to the game Go. Go, being infinitely more complex than chess, was seen as an impossible challenge for computers, as it was believed that without preprogramming all possible moves, no computer could beat the ability of the human mind to consider the countless number of potential moves during a match. Such notions were again dashed in 2016 when the computer AlphaGo beat the world's best Go player by utilizing intricate software that could assess millions of board positions each second, a feat that no human could ever manage. Thus, at least in the realm of board games, computers have already proven themselves to be far more capable than humans.

But what about less specific, more complex tasks than games, such as the ability to hold a conversation? One of the primary factors that separate humans from most other animals, the ability to communicate, is integral to determining the intellectual capacity of an organism, or in this case a machine. While computers are not yet able to express their own personal thoughts, advances in speech algorithms have reached a point where one can go online and attempt to hold a conversation with chatbots who, to their credit, can maintain a basic conversation. Many companies even have customer service chatbots that can aid in diagnosing and presenting solutions to customer questions. Despite the current limitations, most industry experts claim that it is only a matter of time before machines can be developed with fluent speech capabilities.

Of course, both previous arguments fail to address the primary issue of true intelligence, that is, whether a computer can learn from its environment, adapt, and create something entirely new from its acquired knowledge. This has proven to be a large hurdle in the development of AI systems, as most existing computers, even the most advanced among them, require humans to input data to be analyzed before a learning algorithm can begin to work. But this, too, is something that is predicted to change in the near future, as companies such as Microsoft, IBM, and even Facebook are experimenting with developing AI software that can access the internet at will. It can, therefore, be surmised that free-thinking machines are not too far off.

While machines are simply tools of the human mind, the technological singularity, basically the point when computers become smart enough to design superior versions of themselves and surpass humankind as the dominant intelligence in the known universe, may not be far off. Various scientists such as the late Stephen Hawking have already alluded to this possibility, and anyone that has kept up with recent developments in AI technology can attest that believing in the preeminence of human thought over machines cannot be justified for much longer.

53. People who are the most deeply committed to an idea or policy are also the most critical of it. (Discuss how the statement could or could not be true)

It is easy to assume that all people are analytical towards their particular beliefs simply by virtue of being thinking beings and that the more dedicated one is to a certain way of thinking or policy, the greater the level of scrutiny they submit their ideas to. Yet, for most people, this turns out not to be the case for a number of social and psychological reasons.

In behavioral psychology, a concept known as cognitive dissonance states that people will experience discomfort when they possess two contradictory beliefs simultaneously, and will then seek to justify the clashing actions they engage in. Examples of this can be readily observed in politics when a citizen votes for a candidate from his or her preferred party whose policies do not align with the voter's beliefs. Rather than investigating the politician's policies and platform, the voter will follow the party line, and justify the vote by criticizing the candidate's opponent. The 2016 US presidential election was a perfect example of this, wherein many of those who voted for Trump did so out of faith in his rhetoric of helping blue collar workers and removing corrupt politicians. However, when confronted with the policies which Trump supported and involved extensive tax breaks to large corporations and tariffs that caused many blue-collar jobs to leave the country, these voters simply said something to the effect that "at least Hillary did not win", or flat-out denied the facts, stating that such statistics are "fake news".

Even in areas where one would think that subjective beliefs play a minimal role in a person's commitment to an idea, such as the sciences, willful ignorance of objective facts can be seen. For example, in recent years, a growing number of people think that the Earth is flat, rather than a sphere, and vehemently claim that all evidence to the contrary is part of an expansive conspiracy to fool the people of the world. Regardless of how much documentation exists to show that this is false, such as the leftover rocket-boosters from the lunar lander's launch, the video footage from the landing itself, surface samples, and so on, these conspiracy theorists continue to firmly adhere to their belief in a flat earth. Even the logical principle of Occam's Razor, which states that when faced with a myriad of potential explanations for a phenomenon, the explanation that relies on the fewest assumptions is the most likely to be true, is not enough to sway their opinion.

This, of course, does not mean that adamant belief and self-analysis are completely mutually exclusive. The great Greek philosopher Diogenes espoused cynicism, which entailed living a lifestyle devoid of all unnecessary indulgences. Renouncing the wealth of his family and all worldly possessions, he chose to live on the street as a beggar and criticized the wastefulness of contemporary society. Diogenes was so dedicated to his philosophical ideals that when he saw a boy drinking water out of his own hands, he threw away his begging bowl, seeing no real need for it any longer. While his dedication would likely be viewed as insanity, as it was by many of the citizens of the cities in which he lived, his example shows that people are willing to look inward at their own firmly held beliefs and alter their behaviors when faced with inconsistencies.

Extreme examples aside, it is often not the case that one encounters a person that is dedicated to a particular doctrine and at the same time willing to scrutinize such deeply held beliefs. Too often, the social pressure to conform, or simply the self-righteousness associated with a particular ideology, is too intoxicating to warrant an analysis of those ideas.

54. **Some people believe that society should try to save every plant and animal species, despite the expense to humans in effort, time, and financial well-being. Others believe that society need not make extraordinary efforts, especially at a great cost in money and jobs, to save endangered. (Address both views)**

"Humankind has not woven the web of life. We are but one thread within it. Whatever we do to the web, we do to ourselves. All things are bound together. All things connect." This quote by Chief Seattle illustrates the interwoven nature of the human race and the world it lives in. There is no separation; thus, any attempt to save a bird, fern or warthog is in reality an attempt to save ourselves.

Some may argue that society need not make tremendous efforts in terms of cost in jobs and money to save endangered species that do not become so because of anthropogenic activities. When humans are culpable to the destruction, they should be responsible for saving the species. For instance, when runoff from a factory pollutes a river system and begins to kill the plants and animals in the surrounding habitats, humans have an obligation to rectify the damage done. However, when the destruction is a natural process, there is no rationale for humans to save the species at a tremendous cost in terms of jobs and money. The panda is a notable example. It is a picky species when it comes to the food they choose to eat, and they are notoriously apathetic towards mating. If it were not for humans' desire to see them in zoos, there would be little justification for sustaining them at a great cost as they serve no vital function in any ecosystem.

Yet some animals play a large part in the greater food chain and may even provide benefits to humanity if preserved. The horseshoe crab has existed for more than 350 million years. Over the past decade it has become a popular source of live bait for fishermen; it is both easy to catch and apparently very tasty. The mass extinction of the horseshoe crab has left the red knots, the animals most directly reliant on it, in a perilous situation. The horseshoe crab has also opened a new course in viral research using its blue blood. While the retrieval of the blood is still under debate, it can be obtained without killing the animal. The crab's ancient blood will clot around any foreign infection or disease. This simple but powerful immune system could reportedly transform the world of medicine.

The horseshoe crab is not isolated in its symbiotic connection to our world. All creatures fill a commission on this planet. The question then is not whether the animals or plants should be saved, but whether human crusades to save would impair the animals and plants further. First, the encroaching humans would upset the natural laws of survival, either creating a new environment or removing some basic instincts from the species. This danger can already be witnessed as animal rescue teams attempt to place species back in the wild. Second, the intervention would backfire as it would upset the creatures' natural environments to an even greater extent, exposing the animals to human contact and disease.

That said, the damage done by humans to the planet and its species is so grievous that some attempt at rectification is in order. There can be no backpedaling, but the more opportunities found for co-existence and regulation instead of invasion, the greater human redemption will be. In the case of the horseshoe crabs, there has been a ban on using their flesh as bait. This will not restore what was lost, but slowly the crab population will swell; they will lay more eggs, and the red knot will be fat enough to make its journey, hoping that enough will survive in the interim to repopulate the species. This decision has not only helped the horseshoe crab and red knot but will assist humans in their fight against immune attacking diseases.

The attempt to study and support the planet defines human beings in the value they place on life, their ability to move beyond the self-destruction of selfishness, and the level of wisdom which dictates their actions. By showing a strong regard for the environment and attempting to preserve its assets, people show a love for themselves and the future.

55. Some people believe that the purpose of education is to free the mind and the spirit. Others believe that formal education tends to restrain our minds and spirits rather than set them free. (Address both views)

Compulsory education has often been hailed as one of the greatest contributors to the development of nations both socially and economically. However, as beneficial as it may be to society, I contend that formal education is far more likely to crush individuality and innovation more than any other system.

One of the greatest minds of the modern era, Albert Einstein once said, "The only thing that interferes with my learning is my education." A common fact given about Einstein is that he failed primary school. While that is not exactly true, he actually had excellent scores but struggled with some subjects unrelated to math and science, which were his passion. Nonetheless, this quote is insightful, as it implies that he found that the requirements to study subjects he had no interest in limited his ability to focus on what he was good at and enjoyed doing. There is no doubt that numerous other young minds have potentially gone undiscovered in the formal education system due to the limitations placed upon them as a result of their low scores in classes they despise. Nowadays, the strict standardized testing systems in place act as barriers to those seeking higher education in a specialized field they excel in, due to arbitrary course requirements that they wish to ignore.

Another drawback that comes with a formal education is the rigid curriculum, which, with a set of questions with limited acceptable answers, forces students to think one way or be shamed for being rebellious or even stupid. There is little room for free thought when teachers are established to be authoritative sources of knowledge to rely on and not contested under any circumstance. One need only look at the school systems in some countries, where disagreeing with a teacher in class, even if the student is in the right, can lead to punishment and social stigmatism. It is, therefore, no surprise why these countries are criticized time and again for their students' lack of creative thought.

Yet, there is still an argument to be made for the necessity of formal education. As mentioned before, it does provide a minimum educational standard for a country and offers access to learning and knowledge that would otherwise be hard to come by for many people in developing countries. In fact, formal schooling for girls and women in "third-world nations" is listed as one of the greatest contributing factors in lifting the majority of citizens out of poverty. As a result, individuals are set free through their ability to draw on knowledge and skills acquired through formal education, including general skills such as critical thinking and specific skills such as disciplinary thinking. For example, having received a formal education, a person from a poor farming family may apply the mathematics and critical thinking skills to their agricultural process, calculating basic rates of return for certain crops and choosing to plant in such a way that maximizes the return on their harvest.

Aside from this caveat, though, formal schooling does little else beyond providing a minimum standard of education. Students in developed nations, especially in the modern era, are able to access the entirety of human knowledge instantly on the internet, and by all accounts have proven perfectly capable of doing so. One can only imagine how well these young people could pursue their own avenues of innovation and personal development if they could use as they please the time wasted on going to school six or more hours a day. In fact, many have already done so; the number of small businesses started by young adults has exploded since the proliferation of the internet access, and the trend seems only to be more evident as smart devices become cheaper and more powerful.

In conclusion, I think that, while certainly beneficial to some groups where ignorance is endemic, formal schooling is ultimately detrimental to our minds and aspirations. It teaches us only to meet arbitrary course requirements and discourages debate, a practice that is not conducive to the development of individual learning and passion.

56. Some people believe it is often necessary, even desirable, for political leaders to withhold information from the public. Others believe that the public has a right to be fully informed. (Address both views)

The notion of complete political transparency sounds desirable, but the dangers of a full disclosure system are so numerous that it would cripple and disintegrate the political system. It is often necessary for political leaders to withhold sensitive information, but the aim would be to do this with as much transparency as possible.

In the presidential elections some time ago, the full disclosure of contributors to each campaign became a "hot-button" issue. In an effort to validate and account for campaign funds the public was calling for lists of names so that corruption and illegal funding could be avoided. This sounds reasonable; however, the disclosure of names connected to any particular party or activist group creates an instant target for those with or seeking political power. In the 1950's the state of Alabama attempted to force the NAACP to disclose the names of its members in an effort to harass and force them to leave the state. The Supreme Court ruled in favor of the NAACP, saying that in an effort to protect the freedom of association privacy is essential. The same interest in privacy is essential for political parties as well. If supporters found themselves on the losing side, it could lead to IRS audits and other "legal" forms of harassment.

Another platform where full disclosure cannot be sustained is in matters of national security. After 9/11 the vulnerability of the United States was at its peak and those who wished to oppress and cause terror were in a place of power. In an effort to take credit for the bombing, show support to the groups involved, and simply to harass, threats of more heinous suicides were received. This is not uncommon, as the world is full of conspiring men and ideals. If the United States government were to report all incidences of these types of threats it could cause mass hysteria. The general public is not equipped to know which threats are most likely, what signals to look for, and even how to avoid or prevent the tragedies. This is the role of government and in many cases should remain private. When Prince Harry was sent to Afghanistan his location was not revealed as his royal connections would make his whole platoon a target, and this disclosure would lead to destruction instead of freedom.

That said, the transparency of a government, or the right of the public to be fully informed, in matters of an insensitive nature is imperative to fostering a system of trust and integrity, where the corruption of power can remain in check. The Watergate scandal is a prime example. After Nixon's deceit was discovered, he was put on trial and dismissed. His politics were not unsound, and his personal life was tame, but the American public could not trust him. He had not been forthright in his dealings and obtained secret information in a shady and despicable way. When transparency is not the law, corruption and greed become the real politics. To combat issues with non-disclosure the U.S. Senate has to turn in minutes on all non-sensitive items. The President is expected to do the same as a show of good faith and a check for the public to ensure that the politicians are serving the people and not themselves.

To conclude, what is needed is a system of government where the leaders desire to fully inform the public, but judiciously withhold the information that will truly be harmful to the rights and lives of their constituents. If the underlying desire is disclosure, then the information withheld by the leaders, will be in the most capable hands, hands attempting to create a safe and free world order rather than an ignorant one.

57. Claim: Universities should require every student to take a variety of courses outside the student's major field of study.
Reason: Acquiring knowledge of various academic disciplines is the best way to become truly educated. (Claim-Reason)

The speaker claims that a broad curriculum of study is the ideal way to become truly educated and therefore students studying in university should be required to take a variety of courses that are not directly related to their field of study. Yet this raises two important questions: what does it mean to be "truly educated"? Is the purpose of attending university to become "truly educated"?

Taking the claim at face value, we suppose that "truly educated" can be interpreted to mean "knowing about as many fields as possible", based on the given requirement of studying a wide range of courses. However, despite the alleged usefulness of being familiar with a broad spectrum of topics, knowing facts is not necessarily an adequate measure of intellect. Instructors may successfully imprint a large volume of information upon their students yet leave the students unequipped with the ability to apply such knowledge in practical situations. Such is the case in many test-focused education systems in Southeast Asia, where rote memorization does allow students to familiarize themselves with an array of different subjects yet leaves them woefully unable to translate that information into any useful skillset. Thus, the notion of being educated in the context of the claim is far too vague to be of any value to an argument of university education requirements.

If we accept the claim's definition of being "truly educated", there arises the issue of whether the given requirement is conducive to the goals of students who are choosing to attend university. In the context of contemporary society, a university degree has become more of a qualification necessary for employment than the representation of achievement that people in the past sought. Students need a university degree to show their proficiency in a specific area of study that is applicable to a desired job position, not to show that they are "truly educated";

employers need skilled workers, not eclectic intellectuals.

On the other hand, if it is the desire of a student to seek a multi-disciplinary education, the claim and its given reason hold true, as a diverse selection of courses would indeed grant a horizon-broadening education. Alternatively, if the student in question happens to be a polymath or is uniquely motivated in his or her studies to juggle a curriculum laden with unrelated subjects, this would fit in nicely with the current narrative sold by universities that taking courses outside one's major creates a more well-rounded individual. However, just do not put too much stock in employers' thinking the same.

In conclusion, the claim appears to hold true if the interpretation of a "truly educated" individual is quite narrow, yet considering the contemporary job market, this is a highly unrealistic way of viewing a university degree. If a true education means studying a wide variety of subjects, then perhaps university itself is unnecessary in view of the wealth of information available on the internet.

58. Young people should be encouraged to pursue long-term, realistic goals rather than seek immediate fame and recognition. (Discuss how the statement could or could not be true)

People today live in an insanely fast-paced world. The rapid consumption of media, fueled by globalization and the internet, has bombarded the youth of all nations with countless celebrities, all of whom rise and fall with apparent ease. As a result, young people develop a desire to follow in these celebrities' footsteps and make a name for themselves as soon as possible. However, I see danger in this way of thinking, which is why I strongly agree with the statement that young people should instead be encouraged to pursues long-term goals over short-term fame.

A perfect example of the dangers of this attention-seeking behavior can be seen in the rise and fall of various online vloggers, most notably those on the popular website YouTube. It is here that many young people have found fame, even fortune to some extent, by posting their content on the site. A particularly pernicious genre of these videos is prank videos. In such videos various acts, ranging from harmless gags to actions that could be considered assault or harassment were performed for the amusement of viewers. The popularity of these videos and the potential for internet stardom led many young imitators to attempt their own prank videos, with ever more daring pranks. Numerous young people ended up being arrested or prosecuted with criminal charges after acts of vandalism or disturbing the peace occurred. Had these youths been directed to more productive enterprises, they likely would have avoided receiving permanent criminal marks on their records.

An even more convincing argument for impressing the need for long-term goals on young people exists in the inner-city areas of the USA. Here, some young people are entranced with visions of getting rich and infamous quick by becoming notable rappers, gang members, drug dealers, or some combination of the three. Because of this, these communities have consistently ranked among the poorest and most crime-ridden areas of the country. Notable civil rights activist Malcom X even addressed this issue, stating that young men and women in the areas should educate themselves and invest in their communities if they were ever to truly lift themselves out of poverty.

Yet for young people today, it is understandable to seek only short-term fame. After all, the social and economic stratum of most developed countries has solidified, and the unpredictable shifts in the political and economic climates have left little room for any long-term plan to remain viable for more than a few years. All is not lost, however, at least for those enterprising enough to remain constantly adaptable. Numerous new successful startups, especially in the tech sector, are evidence of the merit of goal setting, and the relatively young age of many of these entrepreneurs shows that such goals are achievable. Thus, if people stick to their passions throughout their teens and into their young adult life, there is still a good chance that they too can become the next Mark Zuckerberg or Elon Musk.

To conclude, it would be irresponsible to suggest to young people that seeking immediate fame and recognition is a superior alternative to long-term planning. Unless they plan to die young, they will have to keep on living, and despite the cycle of upheavals that have wracked the world of late, there is still much room for the well-motivated among the planet's youth to create a lasting legacy for themselves.

59. **Governments should not fund any scientific research whose consequences are unclear. (Discuss positive and negative consequences of the policy)**

Since one of the primary functions of governments is to ameliorate quality of life for its citizens, it stands to reason that scientific research should be a top priority when they spend budgets. However, since government spending relies on the tax dollars of its people, there is a limit to how much money can be devoted to research, and thus only those projects with clear goals and results and lacking ethical ambiguity should be approved for funding.

One of the foremost concerns that comes up whenever scientific research is conducted is the moral implications of the discoveries. In fields such as medicine, the results of certain tests may have far reaching effects on the human dignity of patients. For example, one highly controversial research topic has been the development of stem cell therapy. This treatment was and still is considered morally abhorrent in the minds of many people that view the harvesting of stem cells from fetal tissue as desecrating life. They argue that this process effectively commodifies human life, and they are entitled to their civil right to urge their representatives in the government to either make such research illegal, or in terms of this argument, prohibit spending on research into this field that conflicts with their beliefs and has many more repercussions than originally identified.

Also, some kinds of research may reveal knowledge that is too dangerous for anyone to possess. Such knowledge may be unclear before the research, but given the potential dire consequences, governments are not supposed to fund it. Take nuclear weapons as an example. It is undoubtable that numerous ills have been caused by the development of nuclear technology, not only in the cost of human life in the two detonations during WWII, but also in the political tensions between nations in the dispute over who should be allowed to have such weapons. It could therefore be argued that governments should abstain from financially supporting any kind of technology research that could lead to the development of more powerful weapons but unknown consequences so as to avoid further death and conflict.

The blanket policy may place researchers in a dilemma between funding of nothing and funding of everything. Some may argue that one cannot predict the ramifications of developments that come from research, and as such the consequences are never clear. One such piece of evidence for this was the development of the first airplanes thanks to the Wright brothers. They envisioned their creation as something that would promote the quick and convenient transportation of man and goods around the globe, yet they lived to see the descendants of their invention being used as a conveyance for the Hiroshima and Nagasaki nuclear bombings. According to this camp, the government would either have to cease funding of research altogether, or fund all projects equally, which simply is not feasible. In addition, there are certainly areas of research where the potential negative impacts of an experiment are far more numerous than the proposed benefit, as in weapon development or social experiments. This does not mean governments need to stop funding scientific research completely; they need to fund research with well-defined goals and free of ethical risks.

In sum, I believe that when considering the extensive financial burden imposed by scientific research, as well as the ethical responsibility a government has towards its people, it is certainly reasonable for a government to deny funding to scientific research that does not provide a clear benefit or has morally problematic consequences.

60. Knowing about the past cannot help people to make important decisions today. (Discuss how the statement could or could not be true)

Considering that many of the problems that have occurred throughout history came about as a result of an ignorance of past events, it is therefore difficult to agree with the notion that knowing about the past does not contribute to contemporary decision making. World leaders have repeated fatal errors of their predecessors, and otherwise avoidable disasters have ravaged cities – all due to ignorance of historically similar events. Nonetheless, there are also many examples of people studying the failings and mistakes of the past in order to avoid the same pitfalls, proving that a knowledge of history can be applied to important decisions.

Some national leaders have considered themselves to be immune to the repetitive nature of history. For instance, in the ancient world Sparta was a bastion of military might, a nation state of almost unparalleled combat prowess. Several rival nations, including the larger and wealthier city-state of Athens had attempted to conquer Sparta, to no avail. This lesson fell on deaf ears of the Persian Empire, which attempted to bring Sparta to heel in the Peloponnesian war. A small detachment of Spartan warriors backed up by a force of Greek soldiers held a chokepoint and held off a massive Persian army long enough for Sparta and its allies to rally reinforcements and push back the Persian invasion. The Persian king would have done well to have learned from the mistakes of previous generals that faced Sparta when the smaller nation had a tactical advantage. This lesson was applied later by the Macedonian leader, Alexander the Great, who was able to inflict a stunning victory against the Spartans at the battle of Megalopolis, resulting in one of the few decisive military defeats in Spartan history. Thus, the past can be an effective tool in the hands of a leader willing to apply it.

When it comes to suffering from the fierce forces of nature, Japan is near the top of the list. Lying almost directly on one of the most active fault zones in what geologists refer to as the "ring of fire", Japan experiences earthquakes at a frequency unlike that of most other places on earth. On top of this, Japan is an island nation, so it is also an easy target for typhoons, and perhaps worse, tsunamis. Called rough waves, tsunamis have been so prevalent throughout Japan's history that they have left a deep cultural imprint on those Japanese who are brave enough to live in coastal areas. One can even find stone monuments from hundreds of years ago, inscribed with warnings about not building homes or structures within a certain distance of the beach, citing tsunamis as the reason. A monument of this kind was uncovered after the 2011 Tohoku earthquake and tsunami. Even though a few people have ignored these warnings, with disastrous results, the vast majority of coastal residents in Japan have heeded the lessons of the past and kept their residences far enough from the water to avoid the onslaught of the ocean.

However, in numerous instances knowing the events of the past and having the modern tools to solve problems in contemporary circumstances have done extraordinarily little to aid in making significant decisions. For instance, look at the way the USA has handled the COVID-19 pandemic. Despite a wealth of knowledge in epidemiology and several well-known pandemics in history, such as the Spanish Flu, SARS, H1N1, and others, there were still poor decisions made at nearly every level of government that negatively affected the nation as a whole. The number of cases was hardly impacted, and even though the USA is considered one of the most developed nations in the world, it has become the epicenter of the virus. In this case the famous maxim "knowing and not doing is the same as not knowing at all" has been unfortunately true. Still, this is but one instance of people ignoring the lessons of history; many other nations took to heart the dangers of ignoring the past. China was one of the most successful nations at preventing the spread of the COVID-19 virus, learning from its own experience with SARS and mandating masks and lockdowns that quickly ended the virus' impact on the nation.

The past is the past, but this does not mean events that have already occurred are irrelevant to the present. Being willing and able to do historical research to aid with making choices in the modern world can be immensely beneficial to individuals and nations alike. Ignoring history, however, can prove to be fatal.

61. In this age of intensive media coverage, it is no longer possible for a society to regard any living man or woman as a hero. (Discuss how the statement could or could not be true)

Technology has certainly brought media a long way in the past twenty-five years. Devices such as the internet, personal computers, and smartphones have allowed news reporters and journalists to analyze public figures constantly and report any malfeasance immediately. While there have been some shocking revelations about some beloved icons, their fall from grace is no grounds for the statement that no living man or woman can be regarded as a hero. Numerous public figures have integrity and can be seen as role models.

Warren Buffett is a good example of someone who is successful and philanthropic; although the media has spent years covering his life, his company, and his charitable works, he has stayed clean. In fact, it is largely the media coverage itself that led to Warren Buffett being idolized. The publication of his life and achievements was and still is a great motivator for young investors and entrepreneurs. Another celebrity that has avoided scandal is the actor George Clooney. He has been hounded by paparazzi for years, yet he maintains a stellar image. Having no relationship scandals, drunken rants, or other Hollywood drama, Clooney keeps mostly to himself and his family. Malala Yousafzai, the young girl who won a Nobel Peace Prize for her activism in the areas of female education and human rights, has upheld a similarly untarnished reputation despite concentrated coverage and is a role model for young people around the world. Some celebrities have made fools of themselves in the news, but there are still plenty of talented people worthy of being role models.

Also, this claim forgets the resilience of people's opinions. If a public figure is panned or heavily criticized by the media for something they have done, there remains the chance that most people will simply look past it or forgive it, depending on its severity and the following actions of the person. Take American actor Robert Downey Jr. for example. He burned many bridges in the film industry, alienated many fans, and nearly killed his career thanks to his drug addiction. After a stint in rehab and coming to terms with the possibility of never appearing in a film again, Downey Jr. cleaned up and regained his place in audience's hearts, such that he is now one of the highest paid actors in Hollywood. In the case of other famous stars, numerous rappers have been accused and convicted of crimes and their fans cheer for them in spite of that fact. Therefore, I do not think people will stop considering their heroes as such for anything but the most heinous revelations about their character or behavior.

However, it is important to address the fact that media scrutiny has opened the public's eyes to the true nature of some idols that no one expected to have illicit behavior. The famed American comedian Bill Cosby is one such star that has been exposed as somebody far worse than what people thought he was. Beloved by the nation, and sometimes referred to as America's dad, due in part to his role in an extremely popular 80's sitcom, numerous testimonies by women against him in the media unveiled a string of sexual assaults over the years that has now led to a trial and conviction. A man that many looked up to as an inspiration was shown to be a monster. But the important thing to remember is that his actions were his alone; they do not reflect the nature of all people. There will always be those that achieve fame and success in spite of being immoral, just as there will always be good people that can be looked up to.

In sum, the intense coverage by the modern media has exposed many living heroes' flaws, more serious in some cases than in others. However, this does not mean that a society cannot regard them as heroes any more, as there remain many who still deserve the title.

62. **We can usually learn much more from people whose views we share than from people whose views contradict our own. (Discuss how the statement could or could not be true)**

While contradictory views certainly can cause stress and inhibit learning, it is not the case that we usually learn much more from people whose views we share. The statement asserts several implied truths that are not necessarily factual.

First, let us establish the obstacles that prevent people from learning. The issue statement implies that disagreement is a possible inhibitor to the learning process. Disagreement, implied by contradictory views in this context, is a loosely defined term that could be interpreted several ways. Certainly, if disagreement is permitted to become contentious, angry, or malicious, then it certainly will prevent learning. In general terms, learning will be inhibited any time an individual permits strong negative emotion to cloud his or her thoughts. Consider a typical interaction between sports fans of opposing teams. Each fan, being loyal to his or her team, will not be inclined to change positions to match the view of the opposing fan. Additionally, because sporting events are naturally competitive, arguments and contentions are usually near the surface, so it is easy to imagine two individuals becoming angry or even malicious in a debate of which team is superior. Disagreement, if allowed to reach the point of malice, contention, or anger, will create strong emotions in both involved parties that prevent clear, rational thought or learning.

Before we move on to other obstacles that keep people from learning, it should be noted that healthy disagreement, in which individuals act with respect and tolerance, can be extremely beneficial to learning. In the seventeenth century, Czar Peter I of Russia recognized that his nation trailed significantly behind his European neighbors in the arts and sciences. Peter himself took a tour of Europe, meeting with kings and government leaders in several different countries. Certainly, these people were nothing like Peter, but he visited them with the intent to learn from them how to govern his own country more effectively. Because he approached their differences without competitive or malicious attitudes, he learned from them and changed his nation to be more modern and effective.

Another significant obstacle to learning can easily occur when individuals think too much alike. This obstacle is complacency in thought and feeling, a phenomenon that occurs when someone decides that they are "good enough." Without differing ideas and opinions to challenge what an individual considers to be "right" or "good," it is easy for that individual to believe that his or her personal perspective is correct without question. The individual's learning and thoughts then become stagnant, and no progress is made. This effect can sometimes be seen in large corporations that attain some high level of success. The individuals charged with leading the organization, seeing the great success of the corporation, may begin to believe that everything in the corporation is perfect. They will gradually stop challenging the status quo and allow policies and procedures to go unchanged. The corporate leaders' aversion to change will ultimately handicap their potential to learn and take their company further. The negative emotion of complacency can be just as inhibitive to learning as anger or contention.

The types of emotion that can adversely affect learning potential are numerous. One is the anger that can arise from disagreement. Another is the complacency that can arise from similar views. While contradictory views can indeed lead to stress and inhibit learning, this does not necessarily imply that we should surround ourselves with like-minded people if we intend to learn. Each individual must gauge, for himself or herself, which emotions that inhibit learning he or she is susceptible to in a given situation. Having determined that, the individual can make the best decisions to maximize personal learning.

63. The most effective way to understand contemporary culture is to analyze the trends of its youth. (Discuss how the statement could or could not be true)

The trends of the youth are a pertinent, if not all-telling, window into contemporary culture. Youth are in a unique and amplified stage of existence, their desires being mature, but their ability to choose and direct their passions still stunted without a completely developed frontal lobe. Youth is a time of excess and extreme; by taking the excessive currents of teenagers and diluting them, we may achieve a singular look into not only contemporary culture but also the foundations of the culture of tomorrow.

Youth do not just like musicians; they love them. The youth will regale themselves with their favorite artist's paraphernalia and stream their videos until their PC overheats. Music speaks to the youth and becomes an outlet for the passion and freedom they are trying to achieve. Music trends today have greatly shifted. Teenagers were often grouped according to what type of music they were into: rap, emo, pop, or hip-hop. And the music was often segregated along the boundaries of race and gender. Now, however, these barriers of sound are being crossed and the artists considered "superstars" have audiences crossing over race, gender and economic position. Michael Jackson is an iconic example of a cross-over artist. His music transcended all the normal barriers and generation lines as well. With his tragic death his world-wide influence was solidified as millions from all nations and ages took to the streets to show their gratitude. Today, artists like Jay-Z, Miley Cyrus, Carrie Underwood, Eminem and others are showing, through music, that the youth and culture are moving away from segregation and choosing instead to identify with all groups of people by "mixing" their lives the way the DJs mix the records.

The next key aspect of culture is literature. Books have long since been a key indicator of the social climate. In the past two decades the most popular books have been fantasy novels. They are not fantasies of far off worlds, but of this world and the potential of the young. The *Harry Potter* series is one of the best-selling series of all time. This story of a boy wizard who is chosen for greatness has audiences of all ages. A more recent cult hit is the *Twilight* series, where a "friendly" vampire and a human are immortally meant for each other. While these novels are fiction, they show the underlying sense of escapism and destiny that rages through society. People are looking for purpose, direction and a cause worth risking everything for. They want to believe in magic, love and goodness triumphing over evil, not in the unrealistic epics of the past, but in a realistically painful but truthful manner.

Lastly, studying the clothing trends of the youth can grant a glimpse into the economic climate. Clothing trends, since mass production of goods became a standard, have been cyclical, but with some variation. Currently, the style is reverting back to a structured 80's look: hair has more volume, shoulder pads are back and patterns and colors are bigger and bolder. This return to structure comes at a time when the economy is unable to give the youth any sense of security. The structure and control over clothing and hair combat the uncertainty of the future and reveal a healthy sense of rebellion and longing for safety.

The trends of the youth may not reveal every nuance of contemporary culture, but they are able to point out, with their extremism, the values and fears that are the underlying currents of society. The goals, fears and even political climates of the time are not lost on the youth, and it is in their processing of reality that the future will emerge.

64. **People's attitudes are determined more by their immediate situation or surroundings than by society as a whole. (Discuss how the statement could or could not be true)**

The influence of societal norms and expectations can be overwhelming at times. There is no preparation for the curves and twists of life, and even though people often experience the same upsets and accolades the attitude with which they face the world and their own situations can be truly singular. The attitude of a person is not determined by his or her immediate situation or the expectations of society alone but by a merging of the two.

During Hurricane Katrina millions were displaced from their home, losing almost all of their material possessions; the hurricane was no respecter of persons and ravaged the gulf coast with equality, creating refugees of all who lived in its wake. Though the immediate situation was the same people's reactions were not; some people found a reserve of courage while others pillaged and looted the towns. One diabetic woman was found in the attic of a church days after the flood. She survived off the remnants of food in the kitchen and found companionship with a raccoon while awaiting rescue. Once found the woman was in good spirits and was grateful to see friends and family and attempted to help rebuild her community. A couple miles away looters were taking advantage of the distraction ripping down metal guard rails to loot some clothing and jewelry stores. There is also video footage of some police joining in the looting. The immediate situation for these people was the same, and perhaps even the adrenaline released into their bodies was similar, but their choices on how to respond were individual, not unanimously based on social expectations.

Abraham Lincoln was the 16th President of the United States; he grew up in rural Indiana with his father and step-mother. Though he was close to his stepmother Lincoln became distanced himself from his father because of the latter's lack of ambition. Lincoln did not discuss his roots much, considering himself self-made. Most individuals from the backwoods of Indiana and Kentucky remain in similar situations. There was not much in the way of education; Lincoln had less than 2 years of formal education and traveling or self-improvement seemed a daunting task. However, these normal excuses did not hold Lincoln back. He left his father's land and made his own way, giving himself the education he had been denied. Lincoln was definitely influenced by his social upbringing; his anti-slavery position had been taught in his local church, but his response to the challenges was unique and providential for the rest of the United States.

A final example is found in Edith Wharton's *The House of Mirth*. The main character Lily is a socialite looking to marry for money, though she secretly avoids those marriages because she lacks real passion. Lily's financial situation changes along without any great prospects. Then, adding insult to injury Lily is accused of having an affair by an adulterous wife hiding her own indiscretions and she is ruined. At this point Lily has lost her lifestyle, friends, and hope for the future. She does find a job sewing, but she is hopeless at it, and eventually her own toils end as she overdoses on sleeping elixir. Lily's demise is not instantaneous, but slowly she loses chunks of herself without the ability to bounce back; she does not have the internal resources for survival in any world but those of a socialite she was born to. Where others gain strength from toil, Lily just collapses. Once again, her situation is not singular, but her reaction is her own.

Attitudes are not completely determined by society. Instead, immediate situations give people the opportunity to delve into their own soul and choose the way they wish to approach the world.

65. Nations should suspend government funding for the arts when significant numbers of their citizens are hungry or unemployed. (Describe advantageous and disadvantageous circumstances of the recommendation)

While funding for the arts is a noble cause, it has little justification when many citizens are starving or jobless. No example is more striking than the situation of the USA.

Despite the astronomic economic growth of the 20th Century, poverty and ignorance still run rampant throughout the world. Among policies to address such issues, there remain some of the more economically inefficient ones undertaken by governments. Where American Constitutional Law professors seem to stumble regarding the properness of such policies, economists charge in with shouts of "Improper!" Theirs is an argument built upon maximizing marginal gains; money spent on arts programs, they claim, would be better utilized training the poverty stricken because there would be more metaphorical bang for the buck. Although a dollar spent on art can slightly increase the happiness of connoisseurs, a dollar spent training an individual can lead to a lifetime of productivity. According to this argument, whether arts programs have ever clearly established a constitutional mandate for their existence, they utilize funds relatively inefficiently compared to programs aimed at eradicating poverty.

Also, the obvious hypocrisy of supporting the arts while people starve and have no jobs must be challenged. That people could look through a homeless man while studying a publicly subsidized mural remains one of the great testimonies to human selfishness. Art programs, in this contention, exist not to make already pleasant conditions more meaningful but rather to conceal the obvious injustices present in American society. Instead of acting to alleviate hunger and unemployment, the government expends considerable resources to enhance an already enviable existence of some people. This is not only hypocritical, but also violates constitutional provisions for survival over thriving.

Adopting the recommendation would be disadvantageous when a large number of starving or jobless citizens rely for living on government funding for the arts. In the United States, constitutions both legitimize and restrain government actions. Although no wording seems to indicate that government has an obligation to guarantee that the people live well, as opposed to just living, the *14th Amendment* guarantees that life, liberty, and property will not be infringed upon by the states. In the 1930s, Roosevelt commissioned the Works Progress Administration to employ struggling artists. Any action contrary to constitutional law clearly falls under the category of "improper." If the significant number of hungry or unemployed citizens does not depend for survival on government funding for the arts, suspending the funding will be more justified.

The arts, though in themselves highly valuable for maintaining culture, must nevertheless take a back seat to more important concerns. Survival for all trumps beauty for the lucky; any dollar spent on frivolity while suffering yet exists is not only a tragic waste but also an unjustifiable idiocy.

66. All parents should be required to volunteer time to their children's schools. (Describe advantageous and disadvantageous circumstances of the recommendation)

How involved should parents be in the education of their children? Many people argue that once their children are at school, all responsibility for their learning falls upon the educators and administrators. Other people may counter, stating that parents need to take more initiative in regard to their children's education and volunteer at their schools. There is strong evidence to support this latter notion, as it would solve a number of problems that have been plaguing schools throughout the nation.

Having parents volunteer would contribute first and foremost to much needed extra supervision. As it currently stands, the ratio of students to teachers is at least 25 to 1. With so many students in a room with only one teacher, it is hard to maintain discipline by themselves. Students converse with one another freely, ignoring teachers' lectures, and their questions can only be answered to a limited degree because of their number and the limited time available for each class. If parents were made to sit in on classes, they would be able to keep students in line and provide support so that the primary educator can do his or her job with fewer distractions.

Another problem that could be remedied by this recommendation is the growing disconnect between parents and the material being taught to their children, which could allow them to offer better help to their children during their studies. This point is driven home further by the adoption of common core subjects in American primary schools, which have a fundamentally different approach to learning basic math, reading and writing, and other subjects. Common core math has even been featured in the news, where commentators discussed its peculiar methodology that adults have trouble grasping, making it difficult to aid their children that have questions on their homework. It is likely that if parents were made to volunteer at their children's schools, there would be a greater chance of their learning enough about what their children are learning to allow them to help their children with their homework.

Certain reasons against the notion do present themselves. First of all, it is impossible that every parent would have the time to volunteer, a situation that could negate some of the benefits of the suggestion. Also, it would be difficult to practically enforce such a mandate, because of parents' lack of time and the uproar it would cause if any significant punishment were given for not volunteering. However, it is reasonable to assume that most parents would care enough about their children's education to take some time off work to volunteer at their children's schools.

To sum up, the concept of having parents volunteer at their children's schools is a sound one, despite a few potential drawbacks. With its implementation, schools can expect to see a decrease in teacher stress and more well-behaved students overall.

67. **Colleges and universities should require their students to spend at least one semester studying in a foreign country. (Describe advantageous and disadvantageous circumstances of the recommendation)**

In a world that is more globalized than ever before, studying for some time overseas has become an invaluable experience for university students. There are a variety of ways in which having at least a semester abroad may benefit students. It could give them a greater geopolitical awareness and inspire their career ambitions, among other things.

One of the major benefits of studying abroad in a foreign country is the exposure students gain from experiencing different cultures. To this end, a semester or a longer period studying abroad can impart numerous benefits. For example, those studying any form of politics or international relations regarding the country will get firsthand knowledge of the people and culture. Art students can visit museums and galleries in the country they are studying in. These experiences will enable students to gain a broader understanding of international relations and conflicts in the proper context of current and historical events.

Having gone to another country, students can gain further insight into their desired career paths. An engineering student may decide to enter into environmental engineering after seeing the wind farms during a term in Germany. A finance major may decide to apply for a company in Hong Kong after a stint at a local university. Someone studying medicine abroad for at least a semester may decide to relocate to a developing country after seeing the need for their skills there. Such interchange of workers brings a greater diversity to the world's work pool, with larger numbers of workers able to adapt to international conditions.

Adopting the recommendation would not be advantageous if the costs are beyond the means of the students. If students are not financially capable of paying the costs of an exchange program, then they should either be waived from the requirement, or be offered some form of financial aid. Otherwise, such a program would force many students to be unable to continue their education. Such prohibitive practices would likely have a negative impact on the application rate to universities, so some financial safety nets should be set up for students. With the subsidy and waiver in place, such a program would benefit a wide range of students.

In conclusion, if universities require students to study for no less than a term abroad, as long as there are waivers or subsidies offered to financially challenged students, then it will generously benefit the students in the long-term. Also, the overall quality of the world's workers will improve as larger numbers of people gain international work experience.

68. Teachers' salaries should be based on the academic performance of their students. (Describe advantageous and disadvantageous circumstances of the recommendation)

In the attempt to improve the grades and learning of students in schools, the idea has been put forth that the salaries of teachers should be based upon the academic performance of their students. While this may seem reasonable on its face, after further examination of the potential ramifications I cannot agree with this claim.

Firstly, this claim makes no mention of the workload that comes with being a teacher. Perhaps in some countries, or even counties within countries the number of students in a class is small, having only ten to twenty students. However, in other countries such as African nations and East Asia, classes can be composed of over forty students. Taking into account the lesson planning, homework and test assignments, classwork, and grading of all these materials, the teacher in question has almost no time to monitor the individual performance of students, meaning that their performance in class is due mostly to their own studying and the efforts of their parents to ensure they are reviewing daily. Therefore, to base the salary of teachers on the overall performance of their students is unfair, since it does not account for the actual labor they put into their job.

Secondly, students themselves may not be particularly adept at studying or willing to cooperate in class. In fact, in many countries students that tend to perform poorly are often grouped into single classes. Should teachers that are expected to teach these classes be forced to accept a lower pay? Definitely no. In addition, this system would give a coercive power to students that become aware of the pay system, as the sometimes vindictive nature of young students may lead them to perform poorly on purpose to get back at a teacher who they feel wronged them.

I would be remiss if I did not address the potentially beneficial aspect of this kind of pay system. It would certainly motivate many teachers to do their best to teach students effectively, as their livelihood would otherwise literally hang in the balance. For those teachers skilled or lucky enough to have high-performing students, they would be able to turn teaching into a lucrative career. This in turn would create an incentive for them to provide a higher quality education. Through this system, teachers who did not develop effective teaching strategies would be weeded out, leaving the best possible educators, who would in turn receive ample reward for their efforts. After all, one of the reasons for the struggling education systems of many nations is the lack of funding for teacher salaries, which stigmatizes the profession for aspiring educators. However, herein lies a major flaw with a performance-based pay system: corruption and falsification. Under this system, a teacher with a group of under-achieving students tends to be tempted to inflate their students' scores in order to save their pay, and as a result the quality of education may drop, and certainly the quality of students entering universities would fall as well.

In sum, I must disagree with any plan that proposes that we pay teachers based on the scores of their students. At its core, it is unfair for the amount of hard work that teachers must put in just to teach normally, and it offers too much temptation for abuse in the form of inflated grades.

69. It is no longer possible for a society to regard any living man or woman as a hero. (Address challenges to your position)

I do not agree with the notion that it is not possible for society to regard anyone living as a hero anymore. Not only are there a number of examples of famous individuals with a clean record, but also the public is not unanimous in its opinion of media reporting about beloved heroes; even respected people that do get dragged through the mud are still able to make a comeback.

A perfect example of a modern hero with a clean record is Warren Buffett. One of the richest men that have ever lived, after controlling Berkshire Hathaway and investing in other companies, he now contributes to numerous charities and intends to donate 99 percent of his entire fortune before he dies. The media leaves him alone for the most part, as he is often non-controversial. Buffett almost never speaks on hot-button political or social issues; he simply focuses on investment, philanthropy, and his family. Such a man is an ideal role model: rational, hard-working, a loving father and husband, and of course extravagantly rich. He is even a hero that crosses the political divide in the USA, standing for a titan of business for the Republicans, and a generous advocate for workers and the less-privileged for the Democrats. Perhaps he is not a hero in the military sense, but socially, he certainly counts.

Also, this claim forgets the resilience of people's opinions. If a public figure is panned or heavily criticized for something they have done, there remains the chance that most people will simply look past it or forgive it, depending on its severity and the following actions of the person. Take American actor Robert Downey Jr. for example. He burned many bridges in the film industry, alienated many fans, and nearly killed his career thanks to his drug addiction. After a stint in rehab and coming to terms with the possibility of never appearing in a film again, Downey Jr. cleaned up and regained his place in audience's hearts, such that he is now one of the highest paid actors in Hollywood. In the case of other famous stars, numerous rappers have been accused and convicted of crimes and their fans cheer for them in spite of that fact. Therefore, I do not think people will stop considering their heroes as such for anything but the most heinous revelations about their character or behavior.

This is not to say that no person considered to be a hero for people has never been torn asunder in the eyes of their followers by the media. Look at American comedian Bill Cosby. He was once considered to be "America's Dad" for his performance on the acclaimed sitcom *The Cosby Show*, where he as the titular character managed a raucous family to humorous and dramatic effect. Unfortunately, after a number of allegations and court hearings Bill Cosby was found guilty of sexual assault against a number of women over the years, and the backlash against Cosby has forever marred his legacy. Now when people look back on his shows, they see a monster parading as a man; he is no longer an icon to be looked up to. But this is luckily an isolated incident, not a common occurrence among those in the spotlight. There remain a large majority of role models with nigh-pristine records, and thus it would be improper to assume that such is the norm and that there are no heroes anymore.

In conclusion, I do not agree with the statement that no living man or woman can serve as a hero in society anymore. There are still numerous examples of famous people who are not morally or otherwise corrupt and there are those that have recovered. Even if some are abhorrent, this is not evidence of an all-encompassing trend.

70. **Some people believe that in order to thrive, a society must put its own overall success before the well-being of its individual citizens. Others believe that the well-being of a society can only be measured by the general welfare of all its people. (Address both views)**

Both views pit the well-being of a society against the well-being of the individuals within that society, with the first one claiming that the success of the whole is more important than the success of the one and the second one claiming the opposite. I concur with the second view that the wellbeing of the one trumps that of a society, since the first view is flawed in its main assumption that a society could be successful when the citizens are not; this logic cannot stand as the whole is based only on a contract between the individual citizens.

Thomas Paine outlined this collaborative agreement in his pamphlet, *Rights of Man*, claiming that human rights originate in nature and are not subject to political or religious persuasion; he also supported the idea that when the needs of individual citizens are not being met by the society there is a justified reason for revolution. Paine understood that it is the citizens that matter, and the society only exists as a catalyst for individual safety and progression; while there are some sacrifices made in joining a society the sacrifice of personal liberties and choice is not among them, and the idea of the freedom of the masses being placed in the hands of a few is reprehensible indeed.

Those who work in political spheres may accept the statement that leaders can only satisfy some of the people all of the time, all of the people some of the time, but never all of the people all of the time. This is simply because countries are comprised of numerous groups with separate and often conflicting interests. Welfare for the financially challenged, healthcare for the ill, education for the youth, and retirement programs for the elderly, among other things, require vast numbers of resources and citizens to put aside the expectation that all of their individual needs will be met, in order to fulfill the majority of needs for society to function. Thus, a reasonable degree of self-sacrifice for the greater good is an expected requirement in any civilized society. Otherwise, no one's needs are met, and chaos ensues.

On the other hand, even the most liberal and compassionate society has a breaking point insofar as selflessness is concerned. A most famous example can be seen in the founding of the United States of America, wherein the taxes imposed by Britain on the colonists were eventually too much to bear, and the colonial citizens opted for secession rather than the protection of the British Empire. Those taxes may have been justifiable in the context of the amount of money spent by Britain to protect and maintain the colonies, but it was not from the perspective of the revolutionaries whose human rights were being infringed by a tyrannical regime. It can thus be surmised that when individuals are faced with increasingly high burdens to support a supposed society, they will tend to fight back when they reach their limit, leading to the failure of such a system.

In sum, a society is based on a contract between all the individuals it represents; it cannot be considered a success if the citizens are not given the opportunity to succeed. With this proviso, we could then seek a balance between the needs of society and those of the individual.

71. **Claim: Any piece of information referred to as a fact should be mistrusted, since it may well be proven false in the future.**
    Reason: Much of the information that people assume is factual actually turns out to be inaccurate. (Claim-Reason)

The speaker claims that anything called a fact should not be trusted because much of what is considered factual proves to be inaccurate. While the reason has some merit, the claim must be denied, as it would only lead to chaos.

The idea that at any given point in history much of what was viewed as factual was false has been well documented. The notions that the world is flat, bloodletting helps a patient fight an illness, the sun revolves around the earth, bathing too frequently is harmful, a god riding in a chariot causes the sun to rise and women are vixens whose passions must consistently be checked for them to remain pure are just a handful of examples. These "facts" have always been fiction, but it took time and observation for their real nature to be known.

That said, the speaker's assumption that just because a fact might be fiction it should be mistrusted is completely misguided. If this idea were supported on a universal level chaos would ensue. With no consistency the world becomes dangerous and frightening. Who knows whether the sun will rise? Who can be sure their plants will grow? Why worry about prenatal care if a baby might not even be in there? With no facts to count on there is no foundation for reality. With no basic beliefs a world of darkness and fear would prevail. The Mayan civilization believed that the Jaguar of the underworld helped the sun to rise in the morning and to pass through the underworld at night. If the Jaguar decided to sleep then the sun might not rise. Therefore, to appease the Jaguar, who could not be trusted, there were both human and animal sacrifices. In this instance the fear of the unknown evoked a state of instability leading to death and pain.

A world where mistrust reigns can create another problem. If there is no constant, then there is no ability to solve problems. For instance, if a light bulb will not turn on, one would have to accept that this is what happens instead of counting on the idea that the light bulb should turn on when it is in proper working order and there is electricity flowing to it. Without trust all light bulbs would eventually be discarded and society would be forced to make candles or live in the dark, but with trust comes the logical ability to make sure that all of the aspects of the light are in working order. First, check the filament and power source. Next, look into the electrical system, and find a way to make it work using the basic principles of electricity and wiring. This logic is a possibility only if the basic principles of electricity are believed.

Instead of mistrusting all facts people should use their own reasoning to help determine what truths are worth accepting and which ideas should remain in question. One differentiation that can help is the difference between experiential truths and scientific thoughts. An experiential truth is something learned through experience. For example, a plant needs water and sunlight to grow. This event is observed on a normal basis and so it is safe to use it as a fact. These types of facts are also the kind that can give the world a sense of order and regularity. Scientific ideas, on the other hand, are things that people think are true but that cannot always be experienced. The previous example of the earth being thought of as flat was one before telescopes and satellites helped prove otherwise.

Something referred to as a fact may be proven inaccurate. However, just because this is the case does not mean we should be skeptical of everything called a fact. Such a blanket claim would only lead to chaos and uncertainty. Indeed, whatever the fact in question, people must find a balance between questioning the world and taking the opportunity to live in it.

72. **Claim: Nations should suspend government funding for the arts when significant numbers of their citizens are hungry or unemployed.**
Reason: It is inappropriate — and, perhaps, even cruel — to use public resources to fund the arts when people's basic needs are not being met. (Claim-Reason)

The speaker claims that when many citizens starve and have no jobs, the government should not provide funding for the arts anymore, for the reason that meeting people's basic needs takes precedence over public funding for the arts. The reason may be somewhat problematic, but the claim is generally valid.

First, let us establish whether the reason given for the claim is sound. To this end, proper and improper uses of public resources must be clearly dichotomized. In the United States, constitutions both legitimize and restrain government actions. Any action contrary to constitutional law clearly falls under the category of "improper." Indeed, *the US Constitution* grants the Congress the power to make all laws "necessary and proper" for carrying out its constitutionally delineated responsibilities. Any law not rooted in an explicit constitutional mandate exists beyond the legal definition of "proper."

However, the constitutional authorization for programs such as the National Endowment for the Arts remains considerably vague. Although *the 14th Amendment* guarantees that life, liberty, and property will not be infringed upon by the states, no wording seems to indicate that government has an obligation to guarantee that the people live well, as opposed to just living.

Understanding the role of *the Constitution* in shaping arts endowments requires an understanding of the history of such expenditures. Since its inception the US government has expended funds to decorate its buildings in glamorous ways, the capitol dome being an obvious example. In the 1930s, Roosevelt commissioned the Works Progress Administration to employ struggling artists. This program's constitutional grounding, never challenged by the Supreme Court, remained unclear; rather, its existence seemed to supply all the legitimization it required. Even present arts programs exist largely in a paradigm that allows the federal government to spend on any program it deems good.

Although the reason on which the claim is based is somewhat problematic, the claim is usually valid. Despite the astronomic economic growth of the 20th Century, poverty and ignorance still run rampant throughout the world. Among policies to address such issues, there remain some of the more economically inefficient ones undertaken by governments. Where Constitutional Law professors seem to stumble regarding the properness of such policies, economists charge in with shouts of "Improper!" Theirs is an argument built upon maximizing marginal gains; money spent on arts programs, they claim, would be better utilized training the poverty stricken because there would be more metaphorical bang for the buck. Although a dollar spent on art can slightly increase the happiness of connoisseurs, a dollar spent training an individual can lead to a lifetime of productivity. According to this argument, whether arts programs have ever clearly established a constitutional mandate for their existence, they utilize funds relatively inefficiently compared to programs aimed at eradicating poverty.

Also, the obvious hypocrisy of supporting the arts while people starve and have no jobs must be challenged. That people could look through a homeless man while studying a publicly subsidized mural remains one of the great testimonies to human selfishness. Art programs, in this contention, exist not to make already pleasant conditions more meaningful but rather to conceal the obvious injustices present in American society. Instead of acting to alleviate hunger and unemployment, the government expends considerable resources to enhance an already enviable existence of some people. This is not only hypocritical, but also violates constitutional provisions for survival over thriving. While funding for the arts is a noble cause, it has little justification when many citizens are starving and jobless.

All in all, whether addressing people's basic needs should always be put before providing public funding for the arts is debatable. However, it is economically unjustified and hypocritical to provide government funding for the arts when many people go hungry or jobless. Thus, the arts, though in themselves highly valuable for maintaining culture, must nevertheless take a back seat to more important concerns such as survival and suffering.

73. Claim: Many problems of modern society cannot be solved by laws and the legal system.
Reason: Laws cannot change what is in people's hearts or minds. (Claim-Reason)

The speaker claims that laws and the legal system cannot address many problems of modern society for the reason that what is in people's hearts or minds cannot be changed by laws. The claim is certainly true. The reason given is also mostly true. History is rich with examples of people attempting to inculcate morals by restricting action. With few exceptions every conquering power has either explicitly or implicitly attempted to project its ethos and worldview onto the conquered. History, however, has largely demonstrated the futility of these attempts.

Legislated morality from without cannot succeed for several reasons, and understanding those reasons first requires a thorough understanding of the mechanisms such legislation utilizes. These laws attempt to implement an incentive structure to alter behavior, assigning artificial consequences to certain acts that overpower the natural consequences of that deed. A recent example of this has been the mask mandates imposed to deal with the threat of the COVID-19 pandemic. Hefty fines have been levied in many cities to dissuade people from venturing outside without a face mask. The motivation behind this policy is to protect the health of the citizens, but many people perceive it as an attempt to dilute individual freedoms and expand governmental powers.

The logic of this policy stems from the fundamentally flawed assumption that in matters of core belief people will act as value-maximizers. Codified morality assumes that people lack the backbone to stand by their preexistent morality or that they lack any ethos at all. The former assertion hints at the arrogance of policy not grounded in reality, whereas psychologists and sociologists have both repeatedly proven the ridiculousness of the latter claim.

History offers repeated examples of people choosing to fight and die for their fundamental beliefs rather than replace them with those prescribed from without. Examples range in severity from the martyrdom of the Jesuit missionary St. Francis Xavier to the mass pogroms of 19th

Century Europe. However, any encroachment of the established order into the realm of the individual has been met with severe resistance, indicating the degree to which people attach themselves to their ethos.

For people who deny the mask mandates, at least in the USA, their opposition to wearing a mask stems from their belief in individual freedoms. In their hearts they do not view themselves as causing any direct harm to others, and therefore are not under any obligation to inconvenience themselves. When the government attempts to tell them they are wrong, it triggers their defense mechanism against oppressive government, and they become even more entrenched in their defiance.

Any attempt to legislate morality must also battle the hypocrisy attached to such an assertion. Any behavioral restriction comes with a claim to truth regarding proper behavior and belief. This claim has been grounded in various arguments, from the perceived moral superiority of the conqueror over the conquered to the absolute rightness of the majority over the minority. In the end, however, these arguments all boil down to the assertion that "might makes right." However, right, defined as worldview coinciding with reality, exists prior to force and cannot be made known by it alone. Right action cannot be measured by its consequences, and hence cannot be legislated into existence.

It is true that some problems of modern society cannot be addressed by laws and the legal system because legislated morality is futile. However, other problems cannot be solved because laws are outdated and fail to consider changed circumstances. For example, with the advent of the Internet, new laws must be enacted to govern internet-related activities. It is also likely that because laws are not properly enforced, problems persist. For instance, justice governing equality has not always been effectively administered, a situation that tends to perpetuate inequality rather than rectify it.

Although laws that restrict certain behaviors can be made and even enforced, they will probably not be able to change how people think. History has repeatedly demonstrated both the arrogance and futility of such legislation and psychology suggests why this would be so. Even though laws and the legal system cannot solve many problems of modern society, they should not be discarded altogether.

74. **Educators should take students' interests into account when planning the content of the courses they teach. (Describe advantageous and disadvantageous circumstances of the recommendation)**

The speaker claims that teachers should consider the interests of their students when developing their curriculum. I concur with the claim because students are more motivated to learn when they demonstrate interest in the subject they are learning.

Concerning the interests of the students, it is obvious to anyone that has ever gone to school, i.e. the majority of the developed world, that attending a class that one finds boring offers little potential in the way of actual learning. Students that are bored in class will find themselves drifting off to sleep, doodling on their notepads, or becoming otherwise distracted with unproductive activities. In the case of younger students, they cannot be faulted for this, as they already are prone to short attention spans. As for older students, they should not be subjected to this because they are often paying for their education, making it a service which should be tailored to their wants and needs as customers. Thus, teachers that try to make their material more interesting will better guarantee that their students are paying attention and getting their money's worth out of the service they are paying for.

In regard to lesson planning, it is always a good thing when teachers involve their students in the development process, particularly when the latter's interests are incorporated. The traditional method of having the teacher act as an unapproachable bastion of knowledge, one who tells students what is right and wrong and cannot be questioned, is not conducive to learning in a modern world where facts can be accessed instantly on a smartphone. Rather, allowing the students to feel that they have some control over their learning can be very empowering, and can lead to a greater interest in the subject matter, or a development of certainty in what their interests are at the very least. This is a concern that is growing ever more important in modern society, where facts are not as important as competence, which derives from true interest in one's field of study. Therefore, a teacher who allows students to participate, even to a minor extent, by including their interests in the creation of lessons is contributing to individuals that can think for themselves and make better decisions regarding their future education.

One of the biggest problems with modern schooling is the class size and time constraints. A standard class size in most high schools and middle schools is around thirty students per class, and each teacher may have five separate classes to teach. That means each teacher can have at least three-hundred students each semester! Imagine trying to figure out what each individual student wants to learn in each of those five classes and then having to develop a separate curriculum for each class. Sure, the teacher could theoretically simplify it, and have a survey that allows students to choose from a list of topics to include in the curriculum, but that means a portion of students are going to have to learn things that they are not interested in, dooming them to a school year in which they will be bored and therefore more likely to perform poorly on assignments and exams. Even if student opinion is fairly uniform, there is still the issue that students do not exactly know what they need to be learning, that is, why they are in school in the first place. Thus, the unjust workload and unreliable metric of student opinion constitute a damning argument against allowing student input in curriculum development.

In conclusion, while they may find it logistically challenging, teachers should generally take students' interests into consideration when developing their teaching material. Such teachers are more likely to have students that remain engaged during class and develop lasting interest in otherwise boring subjects.

75. The primary goal of technological advancement should be to increase people's efficiency so that they have more leisure time. (Discuss how the statement could or could not be true)

What is the overall purpose of technological advancement? The statement asserts that the main purpose of technological advancement should be to increase the efficiency of people in order to give them more leisure time. I would agree that improving efficiency is a reasonable goal for technological development, but would hesitate to fully support the statement, as there are other clear purposes for innovation aside from just the attainment of greater amounts of leisure time.

The field of medical science, while contributing to a person's efficiency insofar as being healthy is needed for functioning on a daily basis, has little to do with giving people more free time. Instead, medical advances most often aim to treat or cure fatal or debilitating illnesses. To this end progress in medical technology appears to aid people in returning to work more than it does liberate them from it. For example, leg amputees may receive a prosthetic that restores their bipedal faculties, allowing them to walk and in some cases even run, thus returning them to normal human functionality. This may reduce the time they would have otherwise spent living in a wheelchair, but it is a zero-sum equation in terms of their net change in free time. Therefore, unless medical technology reaches a point where it can augment and improve normal human function, it does little to increase people's efficiency in such a way that they experience more free time than usual.

Broader fields of technology such as transportation would appear to be more directly in line with the statement's assertion in favor of increasing efficiency and free time for people. True, the introduction of motor vehicles, locomotives, and air travel has greatly reduced the amount of time required for people to travel or transport goods. But the time that has been made available by such technologies has not been utilized for leisure time. Rather, people have simply used the time saved to work longer hours, as evidenced by the fact that people still tend to work a similar number of hours each week compared with their predecessors. Thus, the question is raised of whether giving people more free time is a meaningful goal of technological progress, as people are unlikely to utilize that time for rest.

There are also certain kinds of technology that do not deal with people in any direct fashion. Take particle physics for example. There are almost no practical applications for the technology required for particle physics research, as the accelerators used are designed for the singular function of smashing atoms together. The science gleaned from studying subatomic explosions tends to wax theoretical, dealing with the so-called "secrets of the universe". If there is any relationship between a kilometers-long particle accelerator and the average person's leisure time, it has yet to be discovered; and until such a discovery is made, the two should remain separate.

While attempting to increase efficiency, and with it, the amount of leisure time people can enjoy, is a part of the goals of some fields of technological advancement, it should not be a factor in all areas of technological research. Some fields, like medical science and more esoteric theoretical fields, have more linear, or abstract, goals when it comes to their intended benefits to humanity.

76. Educators should base their assessment of students' learning not on students' grasp of facts but on the ability to explain the ideas, trends, and concepts that those facts illustrate. (Describe advantageous and disadvantageous circumstances of the recommendation)

A widely accepted notion among experts that study education is the importance of memorization to the learning process. Yet, in the endeavor to assess students' learning there has been some debate over whether the assessment should be based on their acquisition of facts or their ability to elucidate concepts, trends, and ideas demonstrated by the facts; it may be argued that the two are corequisites for effective assessment, with differing focus on either at distinct stages of students' learning.

Evaluation of students' learning should stress mastery of conceptual knowledge and critical thinking skills rather than grasp of facts. Having a natural proclivity for remembering pieces of information is a neat skill that can be used to entertain classmates but is not necessarily evidence of true understanding of the core concepts. After all, not every person who is gifted with rapid mental arithmetic becomes a famous mathematician by virtue of that ability alone. This is due to the fact that mathematics, or any scholastic field for that matter, requires an in-depth understanding of a variety of complex concepts and theories rather than simple rote memorization of multiplication tables. In this vein, when it comes to taking tests, those students who use their ability to quickly memorize bits of information are unable to effectively apply them to questions that are not imitative of the recalled information, nor can such students solve problems in a creative capacity. Therefore, it could be argued that students who rely on memorizing facts alone are hardly educated at all.

Nonetheless, a significant issue with receiving a true education is that concepts, theories, and trends are difficult to learn straight from the outset. When young children begin their education, their learning abilities are far more attuned to memorizing the date that Christopher Columbus arrived in the Americas than grasping the consequences of European expansion for indigenous tribes. It takes an accumulation of pure facts, which can then be pieced together to form a more cohesive whole, before an understanding of complex theories and relationships can occur in a student's mind. This is analogous to a person's ability to fully comprehend a Rembrandt painting's beauty, which can only take place after the person learns the meaning of terms such as "chiaroscuro" and the baroque movement. Therefore, assessment of students' learning cannot ignore their acquisition of facts that exemplify the ideas, trends, and concepts.

Perhaps the most effective assessment would cover facts as well as conceptual knowledge and change its focus with students' learning stage. Teachers often encourage their students to memorize and analyze facts throughout their continuing education. A child's biological advantage to memorizing slices of information is beneficial to acquiring foundational pieces of knowledge and is evident in the reliance on education by rote in the ancient world. However, the law of diminishing returns begins to take effect on using memorization as a crutch with more complex problems that require higher-order thinking skills. Augmenting memorization with analytical skills pays enormous dividends as a student progresses up the academic ladder. Hence, sound evaluation of students' learning needs to involve both facts and conceptual knowledge.

While there are some notable benefits to assessing through ability to master concepts, it does not exist in a state of mutual exclusion with assessing pure fact acquisition. A highly effective assessment will be able to evaluate students' factual knowledge as well as their ability to analyze the overall context and application of those facts within an academic setting.

77. **Unfortunately, in contemporary society, creating an appealing image has become more important than the reality or truth behind that image. (Discuss how the statement could or could not be true)**

The speaker asserts that modern people are more concerned with creating an attractive image than with the substance or truth behind it. I agree with this statement for several reasons: the popularity of social media platforms, specifically image sharing apps, along with the pervasiveness of photo-editing software, makes it evident that most people are obsessed with outward appearances above everything else.

If one were to go to any moderately-populated public area, the chances are high that the people there would be using their smartphones to take pictures of their surroundings, food, or themselves, and immediately posting them on their preferred social media app – not before sending their photo through the adequate number of filters in order to make that flower look brighter, put their latte in focus, or remove age lines in their face. Taglines for each image are always positive and upbeat, even when they are not. The desire for "likes", "hearts", "thumbs-ups", or whatever the icon for confirmation one's app uses seems to be the primary motivating factor behind most of the images posted online. This has even been parodied in the dystopian science-fiction show Black Mirror, wherein the characters of one episode live in a future where one's real-world ability to buy certain items and services, as well as travel to certain areas is limited by their social status online. The people in the episode are shown to be caricatures of contemporary selfie-enthusiasts: all fake smiles and comments of enjoyment, despite the tasteless food and unfair social situations they are forced to experience.

Another example of this obsession with façade can be seen in the world of education and employment. It has become an accepted part of society that a college degree from a noteworthy university is required to obtain a decent job, even though this is not necessarily always the case. Nonetheless, college applications and résumés are endlessly padded with nonsense and fluff to make the candidate seem more appealing. A position as a secretary under the "employment history" section, may, for instance, be amended with a description along the lines of "involved in the management and organization of documents in a professional setting" – a needlessly eloquent way of saying that the candidate filed paperwork. But many people feel that a professional description such as the one previously mentioned is necessary, if not for the appearance, then to show that the candidate is capable of keeping up appearances.

In one area, there has been a consistent concern for the truth behind images: the art industry. For the most part, artists have always tried to paint, carve, write, or otherwise create their work with a deeper meaning behind the images on the canvas or the words on a page. For example, the great masters loved to insert messages into their works, such as the silhouette of god's robes forming a human brain in Michelangelo's "The Creation of Adam", signifying an alternative source of divine knowledge not asserted by the church. Yet in an odd twist, contemporary artists are driven to attach deeper meaning to their creations to the point that they put more effort into contrived explanations than the creation itself. Examples of this range from a white canvas selling for millions of dollars to exhibits of literal trash drawing large crowds; it appears that the desire to maintain an appearance of being a part of the "high art" society has led galleries and collectors to ignore the fact that these works have no value, aesthetic or otherwise.

In sum, the wealth of easily observable evidence largely favors the viewpoint that modern society is far too focused on creating an appealing image to the point that the truth, if there was ever any to begin with, is ignored. While this takes on a counter-intuitive appearance in the realm of art, it is clear from people's behavior on social media.

78. The effectiveness of a country's leaders is best measured by examining the well-being of that country's citizens. (Address challenges to your position)

The speaker argues that the best way to evaluate leaders' effectiveness is to observe the well-being of their country's citizens. While it is hard to disagree outright with this notion, the statement is too vague and absolutist in its stance and calls for some investigation and clarification.

In order to attach the "effective" label to leaders, we need to determine what powers they have to influence legislation and society as a whole, especially whether the well-being of the citizenry will be the metric by which such "effectiveness" is measured. For example, if a country's leader is not afforded any meaningful powers, or has power but no means to apply it, then it would be almost impossible to prove that the current status of the public, whether positive or negative, is the fault of the leader. On the other hand, if the leader is in possession of a consolidated power structure, there would be more connections between their decisions or mandates and the effects of such on the populace with which we determine their efficacy.

From a historical perspective, it is far easier to assess past national leaders in this way, as governments in the past tended to lean toward a centralized system with monarchs as their heads. Hence why there are names for kings such as Alexander the Great, or Ivan the Terrible. Yet even with the benefit of hindsight, such titles do not necessarily stem from the quality of life enjoyed by the people: few historical records describe the relative change in daily life before and after Alexander the Great ascended the throne; his triumphs were primarily military in nature.

This begs an important question: is leaders' effectiveness only judged by the well-being of people during their term as a leader, or by the long-lasting effects of their rule? This is an oft-debated concept in American politics, where incoming leaders blame all current problems on the incumbent and attempt to reap the glory for all of the beneficial policies enacted by the incumbent. This complicates the statement's assertion then, since a current leader may appear to be completely ineffective in the present moment, but may at the same time enact policies that will allow their nation's people to prosper for years to come.

In conclusion, taking the statement at face value would be a bit hasty, as it does not consider the amount of power a leader may hold, nor does it consider the effects a leader's policies may have in the future. With such caveats, it is reasonable to use the well-being of a country's citizens as a metric for determining the effectiveness of their leader.

79. All parents should be required to volunteer time to their children's schools. (Address challenges to your position)

How involved should parents be in the education of their children? Many people argue that once their children are at school, all responsibility for their learning falls upon the educators and administrators. Other people may counter, stating that parents need to take more initiative in regard to their children's education and volunteer at their schools. There is strong evidence to support this latter notion, as it would solve a number of problems that have been plaguing schools throughout the nation.

Having parents volunteer would contribute first and foremost to much needed extra supervision. As it currently stands, the ratio of students to teachers is at least 25 to 1. With so many students in a room with only one teacher, it is hard to maintain discipline by themselves. Students converse with one another freely, ignoring teachers' lectures, and their questions can only be answered to a limited degree because of their number and the limited time available for each class. If parents were made to sit in on classes, they would be able to keep students in line and provide support so that the primary educator can do his or her job with fewer distractions.

Another problem that could be remedied by this recommendation is the growing disconnect between parents and the material being taught to their children, which could allow them to offer better help to their children during their studies. This point is driven home further by the adoption of common core subjects in American primary schools, which have a fundamentally different approach to learning basic math, reading and writing, and other subjects. Common core math has even been featured in the news, where commentators discussed its peculiar methodology that adults have trouble grasping, making it difficult to aid their children that have questions on their homework. It is likely that if parents were made to volunteer at their children's schools, there would be a greater chance of their learning enough about what their children are learning to allow them to help their children with their homework.

Certain reasons against the notion do present themselves. First of all, it is impossible that every parent would have the time to volunteer, a situation that could negate some of the benefits of the suggestion. Also, it would be difficult to practically enforce such a mandate, because of parents' lack of time and the uproar it would cause if any significant punishment were given for not volunteering. However, it is reasonable to assume that most parents would care enough about their children's education to take some time off work to volunteer at their children's schools.

To sum up, the concept of having parents volunteer at their children's schools is a sound one, despite a few potential drawbacks. With its implementation, schools can expect to see a decrease in teacher stress and more well-behaved students overall.

80. A nation should require all of its students to study the same national curriculum until they enter college. (Address challenges to your position)

Decision is not to be made lightly on whether all students of a country should be required to study the same national curriculum preceding entry to college; there are valid points to be made on either side of the argument. Supporters of such a position would posit that it would provide equitable access to quality education and ensure a more robust curriculum created by academic experts on each subject. These points are noble in their own right, yet equally valid is the fact that disregarding a required uniform national curriculum provides a wider range of educational techniques and theories to be applied, which is a superior recipe for a nation's growth and success. Therefore, I do not agree with the statement that a nation should require all of its students to study the same pre-college national curriculum.

A primary source of evidence which contradicts the statement is that the implementation of a mandated national curriculum would stifle the development of a country's talent. Indeed, it is well established that there is not just a single kind of students; every pupil has their own unique hobbies, affinities, and born talents. In this vein, it is very improbable that a uniform curriculum would be effective at fostering the growth of individual strengths, because an academic regimen of this type appeals to the abilities of the lowest common denominator. Those who have specialized interests would be left to fend for themselves. Thus, a variety of curriculums must be made available to suit the needs of individual students.

Additionally, with uniformity comes conformity and the elimination of regional knowledge and culture. As a nation focuses on a singular academic dialogue, little to no room is made for the important cultural traditions that peoples of different areas pass down to future generations. This presents a clear danger of many cultures being pushed to the brink of extinction, which has negative effects on a nation. On the other hand, preserving regional cultures can have a tremendous benefit to a country. For instance, the Harlem neighborhood of New York City in the USA was a traditionally African American neighborhood. There had been attempts for many years in the early to mid 1900's to diversify the area and bring it into the fold of the standard "American Way", which was a euphemism for "White, Anglo-Saxon, Protestantism". Yet the perseverance of the African American community in Harlem led to the Harlem Renaissance, a cultural revolution of art, literature, and music that has had lasting influences in the USA even to the present day. A uniform national curriculum that imparts mainstream culture at the expense of such dynamic culture would be unfair and insipid. Therefore, policies which encourage a rigidly uniform academic curriculum should not be allowed to take the place of the vibrant cultural education that can be found in a country.

Supporters of the statement can, of course, create a level playing field for all students. Yet, an issue with this line of thinking is that, more often than not, the opposite is true. Forcing all students into the same box suffocates those with unique abilities. Their exceptional talents are overshadowed by their apparent lack of aptitude in other areas, and they are left feeling inadequate in the face of a system that rewards mediocrity. This is not fair by any standard, and ultimately leads to self-esteem and confidence issues in students, hardly the desired crop of graduates for any country.

Furthermore, it could be argued that implementing a similar national curriculum would create a more efficient process of designing courses for students. This is undoubtedly true, at least in the context of creating a cookie-cutter model in which topics may be copy-pasted to suit the basic educational requirements for a particular course or semester. Nonetheless, this would render courses completely devoid of meaningful content with which students could prove themselves to be exceptional. The very concept of competitive scores would be made meaningless as everyone would know the same content as everyone else; how then could the cream of the crop be selected? A nation is grown by its leaders, regardless of the field, not the blasé drones.

While implementing a uniform pre-college national curriculum is on its face a beneficial policy, after deeper consideration a less advantageous picture forms. Such a curriculum would exclude academic excellence and effectively eradicate the rich regional knowledge and culture upon which a nation thrives. Therefore, a more diverse range of curricula may be far more beneficial to the students of a nation, and by proxy, the nation itself.

81. Colleges and universities should require their students to spend at least one semester studying in a foreign country. (Address challenges to your position)

In a world that is more globalized than ever before, studying for some time overseas has become an invaluable experience for university students. There are a variety of ways in which having at least a semester abroad may benefit students. It could give them a greater geopolitical awareness and inspire their career ambitions, among other things.

One of the major benefits of studying abroad in a foreign country is the exposure students gain from experiencing different cultures. To this end, a semester or a longer period studying abroad can impart numerous benefits. For example, those studying any form of politics or international relations regarding the country will get firsthand knowledge of the people and culture. Art students can visit museums and galleries in the country they are studying in. These experiences will enable students to gain a broader understanding of international relations and conflicts in the proper context of current and historical events.

Having gone to another country, students can gain further insight into their desired career paths. An engineering student may decide to enter into environmental engineering after seeing the wind farms during a term in Germany. A finance major may decide to apply for a company in Hong Kong after a stint at a local university. Someone studying medicine abroad for at least a semester may decide to relocate to a developing country after seeing the need for their skills there. Such interchange of workers brings a greater diversity to the world's work pool, with larger numbers of workers able to adapt to international conditions.

The most compelling reason that could be used to challenge my position is that the costs will be probably beyond the means of the students. If students are not financially capable of paying the costs of an exchange program, then they should either be waived from the requirement, or be offered some form of financial aid. Otherwise, such a program would force many students to be unable to continue their education. Such prohibitive practices would likely have a negative impact on the application rate to universities, so some financial safety nets should be set up for students. With the subsidy and waiver in place, such a program would benefit a wide range of students.

In conclusion, if universities require students to study for no less than a term abroad, as long as there are waivers or subsidies offered to financially challenged students, then it will generously benefit the students in the long-term. Also, the overall quality of the world's workers will improve as larger numbers of people gain international work experience.

82. Educational institutions should actively encourage their students to choose fields of study in which jobs are plentiful. (Discuss positive and negative consequences of the policy)

The singular purpose of education is to prepare students for their future careers. To this end, it is in the best interest of students if their schools make the effort to encourage them to pursue fields of study that will guarantee many jobs. To do anything less would be a disservice to the incredible investment made by students and their parents when choosing an institution to study at.

It is important to remember that in the highly competitive economic environment in which we live today there is little leeway for mistakes when students choose a field of study and, by proxy, a future career. Since students are usually not as knowledgeable as their adult counterparts in the education administration, it is not always a good idea to allow them to choose whatever field they wish to study. Take liberal arts majors as an example; some of them lead to the lowest paying careers after graduation since few real jobs are available to degree-holders in these areas other than teaching the same subjects which they have studied. There are certainly large sums of money to be made in these fields for those savvy enough to apply their knowledge and skills in the right way, but such skillsets are not often taught in school, but rather learned through experience.

There is no doubt that most students will be initially unhappy with adults advising them to give up what they believe to be their dream jobs in favor of other means of employment, but this preliminary dissatisfaction will often give way to greater overall contentedness once they find that the career path suggested to them will provide a salary which supports a decent lifestyle. In addition, what most people presume is their passion, as with many aspiring musicians and other artists, is often downgraded to a hobby or minor interest when faced with the titanic amount of practice needed to hone their ability, as well as the compromises they must make in order to turn such skills into a profitable means of employment.

One likely negative consequence of implementing the policy is that educational institutions may give the wrong advice: what was initially deemed the fields that promised an abundance of jobs may prove the opposite when students graduate. This has been known to happen before. For instance, in the USA during the early 2000's the law field gained enormous interest as globalization picked up more steam, and as a result there was a projected need for new corporate lawyers and a boom in the legal field in general as the standard of living increased. Thus, academic institutions advertised heavily to encourage students to get legal degrees, not only was the profession highly respected, but it was also very lucrative. Predictably, this boosted law major admissions substantially, but the result was that it became difficult to find a job in the legal field due to the overabundance of law graduates. However, this boom-bust cycle in education and employment opportunities has been heavily researched in recent years, and many colleges and universities now use up-to-date job market analysis to recommend majors to students. In this way, schools can still be reasonably relied upon to persuade students to choose majors in which there are plenty of jobs.

In summary, while it may not be exactly what students want, it is in their best interest to be advised by educational institutions to find a major that would be ideal for finding a job. The financial stability brought about by a better career would, in time, compensate them for the short-term sacrifice of giving up a hobby-oriented major.

83. People's behavior is largely determined by forces not of their own making. (Address challenges to your position)

In determining the source of individuals' actions and personality traits, people debate whether the greater responsibility lies with outside forces or personal choices. While individuals' choice of action certainly plays a role in their behavior, I think that most of what shapes how a person acts is determined by other influences such as genetics and environment.

The theory of "nature vs. nurture" is a frequently discussed dichotomy in behavioral psychology. While it is still undetermined that which of the two is predominant, it is generally accepted by psychologists that both play an important role in behavioral development. We tend to think of ourselves as individuals with full control over all of our faculties, but the truth is that much of who we are is dictated by certain factors, such as genetic predispositions to certain emotions, as well as learned behaviors. For example, recent research has shown that addiction is more of a personality disorder than a result of the contents of a drug. This is not to say that drugs are not themselves addictive, but certain people are genetically prone to addictive behaviors. This is further explained by a look at groups of people who take addictive drugs; some are able to cease using these substances without any adverse psychological reactions aside from normal withdrawal symptoms, while others appear unable to cope with life psychologically without their drugs.

On the nurture side of the issue, it has long been accepted that a person's environment goes a long way toward influencing the actions of a person. The most evident example of this is culture. In different nations, different cultures compel people in certain ways, whether it be as simple as eating etiquette or as complex as interpersonal relationships: what is considered taboo and acceptable is outside the control of the individual. Of course, there are people that choose to go against the grain and play outside the rules of society, but aside from hermits living in isolation, no one is ever fully free from societal influence.

It is important to note that this does not excuse individuals for taking part in taboo or illegal behaviors, especially if they are aware of the nature of their actions. People who grow up in many parts of the world understand that actions such as theft and murder are wrong, even if a violent and criminal upbringing perverted their conscience. When these people steal, they know they are taking that which does not belong to them and that there are other options available. The same goes with murder, a person who kills another knows that a gun or knife or bludgeon used with deadly effect will have no result other than the snuffing out of another's life. There is always a conscious choice, a weighing of conscience or consequence that occurs with each act, not matter how impassioned a person may be. However, attributing all crime and bad behavior solely to individual choice ignores the complex socio-economic histories that created the problems that nations around the world are trying to resolve.

In sum, I consider the actions a person undertakes to be largely the result of behaviors they were either born with or learned from their environment. It is easy to say that someone did something simply because they chose to, but we should be willing to look at the underlying cause of that choice, such as education, upbringing, and genetic predispositions.

84. Colleges and universities should require their students to spend at least one semester studying in a foreign country. (Discuss positive and negative consequences of the policy)

In a world that is more globalized than ever before, studying for some time overseas has become an invaluable experience for university students. There are a variety of ways in which having at least a semester abroad may benefit students. It could give them a greater geopolitical awareness and inspire their career ambitions, among other things.

One of the major benefits of studying abroad in a foreign country is the exposure students gain from experiencing different cultures. To this end, a semester or a longer period studying abroad can impart numerous benefits. For example, those studying any form of politics or international relations regarding the country will get firsthand knowledge of the people and culture. Art students can visit museums and galleries in the country they are studying in. These experiences will enable students to gain a broader understanding of international relations and conflicts in the proper context of current and historical events.

Having gone to another country, students can gain further insight into their desired career paths. An engineering student may decide to enter into environmental engineering after seeing the wind farms during a term in Germany. A finance major may decide to apply for a company in Hong Kong after a stint at a local university. Someone studying medicine abroad for at least a semester may decide to relocate to a developing country after seeing the need for their skills there. Such interchange of workers brings a greater diversity to the world's work pool, with larger numbers of workers able to adapt to international conditions.

Negative consequences of implementing the policy occur when the costs are beyond the means of the students. If students are not financially capable of paying the costs of an exchange program, then they should either be waived from the requirement, or be offered some form of financial aid. Otherwise, such a program would force many students to be unable to continue their education. Such prohibitive practices would likely have a negative impact on the application rate to universities, so some financial safety nets should be set up for students. With the subsidy and waiver in place, such a program would benefit a wide range of students.

In conclusion, if universities require students to study for no less than a term abroad, as long as there are waivers or subsidies offered to financially challenged students, then it will generously benefit the students in the long-term. Also, the overall quality of the world's workers will improve as larger numbers of people gain international work experience.

85. **Although innovations such as video, computers, and the Internet seem to offer schools improved methods for instructing students, these technologies all too often distract from real learning. (Discuss how the statement could or could not be true)**

The assertion here is that technology can assist in teaching some things, but its presence as a whole is more distracting than helpful. While I do feel that technology plays too large a role in the lives of students, I cannot agree with the idea that it inhibits "real learning", especially if the goal of the education is the ability to succeed in the workplace.

Technology is a part of society. There is no getting away from its presence and the powerful way it holds and transmits information. In many ways technology has opened new vistas of learning and created a world where learning can be much more visual and hands on, along with being kinder to the environment. In the medical field doctors can practice surgeries on computer patients who can simulate numerous scenarios and give the training physicians experience without the loss of animal lives. In grade school children can see the animals of Africa running through the desert instead of simply looking at a sketch in a book. College students can look up sources for papers online, type their paper on the computer and often turn it in online. They have at their fingertips greater amounts of information to write more informed responses without killing a single tree. This is only a drop in the ocean opened to students through technology.

Even though technology can accomplish all these amazing things, the speaker asserts that it can distract from "real learning". This claim is difficult to substantiate as the purpose of education is not clearly defined. If the purpose is to prepare students to have a job, then more often than not the exposure to technology and requirement to work with it is one of the most powerful tools students can obtain. It would be a disservice to shield the students from the technology prevalent in the working world, and instead of allowing them to use the education, to set them up to have wonderful thoughts but no avenue for expressing them.

Despite the importance of technology, this vast sea of information is not always conducive to learning. There is something to be said for having your own quiet thoughts, writing things down by hand, going to see something live and reading a book. The pace of these things is so much slower, and the sacrifice is often greater, breeding a more attentive learner. Live productions demand more effort on the audience. First, you have to drive to a theatre, find parking and your seat and then sit in one place for hours. It almost sounds painful, but when the sacrifice is made it can be magical and the energy in the room cannot be replaced by a computer screen. It is these things that students miss when technology overcomes a classroom, the slow things which breed patience and stillness. The real danger to an education drenched in technology is that students will not gain the slow skills. These skills are important not only for academics but also for a person's ability to find peace. Perhaps this is the "real learning" to which the speaker is referring.

Technology is not going away, and our ability to use it to achieve our own goals and purposes will dictate much of our ability to succeed in modern times. Still, technology is not all powerful. It is a tool, and like any tool can do much in the hands of its user. By combining the use of technology in the classroom with more traditional methods of learning, schools will be able to produce more well- rounded students, students who are grounded in the basics but highly competitive in the workplace.

86. Universities should require every student to take a variety of courses outside the student's field of study. (Discuss positive and negative consequences of the policy)

As romantic as the notion of pursuing higher education for education's sake may be, the hard truth of the modern job market is that a university education in a career-related major is a prerequisite for even entry-level jobs. Therefore, I disagree with the statement, because it is unjustifiable for universities to mandate that students must shoulder ever-increasing tuition costs to take a range of courses that do not directly relate to their major.

A common argument in favor of requiring students to take a wide variety of courses is that it creates "well-rounded" people. Not only is this redundant, as most universities are looking for "well-rounded" candidates from high school, but it is also extremely vague. Sure, someone entering the professional world should have a dynamic skillset so as to be adaptable to unexpected challenges that may arise. However, the very fact that such challenges are unexpected, and thus unpredictable in nature means that one cannot fully prepare for them; then, why waste time learning about superfluous subjects when one could put more focus on the actual field of study? Furthermore, when students apply for jobs, most companies ask for a CV, rather than a full résumé, because they are only interested in the skills that specifically apply to the job one is looking for. This is all a part of the specialization of jobs, a system that is designed to address any aforementioned problems by having people with skillsets that are specifically suited for such issues. Therefore, to reiterate, the "well-rounded" argument is a moot point.

On a more practical note, consider the fact that over the past thirty years or so, tuition prices at universities have skyrocketed by over a thousand percent, whereas median incomes have almost stagnated. Add this to the extremely competitive job market, as well as the immense time constraints that most high school graduates have to choose their life paths, and one comes to understand that going to university is a substantial investment. As with any investment, a cost-benefit analysis must be conducted, and in the context that has already been established, there simply is no tangible benefit of paying for classes that fall outside one's major's curriculum. The best example would be from people in STEM fields. Students in these majors are already overburdened with a staggering amount of work for their required classes, which cost more than usual due to the price of each credit and the expensive textbooks that they require; therefore, it is ludicrous to demand that they pay more money for and spend more time on irrelevant courses. This gets worse when one considers that these frivolous classes can keep an otherwise stellar student from graduating if they do not pass them. Thus, not only do mandated courses that fall outside one's major hurt the student, but they also have the potential to hurt a nation's economy as a whole, since it actively limits the number of qualified candidates from entering the job market based on performance in classes that have no relation to that job.

Implementing the policy also has positive consequences. Having a base of college-educated individuals who are well-versed in a wide array of subjects aside from those which directly relate to their major can be very enriching to a society. In an ideal situation, colleges would be attempting to manufacture Renaissance Men and Women, like Da Vinci, who himself was proficient in a variety of fields from anatomy to mechanics. Imagine a population of people who were each in their own way capable of advancing numerous areas of science and art. Yet as with all schemes, there is a catch: Da Vinci himself was an extremely unique individual, whose like is only seen once in a number of generations. Attempting to manufacture people in the same image is simply not efficient, as the majority of people will likely be unwilling to devote their entire lives to constant study in different fields without a very clear financial motivation. Thus, foisting a diverse range of courses upon students who are simply trying to earn a degree to get a career is a waste of resources and has a high chance of leading to failure.

In conclusion, I cannot agree with the statement that universities should require students to take classes other than those required by their field of study. Such classes are a great waste of time and money, do not contribute to their ability to perform their job in any measurable way, and in fact damage their ability to enter their chosen careers.

87. The best ideas arise from a passionate interest in commonplace things. (Discuss how the statement could or could not be true)

Throughout the history of mankind's development, the nature of inspiration has been a frequent topic of debate. Once, great works were credited to divine inspiration; now, the argument is often similar to that of the statement presented above: that the greatest ideas come from long hours of dedicated study of relatively mundane things. In science and most other fields, this is true to a large extent, but there are always unique bursts of thought that seem to arise out of nowhere.

One of the more important discoveries of the modern era, Newton's theory of gravity, is an apt embodiment of the statement's argument. Newton sought an answer to one of the simplest questions in physics at the time: If celestial bodies followed elliptical orbits, as proven by Kepler, why then did objects not simply fly off in tangent lines to their orbits? Or to put it more simply: Why do objects fall towards the Earth at all? Starting from this basic observable fact, Newton conducted his experiments and wrote out his mathematical theorems, until he came to his famous conclusion that there must be a force between all objects known as gravity. It could be argued that Newton's science was far more complex than this, and certainly his math was; however, it all stemmed from the observation of everyday items falling towards the ground.

A more practical invention arose from an even more basic, though equally dogged observation of mundane events: the almanac. Originating around the 12th century, the almanac was an invaluable tool for farmers for centuries, giving weather and seasonal forecasts based on the weather-watching experience of agrarian experts. While almanacs have given way to more advanced meteorological sciences that allow for more accurate weather predictions, the source of the idea likely came from some long-forgotten farmer that noticed a pattern after countless hours of staring at the clouds, season after season, and decided to record it.

Naturally, as science and technology advances, fewer and fewer problems can be solved simply by analysis of the mundane. In a world of complex electrical systems, interwoven networks of roads, wires, and national politics, solutions are rarely so simple. Yet it could be argued that all this complexity merely becomes commonplace to the contemporary man, and that these new systems are the same to him as the clouds were to the ancient farmer. This has been the case for many of the giants of the modern tech industry: Elon Musk found a way to pay for things more easily with his e-commerce app PayPal; Jeff Bezos streamlined shopping and delivery systems; Mark Zuckerberg fundamentally altered how people interact with Facebook. All these people tackled the complexities of modern life by boiling human needs down to their barebones and offered a technological solution to people's inconveniences.

In the end, there is an argument to be made for the statement that great ideas arise from commonplace problems, since it is hard to gain traction among a large number of people with a solution that only benefits a marginal few. In fact, the large number of technological and scientific developments in history has arisen from people keenly looking at the world around them and picking out the patterns and disparate elements to formulate theories and invent machines that could then benefit all mankind.

88. To be an effective leader, a public official must maintain the highest ethical and moral standards. (Address challenges to your position)

Does holding ethical and moral standards to the highest degree of importance determine the effectiveness of a leader? Such a question is not easy to answer, as numerous issues arise when we try to define properly what exactly morality, ethics, and being an effective leader mean. It is, therefore, far easier to approach this question by looking at leadership in three areas: politics, business, and social activism.

With respect to politics, it becomes readily apparent how complex notions of morality and ethical standards become, as such ideals are mired in the amount of power a leader has, and the way in which the leader obtains power. There is also the distinction between the objective morality of the leader and the morality which the leader projects himself or herself as having. Using the United States as an example, it would appear that for all intents and purposes, a presidential candidate's objective morality matters little, insofar as it aligns or conflicts with their voter base, with their projected morality being the paramount focus of their political advertising. Even this has little real influence on their governance, though, as there seems to be a general moral line that is not to be crossed by US politicians. While there are certainly ethical transgressions to be found, most fall within the realm of marital infidelity, or other personal issues, rather than larger scale ethical concerns that could affect the country as a whole. Therefore, a moral compass does seem to be necessary in order to lead a nation, but one need not possess an ivory-tower level of moral fiber to do so.

In the realm of business, the situation is even less clear, and again requires one to define what effectiveness means. If being an effective leader in business solely means earning as much money for the company and shareholders as possible, then it could be argued that ethics and morals are a hindrance instead of a necessity. Maximizing profit in the short term almost always requires a ruthless approach to lay-offs, safety standards, and other company policies, and during the Industrial Revolution, this is exactly what workers experienced under what are now known as the "Robber Barons". Nowadays, with more intense regulations by governments and more awareness on the part of consumers, an effective business leader must tread the line between pleasing shareholders with dividends and maintaining ethical working conditions for employees. Thus, in business, it does not matter whether the leader actually possesses moral or ethical standards; what counts is that they follow those that are laid down by the law.

Only in the realm of social activism does one see a definite need for strong moral and ethical fiber. Leaders of social movements are judged almost exclusively on the beliefs they hold and their willingness to act upon them. When Gandhi espoused his doctrine of nonviolent protest, it was only his example of standing at the front of the protest lines receiving his fair share of beatings doled out by authorities that inspired people to follow him. Similarly, Martin Luther King Jr., the great activist for civil rights in the USA, believed in absolute non-retaliatory protest. He led the marches of his supporters through police dog attacks, wrongful arrests, and various other hate crimes until the hearts of US citizens were swayed toward his cause. It can be surmised, then, that when dealing with society directly, individuals must maintain strong morals if they want other people to follow them.

In summary, from the numerous examples throughout history and the modern world it can be reasonably asserted that in regard to politics and social movements, following a strict set of morals, or at least appearing to, is critical to the success of a leader, whereas in business, a balance must be kept between what earns the most money and what could land the company in legal trouble.

89. Claim: Imagination is a more valuable asset than experience.
   Reason: People who lack experience are free to imagine what is possible without the constraints of established habits and attitudes. (Claim-Reason)

This claim asserts that it is better to have imagination than experience, reasoning that people who lack experience are less limited by preestablished habits or bias, and thus can think more freely and imaginatively. I disagree with this notion, as I believe that it unfairly frames experience as a limiting factor rather than a guide and a shield against harm, though there are admittedly some areas in which an unhindered imagination thrives more than an experienced one.

Consider the various fields of practical science: engineering, chemistry, and so on. While these fields certainly benefited from young open minds during their respective periods of development, the truths about how the laws of nature function that have since been uncovered have led to diminishing returns on unrestrained imagination. Where once Da Vinci imagined a gyrocopter with a spiral-shaped blade, our modern understanding of aerodynamics and flight technology has made the great polymath's ideas seem child-like in their ignorance. As an ardent scientist, had he possessed the knowledge that aerospace engineers have now, he would have conformed his more imaginative flight designs to ones that achieved lift.

This brings up another important factor that experience has over imagination: prudence. An active imagination can contribute much to theoretical sciences by brainstorming possibilities; however, as previously mentioned, we live in a physical world where there are concrete limitations to what can be achieved. Perpetual energy, for example, is a physical impossibility due to entropy, and no amount of imagination can remove that fact. Allowing imagination to take precedence over the wisdom of experience can even be deadly, when the person doing the imagination decides to ignore the laws of nature and it backfires. Take for example the countless stories of children causing harm to themselves or others because they lack experience: a child caused a lightbulb to explode because he wanted to cool it down with a piece of ice, not understanding thermal expansion; a child killed his friend by imitating fighting moves on television, having never been told that they were fake. Both in science and in life, imagination should take a back seat to the better judgement that comes with experience.

There do exist some notable exceptions to my argument, primarily in the arts. Perhaps the most well-known is the composer Mozart, who was a child prodigy. A less known but equally impressive example is Autumn de Forest, who was deemed an artistic genius at only eight years old. However, this argument does not apply to prodigies and other savants, as they are unique products of genetics rather than the application of one mode of thinking being discussed here. Looking more closely at such examples, we find that many of these young open-minded individuals were smothered in the field which they were proclaimed to be naturally gifted in. Mozart, for example, was indeed naturally talented, but people often forget that his father, Leopold Mozart, was already a highly respected composer, conductor, and musical educator. It would be difficult to argue that this did not have any bearing on Wolfgang's upbringing and musical development. It can be asserted, therefore, that while an open mind is useful for expressing one's talents, such talents require nurturing from the more experienced among us.

To conclude, imagination is not necessarily more valuable than experience. In science, being imaginative can bolster theoretical design, but in the end the design must fit within the natural laws of the universe that one can only know through years of study and experience. In art, an open mind that lacks experience is like a flexible metal alloy before tempering: it is flexible and can be shaped, but lacking hardness, it is without practical use.

90. In most professions and academic fields, imagination is more important than knowledge. (Discuss how the statement could or could not be true)

The speaker asserts that imagination supersedes knowledge in importance in most academic fields and professions. I find this notion to be utterly indefensible, as it is both naïve and overly optimistic about how imagination works and how the search for knowledge functions.

I describe the statement as naïve for two main reasons. The first is that it implies that nature bends to the will of one's mind, and the second is that imagination is equally valued by employers. Children are often told that they can accomplish anything if they put their minds to it, and while this is intended to develop a strong work ethic, many misconstrue it as meaning that anything is possible. The problem with this mode of thinking is that not everything is possible. We live in a finite physical universe with very real limitations, limitations that cannot simply be imagined away.

To speak more directly to the point, many difficulties in the academic and working world that require solutions may call for some critical thinking, but being too imaginative can be impractical, or even harmful. Take finance and accounting for example: If there are inconsistencies with a company's financial records, there is a strict protocol to follow in attempting to correct or report such findings. Being "imaginative" in this situation is tantamount to committing fraud, as proper records are legally required to do business. Thus, in this case knowledge of financial law and accounting procedures is far more important than an imagination.

In the realms of science, too many examples prove that knowledge is more important than imagination. Science itself is a process for finding truth in the universe we live in; thus, imagination must always bow to the facts. An example of this can be seen in the almost disastrous Apollo 13 Lunar mission, where an electrical malfunction caused one of the pod's oxygen tanks to explode, damaging their computer and other life-support systems. It is here that one could make the argument in favor of imagination being important, as teams of earth-side engineers worked non-stop to come up with a solution to bring the crew home safely, using only items they had on board the space craft. A jury-rigged device was developed, using tubes and air-filter parts from their space suits; however, this remedy was born not purely out of imagination, but also out of the decades of combined experience of a number of scientists working with all their might. It was the knowledge these people possessed of the various systems and capabilities of every item on the vessel that allowed them to come up with the quick fix that saved four men's lives.

When it comes to academics, there is a bit more leeway for imagination to play a greater role, but it strongly depends on which field one is studying. There are the arts, of course: song, dance, painting, and others. In these a strong imagination is critical for developing new and more interesting modes of expression. Knowledge has its role in color theory, biodynamics, and music theory, but is not as necessary as in other fields. However, even in non-STEM fields, knowledge takes precedence. History, for example, requires a large collection of knowledge in order to be understood. Imagination has no place other than in the colorful ways historical events can be described, but as for what happened, the goal of history is to find hard evidence proving or disproving various historical occurrences instead of making them up. Using one's imagination in this way is considered falsification or revisionist and is highly frowned upon in the academic community.

While imagination does have its uses in sparking ideas, it can be seen in both professional and academic scenarios that knowledge is more useful for solving problems and performing work effectively. Without the knowledge with which to imagine, the most that can come out of a brainstorming session will be something too abstract to be applicable to any real situation.

91. To be an effective leader, a public official must maintain the highest ethical and moral standards. (Discuss how the statement could or could not be true)

Does holding ethical and moral standards to the highest degree of importance determine the effectiveness of a leader? Such a question is not easy to answer, as numerous issues arise when we try to define properly what exactly morality, ethics, and being an effective leader mean. It is, therefore, far easier to approach this question by looking at leadership in three areas: politics, business, and social activism.

With respect to politics, it becomes readily apparent how complex notions of morality and ethical standards become, as such ideals are mired in the amount of power a leader has, and the way in which the leader obtains power. There is also the distinction between the objective morality of the leader and the morality which the leader projects himself or herself as having. Using the United States as an example, it would appear that for all intents and purposes, a presidential candidate's objective morality matters little, insofar as it aligns or conflicts with their voter base, with their projected morality being the paramount focus of their political advertising. Even this has little real influence on their governance, though, as there seems to be a general moral line that is not to be crossed by US politicians. While there are certainly ethical transgressions to be found, most fall within the realm of marital infidelity, or other personal issues, rather than larger scale ethical concerns that could affect the country as a whole. Therefore, a moral compass does seem to be necessary in order to lead a nation, but one need not possess an ivory-tower level of moral fiber to do so.

In the realm of business, the situation is even less clear, and again requires one to define what effectiveness means. If being an effective leader in business solely means earning as much money for the company and shareholders as possible, then it could be argued that ethics and morals are a hindrance instead of a necessity. Maximizing profit in the short term almost always requires a ruthless approach to lay-offs, safety standards, and other company policies, and during the Industrial Revolution, this is exactly what workers experienced under what are now known as the "Robber Barons". Nowadays, with more intense regulations by governments and more awareness on the part of consumers, an effective business leader must tread the line between pleasing shareholders with dividends and maintaining ethical working conditions for employees. Thus, in business, it does not matter whether the leader actually possesses moral or ethical standards; what counts is that they follow those that are laid down by the law.

Only in the realm of social activism does one see a definite need for strong moral and ethical fiber. Leaders of social movements are judged almost exclusively on the beliefs they hold and their willingness to act upon them. When Gandhi espoused his doctrine of nonviolent protest, it was only his example of standing at the front of the protest lines receiving his fair share of beatings doled out by authorities that inspired people to follow him. Similarly, Martin Luther King Jr., the great activist for civil rights in the USA, believed in absolute non-retaliatory protest. He led the marches of his supporters through police dog attacks, wrongful arrests, and various other hate crimes until the hearts of US citizens were swayed toward his cause. It can be surmised, then, that when dealing with society directly, individuals must maintain strong morals if they want other people to follow them.

In summary, from the numerous examples throughout history and the modern world it can be reasonably asserted that in regard to politics and social movements, following a strict set of morals, or at least appearing to, is critical to the success of a leader, whereas in business, a balance must be kept between what earns the most money and what could land the company in legal trouble.

92. Critical judgment of work in any given field has little value unless it comes from someone who is an expert in that field. (Discuss how the statement could or could not be true)

Here the speaker posits that no critical judgement of work in any field is valid unless the critic is an expert in that field. While this does make a modicum of sense, the truth of this statement depends on both the field in question and the type of judgement being made.

Dealing first with the relative value of the statement across different fields, I think that for many of the STEM fields, the statement holds true, while for many of the social sciences it does not. For example, an engineer's designs for a new engine require a specific set of skills and a particular knowledge of thermodynamics, material science, and mechanics in order to understand them properly. An artist, unversed in any of the aforementioned sciences, would be unable to offer any meaningful criticism to the engineer on improving the design or pointing out mistakes. Similarly, a surgeon would not take advice on medical procedures from anyone that has not extensively studied medicine and anatomy, as it could lead to the death of their patient.

On the other hand, more subjective fields, as are found among the arts, can be criticized by those not necessarily knowledgeable about the finer details of the subject. For example, a person viewing Michelangelo's Statue of David need not know all the intricacies of stone masonry and carving or proportions and the particular difficulties Michelangelo had with the flawed marble he used for the piece, to appreciate its beauty. Any person can, upon looking at David, see the amount of time and effort that went into making sure every feature was distinct, realistic, and impactful. Alternatively, the works of Jackson Pollock are often criticized by laymen and art aficionados alike for their lack of any defining features other than his drip-method painting, being disorganized collages of color without form. Thus, an understanding of the details of the craft may lend a finer appreciation of a piece of art, but is not needed for criticism.

Here we touch upon the kind of criticism being levied at the field. In the example of the engineer and the surgeon, certainly no one without the necessary knowledge and experience could critique the technical parts of their work. However, in the engine design example, an artist could add their ideas on aesthetics to alter, within reason, the style of certain parts of the machine to make it more visually appealing. As for the surgeon, while no one would dare question his or her skill with a knife, a biomechanical engineer could propose a new prosthesis to make the surgery more efficient and effective. Therefore, it can be said that as long as the criticism is one where the critic's relevant experience can be applied, such judgements are valid, whereas otherwise they would not be.

All in all, I agree that the statement holds true for the most part. If an expert decides or creates something that requires a high degree of technical knowledge to understand, then those who do not possess such knowledge should not try to make criticisms that require it. Critics can, however, use the knowledge they do possess and is significantly related to the field in question to make valid observations about improving the work.

93. **Some people believe that scientific discoveries have given us a much better understanding of the world around us. Others believe that science has revealed to us that the world is infinitely more complex than we ever realized. (Address both views)**

The steady march of human progress has led to countless discoveries that have been instrumental in advancing our understanding of the universe. Yet it has been said that with each scientific finding, the scale and scope of our ignorance is revealed. I think that this is true to a certain extent. Some scientific fields have ever-expanding ranges of knowledge based upon the sheer lack of information we have on those subjects. However, other areas of scientific inquiry are very clearly understood and have little in the way of further discovery.

It can be argued that the fields of astronomy and physics are amongst the most open-ended fields of human understanding. The cosmos is vast, and we have only observed a tiny fraction of the stars and other celestial phenomena. With each new sector photographed and analyzed, thousands of new stars, galaxies and other bodies are discovered, each with unique characteristics and features that give insight into the endless possibilities of form and composition of matter in the universe. Similarly, physics as a function of the motion and interaction of bodies in space is recontextualized with the discovery of new masses and gravitational forces. For instance, when evidence of black holes was first observed, scientists had to reconsider how gravity and inertia functioned as a result. Even now experts struggle to understand the source and function of black holes, and the introduction of the theory of dark matter has only made the issue more complicated. Indeed, with each bit of information we glean about space and the physics that govern it, we have more complexities, many of which are beyond imagination, to address.

However, astronomy and physics are fields which deal with vast parts of the natural world and the unknown. When it comes to applied sciences, far less is available in terms of the possibilities of new discoveries. This means that scientific discoveries in such fields have led us to a much better understanding of the world around us. For example, in mechanics and engineering, the foundational theories are virtually set in stone already. Our knowledge of gears, springs, and electric motors has been established, and now all new developments with respect to this field rely solely upon the discovery of new materials which help to overcome limitations of stress, heat, and efficiency. An example of this can be seen in the internal combustion engine of a car. For the most part, the overall design has changed little in terms of layout and function: a chamber is injected with combustible fuel, which when ignited moves a piston that drives the shaft to the powertrain. There has not been a significant change in understanding how this process functions; instead, we have made engines safer, faster, more powerful, and more fuel-efficient through the development of more durable materials and advanced fuel. The major scientific discoveries of mechanical science have already been established; at this point we are simply refining them to work best with the tools and resources available to us. Thus, scientific discoveries in mechanics have given us such a good understanding of the world around us that it has become a well-mapped area of science with little room for further advancement from a fundamental perspective.

In addition, the notion that new discoveries in science reveal a massive lack of understanding discredits the tremendous good that such discoveries have done for mankind; it implies a sort of luddite mentality that serves no real purpose other than to be contrarian for argument's sake. Do the new questions raised by the finding of a new organ function in the human body negate the understanding of anatomy and physiology? Certainly not. It simply adds to the diagnostic and prognostic power that doctors now have in treating their patients. If anything, new scientific discoveries can simplify the way we think about the world around us. In previous eras, we had only questions about how things worked, the answers to which we filled in with fantastical theories of gods, spirits, humors, and other archaic nonsense. Any real attempt at scientific inquiry was impossible due to the sheer dearth of knowledge we had. But now we have solid foundations of evidence and data about the universe upon which we can build, making it far easier to analyze the new bits of information we discover.

While new scientific discoveries open up further lines of questioning of the nature and function of the universe, it does not necessarily imply that mankind's understanding will be perpetually insufficient. In a seemingly infinite plane of existence, as long as we are able to surpass the limits of our natural perception, there will always be new questions to be investigated by science. Nevertheless, regardless of how much we discover, certain physical limitations in our world render further lines of questioning moot, as in the example given of mechanics, since only so much can be done within the confines of the physical world.

94. Critical judgment of work in any given field has little value unless it comes from someone who is an expert in that field. (Address challenges to your position)

Here the speaker posits that no critical judgement of work in any field is valid unless the critic is an expert in that field. While this does make a modicum of sense, the truth of this statement depends on both the field in question and the type of judgement being made.

Dealing first with the relative value of the statement across different fields, I think that for many of the STEM fields, the statement holds true, while for many of the social sciences it does not. For example, an engineer's designs for a new engine require a specific set of skills and a particular knowledge of thermodynamics, material science, and mechanics in order to understand them properly. An artist, unversed in any of the aforementioned sciences, would be unable to offer any meaningful criticism to the engineer on improving the design or pointing out mistakes. Similarly, a surgeon would not take advice on medical procedures from anyone that has not extensively studied medicine and anatomy, as it could lead to the death of their patient.

On the other hand, more subjective fields, as are found among the arts, can be criticized by those not necessarily knowledgeable about the finer details of the subject. For example, a person viewing Michelangelo's Statue of David need not know all the intricacies of stone masonry and carving or proportions and the particular difficulties Michelangelo had with the flawed marble he used for the piece, to appreciate its beauty. Any person can, upon looking at David, see the amount of time and effort that went into making sure every feature was distinct, realistic, and impactful. Alternatively, the works of Jackson Pollock are often criticized by laymen and art aficionados alike for their lack of any defining features other than his drip-method painting, being disorganized collages of color without form. Thus, an understanding of the details of the craft may lend a finer appreciation of a piece of art, but is not needed for criticism.

Here we touch upon the kind of criticism being levied at the field. In the example of the engineer and the surgeon, certainly no one without the necessary knowledge and experience could critique the technical parts of their work. However, in the engine design example, an artist could add their ideas on aesthetics to alter, within reason, the style of certain parts of the machine to make it more visually appealing. As for the surgeon, while no one would dare question his or her skill with a knife, a biomechanical engineer could propose a new prosthesis to make the surgery more efficient and effective. Therefore, it can be said that as long as the criticism is one where the critic's relevant experience can be applied, such judgements are valid, whereas otherwise they would not be.

All in all, I agree that the statement holds true for the most part. If an expert decides or creates something that requires a high degree of technical knowledge to understand, then those who do not possess such knowledge should not try to make criticisms that require it. Critics can, however, use the knowledge they do possess and is significantly related to the field in question to make valid observations about improving the work.

95. In any profession — business, politics, education, government — those in power should step down after five years. (Address challenges to your position)

While it may be tempting to allow a seemingly faultless leader to continue to rule, a change in administration is absolutely necessary after a term of five years, regardless of the field. In this way, success is all but guaranteed, as obsolete ideas can be replaced with new ones, reducing the probability of stagnation and failure.

There have been plenty of instances in which a long-serving singular ruler, though initially competent and even highly regarded, has brought ruin upon those they had hoped to benefit. Frederick the Great of Prussia was and still is hailed as one of the few 'enlightened despots', a wise and intelligent leader that brought Prussia out of the Seven Year war during the mid-1700's. He made various contributions that allowed the arts and sciences of his nation to flourish during his reign, but ultimately his militaristic and nationalistic ideals promoted the expansionist mindset, which he applied for the entire 46 years of his reign and led to the destruction and partitioning of Prussia in the 19th century. His continued annexation of neighboring territories throughout his many years in power gave rise to much animosity of other powers, such that his death marked a power vacuum which was readily exploited. Had Frederick served a shorter period of rule, perhaps his militaristic inclinations would not have left such a sour taste in the mouth of Prussia's rivals, and they would not have been so eager to see his empire fall.

The dangers of endless leadership are not owned by politics alone but may also be seen in the realm of business. Steve Jobs is famous for his founding of Apple, the tech giant that has been a revolutionary force in consumer electronics for decades. However, Jobs' extended leadership between 1976 and 1985 was fraught with controversy, and his poor business decisions, along with his often-violent mood swings, forced the company to strip him of his executive powers in the late eighties. The board had felt that Jobs had, after experiencing so many years of unfettered creative control, become too arrogant in his position and feared that he would rather see the company ruined than give up his own personal vision for the products Apple created. It was only after he resigned that Apple was able to achieve the success, however lukewarm it might have been, in the nineties, which set the stage for his return and subsequent fresh ideas to turn the company into the international juggernaut we know today.

However, there is no guarantee that new leadership will most assuredly lead to success. The need for new leadership can be seen in the current education system in the USA, where the federal administration has seen little real change in decades. Sure, there have been new department heads, but the majority of them tout the same line of policies such as standardized testing and budget cuts. This has led to a severe stagnation of education quality in US public schools, contributing to a disparity between subsidized education and private schooling that was not as much of an issue in previous years. There is a growing sentiment that the fall in international education rankings, which has been steadily becoming more dramatic, is a direct consequence of hiring the same kind of educational administrators over and over, despite the fact that they replace former leaders.

In conclusion, in order to ensure the long-term success of any organization, whether it be a nation, company or other collective, a regular change in leadership is vital. Even though this may not be the most reliable path to prosperity, doing so allows new ideas to be implemented and tested, while stagnation is avoided.

96. Requiring university students to take a variety of courses outside their major fields of study is the best way to ensure that students become truly educated. (Discuss how the statement could or could not be true)

The speaker claims that a broad curriculum of study is the ideal way to become truly educated. Yet this raises two important questions: what does it mean to be "truly educated"? Is the purpose of attending university to become "truly educated"?

Taking the claim at face value, we suppose that "truly educated" can be interpreted to mean "knowing about as many fields as possible", based on the given requirement of studying a wide range of courses. However, despite the alleged usefulness of being familiar with a broad spectrum of topics, knowing facts is not necessarily an adequate measure of intellect. Instructors may successfully imprint a large volume of information upon their students, yet leave the students unequipped with the ability to apply such knowledge in practical situations. Such is the case in many test-focused education systems in Southeast Asia, where rote memorization does allow students to familiarize themselves with an array of different subjects yet leaves them woefully unable to translate that information into any useful skillset. Thus, the notion of being educated in the context of the claim is far too vague to be of any value to an argument of university education requirements.

If we accept the claim's definition of being "truly educated", there arises the issue of whether the given requirement is conducive to the goals of students who are choosing to attend university. In the context of contemporary society, a university degree has become more of a qualification necessary for employment than the representation of achievement that people in the past sought. Students need a university degree to show their proficiency in a specific area of study that is applicable to a desired job position, not to show that they are "truly educated"; employers need skilled workers, not eclectic intellectuals.

On the other hand, if it is the desire of a student to seek a multi-disciplinary education, the claim holds true, as a diverse selection of courses would indeed grant a horizon-broadening education. Alternatively, if the student in question happens to be a polymath or is uniquely motivated in his or her studies to juggle a curriculum laden with unrelated subjects, this would fit in nicely with the current narrative sold by universities that taking courses outside one's major creates a more well-rounded individual. However, just do not put too much stock in employers' thinking the same.

In conclusion, the claim appears to hold true if the interpretation of a "truly educated" individual is quite narrow, yet considering the contemporary job market, this is a highly unrealistic way of viewing a university degree. If a true education means studying a wide variety of subjects, then perhaps university itself is unnecessary in view of the wealth of information available on the internet.

97. **Claim: The surest indicator of a great nation is not the achievements of its rulers, artists, or scientists.**
Reason: The surest indicator of a great nation is actually the welfare of all its people. (Claim-Reason)

Throughout history, those nations that we look back upon as prime civilizations have always been admired for the singular achievements of their scientists, artists, and leaders. Yet, as the claim states, those great people's achievements are not the best indication of their nation's success and status. A nation's greatness involves far more than the accomplishments of a few successful individuals. Rather, as the reason points out, it is the well-being of a country's citizens as a whole which determines whether the country flourishes and is held in high esteem by its neighbors.

First of all, it should be noted that genius can come from almost anywhere. Even the least developed nations have had their own great minds arising from their populations, but this does not make the nation great. For example, the great civil rights leader Mahatma Gandhi is an icon of political thought and protest, yet India could not be considered a great nation during his lifetime. In Gandhi's time, India was still a colony of Britain, and the oppressive regime there had stifled the economic development of almost the whole country. Poverty and famine were rampant, and no matter how impactful Gandhi's words and actions may have been on the future of India, the nation itself during Gandhi's time was not considered great. Now, however, things have changed drastically, in terms of technological and economic development India's people have flourished, and the nation is now considered one of the most powerful on the world stage.

Another example can be seen in the self-proclaimed great nation of Nazi Germany. A large portion of scientific discoveries from the 1940's and 1950's was made by or with the help of German and Austrian scientists fleeing the Nazi regime. If the nation had truly been as great as it alleged itself to be, then there would not have been so many great minds that left it. At the time, persecution of a variety of categories was common; political, religious, social, and virtually all other aspects of life that may have posed a threat to the regime were ruthlessly culled by the Gestapo secret police. The country was still unsustainable from an industrial standpoint; the entire Sudetenland annexation was planned in order to seize the natural resources and utilize the labor force of nearby nations to feed the German economy. As a result, the revolutionary discoveries of Nazi Germany's scientists were almost completely overlooked in most cases since their achievements did little to improve the nation's overall well-being.

One way in which the claim may need qualification involves the fact that the general welfare of a great nation is often inextricably intertwined with the accomplishments of its rulers, artists, and scientists. In other words, the general well-being of a great nation is almost impossible without competent rulers and difficult to achieve without notable artists or scientists. This means that the achievements of such eminent people do demonstrate that the nation is great. A historical example can be seen in Tang Dynasty China, the era which is generally accepted as one of the nation's greatest premodern periods of cultural and scientific development. The people in China at the time were extremely well-cared for as compared to previous eras, and some of the most iconic Chinese poets, such as Li Bai and Du Fu, became ensconced in the annals of cultural greatness. To this day, the people of China still look back to the Tang Dynasty as a period to be emulated in regard to its artistic accomplishments as well as the welfare of the people: accessible education, cultural enrichment, available food, and other resources; the list goes on.

In conclusion, it is justified to claim that a nation's greatness is not gauged by achievements of its notable leaders, artists, or scientists because it is determined by the well-being of its people. Truly outstanding countries have been, with almost no exception, those in which most of the population enjoyed a relatively high standard of living.

98. Any leader who is quickly and easily influenced by shifts in popular opinion will accomplish little. (Discuss how the statement could or could not be true)

Effective political leaders differ from scholars and artists in that they must represent and even make choices for an entire group. This responsibility should shift the focus of political leaders from a singular view on voting and progress to a more holistic one. While their outlook should be holistic and choices should be made with their constituents in mind, this does not mean that politicians should abandon their own principles for their people. Instead, politicians must carefully determine what is best for their constituents while remaining true to themselves.

There are certainly situations where politicians can achieve much by following the tides of public opinion. For instance, when the political system relies on popular vote, then being able to quickly address and match the opinions of the masses is of great importance to accomplishing anything. Specifically, look at the relationship between the U.S. executive and legislative branches. Any sitting president wishing to enact the policies they pledged to uphold while running for office must be keenly aware of the opinions of the members of the Senate and House of Representatives. Otherwise, passing any law through either house would be nearly impossible as the bill would be struck down almost immediately. A president who can read the motives of Congress and proactively change his platform to match such views can enact a host of legislation in a relatively short period of time. Yet, such a strategy has an ironic consequence: the more it is used, the less trust people will have in the leader in question. Shifting views so often just to get things done, while practical, could be seen as disingenuous, and lead to the loss of the public trust in the leader. Therefore, even though it may limit the full potential of what a leader could accomplish, the better strategy could be picking a platform and sticking with it regardless of the whims of the public.

Indeed, in most cases politicians must abide by principle. The decision to act on principle, even though it might defame the people and country represented, must be grueling for any political leader; yet, following principle and truth will always serve the people better than ignoring them. In 1942, the French police, under Nazi orders, rounded up 10,000 Jews, placed them in the Vélodrome d'Hiver under horrible conditions, and then sent them to a French work camp and on to Auschwitz. Though the orders came from the Nazi regime, it was French policemen and the French government who carried them out. For decades, the role that the French played in this horrific event was covered up, until President Jacques Chirac officially apologized for the complicit role the French had played in the extermination of the French Jews, many of whom had been born in France. His acknowledgement of and public apology for these horrors could have tainted the reputation of his country; yet, Chirac acted on principle, attempting to do right for all who were involved in this tragedy. Chirac was not betraying his constituents with his candor; instead, he was demonstrating the integrity of his people through his own words.

Gandhi was another powerful political leader who was unwilling to abandon his principles despite pressure from his constituents. Gandhi's practice of non-violence was not popular among many Indian politicians. India had often been treated as a commodity under British rule and a more aggressive and forceful approach was supported by many of Gandhi's counterparts. While compromise could play a role in this disagreement, Gandhi did not waiver from his stance not to use violence, even after enduring long fasts that weakened his body. In the end, it was Gandhi's method of non-violence that was given credit for the emancipation of India. His dedication to his own principles changed the fate of his country and set an example for the world of the power of peace and self-sacrifice.

To conclude, politicians must lead through their examples, and the greatest example they can impart is one of integrity and truth. This might never win an election, but the decisions made based on these principles will at least be done in honesty and not influenced by fear. Thus, I feel that leaders should remain true to their principles and lead with the authority imparted to them by the people, with the caveat that their decisions should take public opinion into account.

99. Government officials should rely on their own judgment rather than unquestioningly carry out the will of the people whom they serve. (Discuss how the statement could or could not be true)

The role of government workers as public officials is fraught with difficult decisions. Should they execute their duty according to their own interpretation of the law, or should they follow the commands of public opinion? If one were to ask my opinion, I would have to say that government officials should use their own discretion rather than march in lockstep to the drumbeat of the common people.

Across the span of human history, one of the most vivid lessons is that people in groups commit some of the most horrific crimes against their fellow men, with unquestioning officials acting as the instrument of such abuses. A most visceral example can be witnessed during the French Revolution when Maximilien Robespierre was in power. It was during this period that thousands of people were officially sentenced to death by guillotine at the demands of the revolutionary masses who opposed the privileged classes. Dissent by public officials was nearly nonexistent throughout this morbid affair, as any opposition was seen as an attack on the government founded on the general good. With men of conscience in such short supply in positions of power, the Reign of Terror, as it became known, stained the streets of Paris red.

For a less macabre example of the specious nature of public influence on politics, one must fast forward to the present-day USA. Here one sees a polarized society, where the parties in power cater to the demands of their voter base, for better or for worse. On the conservative front, blue collar workers and WASPs from America's heartland cry out for deportations of illegal immigrants, and President Trump, who rose to power by riding a wave of populism pushed forth by these people, happily obliges. Officers of U.S. Immigration and Customs Enforcement separate and detain immigrant children, many of whom have been kept in camps while their parents are processed and sent back to their home countries without them. Even those in office that know such actions are immoral stand idly by while families are torn apart in the land of the free.

There are certainly situations in which the proper course for civil servants is to put aside their own opinions and bend to the will of the public at large. If we put contemporary America in the spotlight once more, the area of police brutality is a prime example of when those in office should lend an ear to their constituents. Too often occurs blue fraternity, the colloquial term for the protectionism practiced by officers in cases where unjustified use of force is suspected, used to allow aggressive officers to escape punishment. The uncomfortably high numbers of videos released online of young men of color being shot by police with itchy trigger fingers, followed by a lukewarm internal investigation that results in mere wrist-slapping, more than earn the public outcry that has come as response. As the demands of the public in this regard are ignored, society splits in twain even more than before, and public trust in government evaporates. Yet even this is not itself justification for mob rule. Public officials must engage in reasonable analysis on a case-by-case basis, lest the rule of law be undermined completely.

In conclusion, officials in government must tend to their duties first according to their own judgement and then according to the demands of the public. Otherwise, government descends into little more than mob rule, and anybody who disagrees may be at the mercy of unrestrained retribution.

100. A nation should require all of its students to study the same national curriculum until they enter college. (Discuss how the statement could or could not be true)

Decision is not to be made lightly on whether all students of a country should be required to study the same national curriculum preceding entry to college; there are valid points to be made on either side of the argument. Supporters of such a mandate would posit that it would provide equitable access to quality education and ensure a more robust curriculum created by academic experts on each subject. These points are noble in their own right, yet equally valid is the fact that disregarding a required uniform national curriculum provides a wider range of educational techniques and theories to be applied, which is a superior recipe for a nation's growth and success. Therefore, I do not agree with the statement that a nation should require all of its students to study the same pre-college national curriculum.

A primary source of evidence which contradicts the statement is that the implementation of a mandated national curriculum would stifle the development of a country's talent. Indeed, it is well established that there is not just a single kind of students; every pupil has their own unique hobbies, affinities, and born talents. In this vein, it is very improbable that a uniform curriculum would be effective at fostering the growth of individual strengths, because an academic regimen of this type appeals to the abilities of the lowest common denominator. Those who have specialized interests would be left to fend for themselves. Thus, a variety of curriculums must be made available to suit the needs of individual students.

Additionally, with uniformity comes conformity and the elimination of regional knowledge and culture. As a nation focuses on a singular academic dialogue, little to no room is made for the important cultural traditions that peoples of different areas pass down to future generations. This presents a clear danger of many cultures being pushed to the brink of extinction, which has negative effects on a nation. On the other hand, preserving regional cultures can have a tremendous benefit to a country. For instance, the Harlem neighborhood of New York City in the USA was a traditionally African American neighborhood. There had been attempts for many years in the early to mid 1900's to diversify the area and bring it into the fold of the standard "American Way", which was a euphemism for "White, Anglo-Saxon, Protestantism". Yet the perseverance of the African American community in Harlem led to the Harlem Renaissance, a cultural revolution of art, literature, and music that has had lasting influences in the USA even to the present day. A uniform national curriculum that imparts mainstream culture at the expense of such dynamic culture would be unfair and insipid. Therefore, policies which encourage a rigidly uniform academic curriculum should not be allowed to take the place of the vibrant cultural education that can be found in a country.

Supporters of the statement can, of course, create a level playing field for all students. Yet, an issue with this line of thinking is that, more often than not, the opposite is true. Forcing all students into the same box suffocates those with unique abilities. Their exceptional talents are overshadowed by their apparent lack of aptitude in other areas, and they are left feeling inadequate in the face of a system that rewards mediocrity. This is not fair by any standard, and ultimately leads to self-esteem and confidence issues in students, hardly the desired crop of graduates for any country.

Furthermore, it could be argued that implementing a similar national curriculum would create a more efficient process of designing courses for students. This is undoubtedly true, at least in the context of creating a cookie-cutter model in which topics may be copy-pasted to suit the basic educational requirements for a particular course or semester. Nonetheless, this would render courses completely devoid of meaningful content with which students could prove themselves to be exceptional. The very concept of competitive scores would be made meaningless as everyone would know the same content as everyone else; how then could the cream of the crop be selected? A nation is grown by its leaders, regardless of the field, not the blasé drones.

While implementing a uniform pre-college national curriculum is on its face a beneficial policy, after deeper consideration a less advantageous picture forms. Such a curriculum would exclude academic excellence and effectively eradicate the rich regional knowledge and culture upon which a nation thrives. Therefore, a more diverse range of curricula may be far more beneficial to the students of a nation, and by proxy, the nation itself.

101. It is primarily in cities that a nation's cultural traditions are generated and preserved. (Discuss how the statement could or could not be true)

The melting pot of urban areas is unique in its mixture of cultures and traditions. While they can be the breeding ground for new traditions, they are definitely not the place where preservation is most likely to occur.

Cities are saturated with diverse cultures, languages and ideals. Unlike agrarian areas people cannot normally survive off the land or without constant interaction in the world around them. As men and some women are forced to take jobs in the public sector, they begin to make sacrifices and also to change. In a city there are no communal days off; there is a lack of traditional places of worship and the children in the city are constantly being influenced by the media, their friends and the language revolving around them. These conditions are not suitable for maintenance of a culture, but only for change. In the play *Fiddler on the Roof* the father Tevye is thrust into cultural calamity when Russian officers begin living in his Jewish settlement. The influence of these "outsiders" is often scary for the town, but the real impact for Tevye comes in the marriages of his three daughters: the oldest daughter chooses her own husband, the second marries a scholar and leaves her family and the third does not even ask her father's permission when she marries a Russian man, cutting her off from her family and faith. No! Mixing cultures and people does not lend itself to preserving tradition.

Cities may not preserve tradition, but they can be hot-beds of cultural generation. When groups of people meet and interact in city new traditions and cultures are formed. New York City, one of the infamous melting pots of the world, has become its own sub-culture, complete with accent, traditions, foods, and stereotypes. In the popular sitcom *Seinfeld*, the main characters take a humorous look at the singular culture of a New Yorker. The generating of tradition becomes apparent as Jerry, Elaine, George, and Kramer form their own modern family: eating at the same café, discussing life's taboo topics and navigating their own idiosyncrasies with the help of their friends. The stereotypical lack of empathy and display of all the unique characters inhabiting New York create an entertaining display. Cities can also bond groups of the same culture in modern ways. Cities are often stratified by ethnicity, forming a mini version of the country of origin. The people might not even come from the same region, but this new society thrusts them together and they learn to depend on each other for camaraderie and often employment. Though they do not preserve tradition cities exemplify the unique ability of the human spirit to thrive in a new and shifting environment.

Cultures shift and change with exposure. If the government wishes to preserve existing cultures, it needs to safeguard the areas of least exposure while allowing the city to generate new traditions of its own accord.

102. We can learn much more from people whose views we share than from people whose views contradict our own. (Discuss how the statement could or could not be true)

While contradictory views certainly can cause stress and inhibit learning, it is not the case that we usually learn much more from people whose views we share. The statement asserts several implied truths that are not necessarily factual.

First, let us establish the obstacles that prevent people from learning. The issue statement implies that disagreement is a possible inhibitor to the learning process. Disagreement, implied by contradictory views in this context, is a loosely defined term that could be interpreted several ways. Certainly, if disagreement is permitted to become contentious, angry, or m....++alicious, then it certainly will prevent learning. In general terms, learning will be inhibited any time an individual permits strong negative emotion to cloud his or her thoughts. Consider a typical interaction between sports fans of opposing teams. Each fan, being loyal to his or her team, will not be inclined to change positions to match the view of the opposing fan. Additionally, because sporting events are naturally competitive, arguments and contentions are usually near the surface, so it is easy to imagine two individuals becoming angry or even malicious in a debate of which team is superior. Disagreement, if allowed to reach the point of malice, contention, or anger, will create strong emotions in both parties involved that prevent clear, rational thought or learning.

Before we move on to other obstacles that keep people from learning, it should be noted that healthy disagreement, in which individuals act with respect and tolerance, can be extremely beneficial to learning. In the seventeenth century, Czar Peter I of Russia recognized that his nation trailed significantly behind his European neighbors in the arts and sciences. Peter himself took a tour of Europe, meeting with kings and government leaders in several different countries. Certainly, these people were nothing like Peter, but he visited them with the intent to learn from them how to govern his own country more effectively. Because he approached their differences without competitive or malicious attitudes, he learned from them and changed his nation to be more modern and effective.

Another significant obstacle to learning can easily occur when individuals think too much alike. This obstacle is complacency in thought and feeling, a phenomenon that occurs when someone decides that they are "good enough." Without differing ideas and opinions to challenge what an individual considers to be "right" or "good," it is easy for that individual to believe that his or her personal perspective is correct without question. The individual's learning and thoughts then become stagnant, and no progress is made. This effect can sometimes be seen in large corporations that attain some high level of success. The individuals charged with leading the organization, seeing the great success of the corporation, may begin to believe that everything in the corporation is perfect. They will gradually stop challenging the status quo and allow policies and procedures to go unchanged. The corporate leaders' aversion to change will ultimately handicap their potential to learn and take their company further. The negative emotion of complacency can be just as inhibitive to learning as anger or contention.

The types of emotion that can adversely affect learning potential are numerous. One is the anger that can arise from disagreement. Another is the complacency that can arise from similar views. While contradictory views can indeed lead to stress and inhibit learning, this does not necessarily imply that we should surround ourselves with like-minded people if we intend to learn. Each individual must gauge, for himself or herself, which emotions that inhibit learning he or she is susceptible to in a given situation. Having determined that, the individual can make the best decisions to maximize personal learning.

103. When old buildings stand on ground that modern planners feel could be better used for modern purposes, modern development should be given precedence over the preservation of historic buildings. (Discuss how the statement could or could not be true)

When we plan urban development, a common issue which arises is what to do with historic buildings. Should they be demolished to make way for modern structures, or should they be preserved for future generations? Despite endless debate, tackling this dilemma is rarely cut and dry; therefore, city planners must consider the unique factors surrounding each historic structure.

It goes without saying that new buildings are an inevitable requirement of any healthy city. As the population of a city increases, so does the need for accommodation and business space. In fact, a city's size exacerbates this problem, for the more people that live in an area, the faster the population increases in size as a result of new births alone. Thus, the larger a city gets, the more likely the case is that older buildings with smaller capacities must be removed to make way for larger structures that can meet the needs of the numerous urbanites.

Yet, the significance of old structures to a city's culture and history cannot be so easily overlooked simply out of utilitarianism. Certain structures, such as the White House or the Brooklyn Bridge, may not be as practical as a larger, more advanced modern construction, but the iconic nature of their presence and their significance to historical events imbue them with a citizenship of their own within their locale. To remove and replace such structures would be akin to stripping a person's body of a vital organ, leaving a gaping wound in the consciousness of the cities they enriched. How could a glass monstrosity of an office building replace the grandeur of the White House? How could a soulless steel lattice compensate the mammoth tribute to industrialism that is the Brooklyn Bridge? This is simply not possible.

Thus, there should be no question about the need to protect historic buildings and other old structures as much as possible, and we can only surrender them to the wrecking ball if all other routes have been exhausted. City planners should consider every other possible site of development first, taking into account underutilized land and dilapidated structures without historical or cultural significance as the immediate options to be culled. If there is no choice but to remove a building of great importance, then at the very least its replacement can be adorned with a façade or other stylistic embellishments reminiscent of its predecessor to pay homage and preserve its memory.

In short, the replacement of old buildings with new ones is a necessary evil. Such a task should be undertaken with the greatest diligence to ensure that every effort is made to conserve the history and culture that a structure possesses, whether through the continued maintenance of the building itself, or by imbuing its replacement with the trappings of the past as a token of remembrance.

104. Claim: The surest indicator of a great nation must be the achievements of its rulers, artists, or scientists.
Reason: Great achievements by a nation's rulers, artists, or scientists will ensure a good life for the majority of that nation's people. (Claim-Reason)

Throughout history, those nations that we look back upon as prime civilizations have always been admired for the singular achievements of their scientists, artists, and leaders. The speaker claims that this is the case, reasoning that a nation's great rulers, scientists, and artists will provide a better life for most of its people. However, I do not agree with the claim or the reason for a number of considerations.

First of all, it should be noted that genius can come from almost anywhere. Even the least developed nations have had their own great minds arising from their populations, but this did not make the nation great. In fact, it is often the case that minds such as these will not achieve significant change within their lifetimes, so while their actions may bring about many benefits for people in the future, they do not necessarily contribute to their countries' greatness while they are alive. For example, the great civil rights leader Mahatma Gandhi is an icon of political thought and protest, yet India could not be considered a great nation during his lifetime. Furthermore, India's current status as a powerful nation could hardly be attributed to the accomplishments of Gandhi alone, or those of any other individual for that matter. It is the toil of countless common people working towards a common goal that eventually has built India and numerous other impoverished nations into places where most citizens could enjoy a comfortable standard of living.

Another example can be seen in the self-proclaimed great nation of Nazi Germany. A large portion of scientific discoveries from the 1940's and 1950's was achieved by or with the help of German and Austrian scientists fleeing the Nazi regime. These scientists did little to bolster the standard of living for their national contemporaries; more often their discoveries were turned into weapons of destruction. If the nation had truly been as great as it alleged itself to be, then there would not have been so many great minds that left it. This exemplifies the fact that the origin of a scientist, leader, or artist is irrelevant, and what really matters is to whom they give their discoveries. The discoveries of many German scientists in the 1940's and 1950's ended up being utilized by the countries to which they fled, which were in fact enemies of the Nazi regime. Had the Reich focused more on genuine improvements in the overall well-being of its people instead of funding scientific and industrial showpieces and brutally oppressing dissidents, then perhaps the discoveries of these scientists could have in fact contributed to Germany's greatness.

It is true that many nations take great pride in their famous artists and the works they created. However, it should be remembered that, at the time of their creation, many of the great works we appreciate in galleries today were not intended for the public. Many works of the great masters were commissioned by extremely wealthy merchants for private collections, or by royalty seeking new palace décor. If anything, the creation of these masterpieces was detrimental to the public, as countless people suffered in hazardous working conditions to mine the stone and mix the chemicals and dyes to make paint, among other things. Therefore, it is only when artistic works are created for public consumption that they can be clearly termed as benefiting the nation as a whole.

In conclusion, I do not agree with the reasoning of the claim that a nation's greatness is determined by the achievements of its rulers, scientists, and artists. Not every leader, scientist, or artist is able to accomplish their goals in life, nor are their accomplishments always appreciated while they are alive. Furthermore, scientists and creators are not always tied to their nationality and will emigrate when necessary, taking their talents with them.

105. Some people claim that you can tell whether a nation is great by looking at the achievements of its rulers, artists, or scientists. Others argue that the surest indicator of a great nation is, in fact, the general welfare of all its people. (Address both views)

Throughout history, those nations that we look back upon as prime civilizations have always been admired for the singular achievements of their scientists, artists, and leaders. Yet these achievements were not necessarily what made the nations themselves great. Rather, it was the well-being of their citizens that determined whether the country flourished and was held in high esteem by its neighbors.

Some may argue that we can determine whether a nation is great by examining the achievements of its rulers, artists, or scientists. Looking back on renowned civilizations, we can see that the populace was generally uneducated. Thus, the contributions of unique individuals were far more impactful than in modern societies. The Mongolian conqueror Genghis Khan is a notable example. He took a scattered group of nomadic peoples and united them into the greatest military empire of his era. Through his keen military and political strategies, which included previously neglected concepts such as meritocracy and the adoption of a wide variety of technological developments, he forever altered the entire Eurasian continent and built a legacy for his people that lasted hundreds of years. Similarly, the Greek philosopher and inventor Archimedes developed many principles of physics and philosophy that were revolutionary during his time. The famous example is that of the eponymous Archimedes' principle, a method of measuring buoyancy and mass of objects, which is still taught as a foundational theory in physics. Therefore, he is an exemplary icon of the greatness of ancient Greece.

However, it should be noted that genius can come from almost anywhere. Even the least developed nations have had their own great minds arising from their populations, but this does not make the nation great. For example, the great civil rights leader Mahatma Gandhi is an icon of political thought and protest, yet India could not be considered a great nation during his lifetime. In Gandhi's time, India was still a colony of Britain, and the oppressive regime there had stifled the economic development of almost the whole country. Poverty and famine were rampant, and no matter how impactful Gandhi's words and actions may have been on the future of India, the nation itself during Gandhi's time was not considered great.

Another example can be seen in the self-proclaimed great nation of Nazi Germany. A large portion of scientific discoveries from the 1940's and 1950's was made by or with the help of German and Austrian scientists fleeing the Nazi regime. If the nation had truly been as great as it alleged itself to be, then there would not have been so many great minds that left it. The national pedigree of those scientists is almost completely overlooked in most cases. In fact, stories of life in Germany at the time indicate the harsh reality of life under the Nazi regime. Political oppression was constant, as the fascist regime brooked no disagreement with its policies in any form. There was also strict rationing of food and other goods for common people in order to support the military, a far cry from Hitler's promised utopia. No number of advancements in the scientific fields were sufficient to mask the atrocities committed during the Holocaust. Had the Nazi government focused more on improving the life of its people in practical ways, instead of rooting out all non-believers of the Third Reich, the people of Germany might have thrived and contributed to a great nation.

While there are certainly examples in history of nations that owed their greatness to the achievements or abilities of exceptional leaders or thinkers, such cases are few and far between and could be attributed more to the general lack of knowledge or ability at the time than to the true strength of the individuals. It can instead be surmised that, in the context of a great nation, the achievements of the few are secondary to the welfare of the people as whole. If most of the population is suffering, then no number of leadership qualities or scientific discoveries can compensate.

106. The best way to understand the character of a society is to examine the character of the men and women that the society chooses as its heroes or its role models. (Address challenges to your position)

The speaker declares that examining the character of the people chosen by a society as its "heroes" or "role models" is the best way of understanding the society. I disagree with this statement, because studying a society's heroes or role models only reveals the ideals rather than the realities of a society. Indeed, the nature of heroism is about celebrating the finer attributes of certain people and ignoring their weaknesses and failings, rather than acknowledging the full spectrum of attributes composing any person.

The great classical God-heroes of Greece and Rome had strengths and weaknesses, although it is most often their strengths that are celebrated and emulated. These Greek and Roman gods and demi-gods are reputed to have saved mankind and even helped form modern society. The etymological Greek and Latin roots of the word "hero" refer to people of divine descent. This evokes thoughts of perfection and true nobility; while there are those who perform amazing feats and act in noble ways, all heroes have faults. These faults, which are depicted in mythology as "tragic," set up the hero to fail despite his or her wonderful attributes. For example, the great warrior, Achilles, was invincible aside from a small spot on his heel. Despite his valor, he died when he was shot in the heel. Achilles becomes a type for heroes; all heroes have flaws which would be expected and looked over in normal people, but for a hero, any minor flaw can lead to social, spiritual, or physical downfall. Thus, the pressure of being labeled as a "hero" seems too great a weight for anyone—even a demi-god—to bear, and we should be wary of trying to analyze the realities of ancient Greece or Rome through the prism of such figures who represent a society's ideals.

Mythology aside, history is rife with examples of people who are extolled as heroes or role models by their society and subsequent generations, yet whose character flaws should not be imputed to an entire society. Some people consider the conqueror, Genghis Khan, to be a hero; he had an amazing ability to assemble many tribes into one empire, yet he was ruthless in warfare and had no mercy for his enemies. One cannot assume that because Genghis Khan acted in this manner all of Mongolian society followed suit. A more modern example of the dual nature of most heroes is Thomas Jefferson, the author of the American *Declaration of Independence*. Jefferson had a legendary mind and was a scholar of many disciplines: he was a farmer, a lawyer, and later the President of the United States. However, he held slaves and is believed to have fathered children with at least one of his slaves. It has only been in recent years that the less attractive components of Jefferson's life have been widely acknowledged, and that Jefferson has been viewed as a man rather than as a reflection of early Americans.

Finally, the true pulse of a society's character is found in the masses of commoners, rather than in the heroes or role models who belong to the small elite. Christopher Dyer, in his research on the population of medieval England, has revealed that the vast majority of people in England were involved in the wool trade: spinning, carding, and weaving. But it was the knights in armor that were lauded as the heroes of the time. Thus, to truly understand the character of medieval English society it is more important to study those involved with sheep than those involved in war. That is, the character of any society is found in its body rather than its head.

To conclude, understanding of the character of a particular society should not be attempted through an examination of that society's heroes or role models. Such heroes or role models reflect merely the narrowest ideals of any society. Moreover, every hero has flaws, and these flaws cannot fairly be imputed to every member of that society. From a statistical standpoint, the character of a society is more likely to be found through an analysis of the myriad common people, rather than a select few.

107. All college and university students would benefit from spending at least one semester studying in a foreign country. (Discuss how the statement could or could not be true)

In a world that is more globalized than ever before, studying for some time overseas has become an invaluable experience for university students. There are a variety of ways in which having at least a semester abroad may benefit students. It could give them a greater geopolitical awareness and inspire their career ambitions, among other things.

One of the major benefits of studying abroad in a foreign country is the exposure students gain from experiencing different cultures. To this end, a semester or a longer period studying abroad can impart numerous benefits. For example, those studying any form of politics or international relations regarding the country will get firsthand knowledge of the people and culture. Art students can visit museums and galleries in the country they are studying in. These experiences will enable students to gain a broader understanding of international relations and conflicts in the proper context of current and historical events.

Having gone to another country, students can gain further insight into their desired career paths. An engineering student may decide to enter into environmental engineering after seeing the wind farms during a term in Germany. A finance major may decide to apply for a company in Hong Kong after a stint at a local university. Someone studying medicine abroad for at least a semester may decide to relocate to a developing country after seeing the need for their skills there. Such interchange of workers brings a greater diversity to the world's work pool, with larger numbers of workers able to adapt to international conditions.

The statement might not hold true when the costs are beyond the means of the students. If students are not financially capable of paying the costs of an exchange program, then they should either be waived from the requirement, or be offered some form of financial aid. Otherwise, such a program would force many students to be unable to continue their education. Such prohibitive practices would likely have a negative impact on the application rate to universities, so some financial safety nets should be set up for students. With the subsidy and waiver in place, such a program would benefit a wide range of students.

In conclusion, if universities require students to study for no less than a term abroad, as long as there are waivers or subsidies offered to financially challenged students, then it will generously benefit the students in the long-term. Also, the overall quality of the world's workers will improve as larger numbers of people gain international work experience.

108. Some people claim that a nation's government should preserve its wilderness areas in their natural state. Others argue that these areas should be developed for potential economic gain. (Address both views)

One of the more pressing environmental issues currently facing the world is the loss of forests and other wilderness areas to development. Therefore, I believe it is necessary for governments to keep their nations' wilderness areas intact, even at the cost of losing out on the economic gains that could be garnered by development of such areas. It is my firm belief that this is the only way to effectively halt the destruction of habitats and return some semblance of homeostasis to the environment.

An important part of this argument that must be considered is the current rate of habitat loss that is occurring even at this very moment and the harm it poses to human life. Most of the breathable oxygen on our planet is generated by rainforests such as the Amazon. Yet, every year nearly 80 million acres of the Amazon is burned to make way for development. It is therefore no surprise that the air quality of Brazil's major cities has declined over time. Conserving the

Amazon and other rainforests in their natural state would not only serve to protect the many endangered species that call these habitats home but would also aid in improving the air quality of nearby cities. Naturally, it would prove to be an inconvenience to farmers and other developers hoping to turn rainforest land into valuable real-estate, but the long-term benefits of conservation far outweigh the short-term greed.

If it is monetary gain that drives much of the destruction of natural habitats, then promoting conservation for the purposes of eco-tourism would be a win-win for both sides. Many wilderness areas are places of astounding beauty, such as the icy northern reaches of Alaska and the arid desert regions of the Midwest USA, which also boast unique indigenous cultures. Certainly, if these regions were legally protected, then they would prove to be valuable sources of revenue for the local people, who can sell their native crafts, and the tax coffers by proxy. There are already similar programs in place, the famous Yellowstone National Parks being the most famous. Every year, thousands of people pay for hunting licenses, tour trips, and other tourist activities to the parks, which in turn finance their continued conservation. This not only incentivizes their continued upkeep but also makes it difficult for developers to match the financial gains that they could offer in lieu of the annual tourist revenue. Thus, conserving wilderness habitats not only preserves the wealth of natural beauty these places offer, but also contributes real wealth to the government through tourism.

Of course, many industrialists argue that it is a waste to leave the untapped resources of the wilderness undeveloped. A contemporary example is the desire of large oil companies to drill in the Arctic regions of North America. The oil companies argue that the regions are mostly uninhabited and thus their drilling would pose little threat to ecosystems. However, their arguments are misleading, as the Arctic regions are an important part of seasonal migration for caribou and other forms of wildlife, the destruction of which would cause a negative chain reaction throughout several distant ecosystems. Additionally, the amount of oil that would be extracted from these regions would be an insignificant percentage of the nation's oil consumption. Protecting these regions would ensure that the ecosystems which rely on the animals that migrate through the Arctic would remain intact, and prevent the often irreparable damage that follows industrial development.

In conclusion, I think that governments' preserving forests and other wilderness areas in their natural state is both necessary and beneficial. Not only does this protect ecosystems from annihilation, but the natural havens which are preserved can still benefit humanity health-wise, and even economically in some cases.

109. In most professions and academic fields, imagination is more important than knowledge. (Address challenges to your position)

The speaker asserts that imagination supersedes knowledge in importance in most academic fields and professions. I find this notion to be utterly indefensible, as it is both naïve and overly optimistic about how imagination works and how the search for knowledge functions.

I describe the statement as naïve for two main reasons. The first is that it implies that nature bends to the will of one's mind, and the second is that imagination is equally valued by employers. Children are often told that they can accomplish anything if they put their minds to it, and while this is intended to develop a strong work ethic, many misconstrue it as meaning that anything is possible. The problem with this mode of thinking is that not everything is possible. We live in a finite physical universe with very real limitations, limitations that cannot simply be imagined away.

To speak more directly to the point, many difficulties in the academic and working world that require solutions may call for some critical thinking, but being too imaginative can be impractical, or even harmful. Take finance and accounting for example. If there are inconsistencies with a company's financial records, there is a strict protocol to follow in attempting to correct or report such findings. Being "imaginative" in this situation is tantamount to committing fraud, as proper records are legally required to do business. Thus, in this case knowledge of financial law and accounting procedures is far more important than an imagination.

In the realms of science, too many examples prove that knowledge is more important than imagination. Science itself is a process for finding truth in the universe we live in; thus, imagination must always bow to the facts. An example of this can be seen in the almost disastrous Apollo 13 Lunar mission, where an electrical malfunction caused one of the pod's oxygen tanks to explode, damaging their computer and other life-support systems. It is here that one could make the argument in favor of imagination being important, as teams of earth-side engineers worked non-stop to come up with a solution to bring the crew home safely, using only items they had on board the space craft. A jury-rigged device was developed, using tubes and air-filter parts from their space suits; however, this remedy was born not purely out of imagination, but also out of the decades of combined experience of a number of scientists working with all their might. It was the knowledge these people possessed of the various systems and capabilities of every item on the vessel that allowed them to come up with the quick fix that saved four men's lives.

When it comes to academics, there is a bit more leeway for imagination to play a greater role, but it strongly depends on which field one is studying. There are the arts, of course: song, dance, painting, and others. In these a strong imagination is critical for developing new and more interesting modes of expression. Knowledge has its role in color theory, biodynamics, and music theory, but is not as necessary as in other fields. However, even in non-STEM fields, knowledge takes precedence. History, for example, requires a large collection of knowledge in order to be understood. Imagination has no place other than in the colorful ways historical events can be described, but as for what happened, the goal of history is to find hard evidence proving or disproving various historical occurrences instead of making them up. Using one's imagination in this way is considered falsification or revisionist and is highly frowned upon in the academic community.

While imagination does have its uses in sparking ideas, it can be seen in both professional and academic scenarios that knowledge is more useful for solving problems and performing work effectively. Without the knowledge with which to imagine, the most that can come out of a brainstorming session will be something too abstract to be applicable to any real situation.

110. The surest indicator of a great nation is not the achievements of its rulers, artists, or scientists, but the general well-being of all its people. (Address challenges to your position)

Throughout history, those nations that we look back upon as prime civilizations have always been admired for the singular achievements of their scientists, artists, and leaders. Yet these achievements were not necessarily what made the nations themselves great. Rather, it was the well-being of their citizens that determined whether the country flourished and was held in high esteem by its neighbors.

First of all, it should be noted that genius can come from almost anywhere. Even the least developed nations have had their own great minds arising from their populations, but this does not make the nation great. For example, the great civil rights leader Mahatma Gandhi is an icon of political thought and protest, yet India could not be considered a great nation during his lifetime. In Gandhi's time, India was still a colony of Britain, and the oppressive regime there had stifled the economic development of almost the whole country. Poverty and famine were rampant, and no matter how impactful Gandhi's words and actions may have been on the future of India, the nation itself during Gandhi's time was not considered great. Now, however, things have changed drastically, in terms of technological and economic development India's people have flourished, and the nation is now considered one of the most powerful on the world stage.

Another example can be seen in the self-proclaimed great nation of Nazi Germany. A large portion of scientific discoveries from the 1940's and 1950's was made by or with the help of German and Austrian scientists fleeing the Nazi regime. If the nation had truly been as great as it alleged itself to be, then there would not have been so many great minds that left it. At the time, persecution of a variety of categories was common; political, religious, social, and virtually all other aspects of life that may have posed a threat to the regime were ruthlessly culled by the Gestapo secret police. The country was still unsustainable from an industrial standpoint; the entire Sudetenland annexation was planned in order to seize the natural resources and utilize the labor force of nearby nations to feed the German economy. As a result, the revolutionary discoveries of Nazi Germany's scientists were almost completely overlooked in most cases since their achievements did little to improve the nation's overall well-being.

The most convincing reason that could be used to poke holes in my argument is that the general welfare of a great nation is often inextricably intertwined with the accomplishments of its rulers, artists, and scientists. In other words, the general well-being of a great nation is almost impossible without competent rulers and difficult to achieve without notable artists or scientists. This means that the achievements of such eminent people do demonstrate that the nation is great. A historical example can be seen in Tang Dynasty China, the era which is generally accepted as one of the nation's greatest premodern periods of cultural and scientific development. The people in China at the time were extremely well-cared for as compared to previous eras, and some of the most iconic Chinese poets, such as Li Bai and Du Fu, became ensconced in the annals of cultural greatness. To this day, the people of China still look back to the Tang Dynasty as a period to be emulated in regard to its artistic accomplishments as well as the welfare of the people: accessible education, cultural enrichment, available food, and other resources; the list goes on.

In conclusion, I believe the only relevant factor for a great nation is the welfare of its people, for without it, not only are great minds less likely to thrive, but the nation itself will suffer and in all likelihood cease to exist.

111. **Some people argue that successful leaders in government, industry, or other fields must be highly competitive. Other people claim that in order to be successful, a leader must be willing and able to cooperate with others. (Address both views)**

Career and life preparation are a natural product of the human desire to succeed. Most people want to succeed; it is common to meet someone who wants to "make it to the top," but far less common to meet someone who wants to fail at every endeavor they make in life. This then begs the question—What skills, attributes, or characteristics lead a person to success? Cultivating a spirit of competition can prepare a person to want to "be the best" in everything he or she does, but if this attitude is carried too far it can be harmful. Learning skills of cooperation, on the other hand, teaches an individual to work well in teams, but if this trait is taken too far it can lead to complacency. The ideal leader, then, is one who possesses a strong internal drive to excel while still maintaining an ability to work well with others.

A strong competitive desire, in essence a driving motivation to be "better" or the "best" in a group of people, is dangerous if it supersedes the ability of leaders to manage their nation effectively. Look at the polarized politics of the USA as an example. Currently, the two ruling parties, the Democrats and the Republicans, vie for power in the three branches of government. Due to the increasing level of combativeness between the two, whenever one party controls the legislative body whereas one member of the other party serves as President, as can be seen during the most recent term of President Trump, it becomes difficult to implement productive policies. Indeed, the competition for public opinion or continuing power in government makes many policy debates an exercise in mudslinging and ad hominem attacks rather than thoughtful discussions of the viability of the policies in question. Thus, competition detracts from the overall purpose of leadership in government and is detrimental to a nation as a whole; a good leader of government should be able to cross the lines of factional competition and collaborate with his or her peers in office.

Pure competition can rip a team apart, but can pure cooperation keep a team together? The answer, again, is no. A spirit of cooperation carried too far can also destroy productivity and prevent a leader's success. This phenomenon can be seen in the management of some modern companies. An over-cooperative executive in a corporation could become so occupied helping other directors in the company fulfill their responsibilities that he or she fails to take care of his or her own responsibilities directing the company. Similarly, a project manager who wants to make a name for himself or herself on a big project may attempt to receive input from all parties involved; this is not a bad idea, considering the number of different fields that must come together for the task at hand. However, if the manager gives too much attention to simply listening to the opinions of others and does not delegate responsibilities and manage the team, he or she may find no success at all. Thus, cooperation will be misplaced whenever its practice comes at the expense of individual responsibilities.

It seems, then, that there should be some level of healthy balance between the two extremes. The best leaders are able to cultivate and maintain a strong desire for individual excellence and accomplishment while still working together with others. Leaders of a nation must put aside their political inclinations and work with other members of the government despite their differing opinions on policy or political theory in order to foster the common good of the nation. On the other hand, the over-cooperative project manager could recognize that the need for his or her leadership cannot be neglected in favor of accepting everyone else's opinions. In this way, a truly great leader can be made.

112. College students should base their choice of a field of study on the availability of jobs in that field. (Describe advantageous and disadvantageous circumstances of the recommendation)

The question of which major should be chosen when students enter college is never an easy one. Should one seek a field that would provide the greatest opportunity for gainful employment after graduation? My answer is a resounding "Yes."

A central point that is often forgotten in the debate over educational choices is that the primary purpose of attending college is to develop the skills needed to acquire a job. In the modern era, this fact is obscured by the accessibility and low cost of going to university relative to previous centuries when only the extremely wealthy elites could attend higher education institutions. Nevertheless, the simple truth of the matter is that the only real purpose for going to school is to get a degree that qualifies one for a position at a company. After all, if companies did not have education requirements, one could be reasonably certain that few people, if any at all, would bother to attend colleges or universities.

Choosing a major that promises an abundance of jobs after graduation from college may also help students save time and money. When focusing on a major with a broad scope of careers in mind, students can target courses which develop relevant skills that are applicable to certain jobs. Too often, students choose a major that does not have a direct correlation to any particular job. As a result, they fill their semesters with classes that cost significant amounts of time and money, which results in a tragic waste of energy. For instance, a degree in philosophy will probably lead a student to take numerous classes on literature and schools of thought, few of which may be readily useful in any workplace setting. Also, such courses are rarely transferrable as college credit to other majors if students have second thoughts and decide to change their field of study. Thus, selecting a major related to specific jobs ensures that students are making the most of the considerable chunk of their lives and bank accounts in their university education.

However, I do not want anyone to think that they should immediately give up on their dreams to settle for a major that is in high demand. After all, job markets can shift radically with new developments in technology. A good example can be seen in the dot-com bubble in USA in the early 2000's. In this period, with the advent of the Internet, speculation around the potential economic benefits of tech companies led to a glut of those pursuing degrees in IT and other fields related to internet technology after the bubble burst. Anyone who had wanted to cash in on the bubble by sacrificing their passions was sorely disappointed. Yet this is a rather isolated incident, and in general, a person who stays well informed on employment trends and the state of the world economy should be able to avoid such mistakes.

To sum up, college students are often better off choosing a major that may guarantees a job after graduation because this is the purpose of a college education. While it is a nice idea to follow one's dream when one chooses a major, to do so is a risk not worth taking in a job market that is increasingly competitive.

113. Some people believe that corporations have a responsibility to promote the well-being of the societies and environments in which they operate. Others believe that the only responsibility of corporations, provided they operate within the law, is to make as much money as possible. (Address both views)

The place of businesses in nations and society has long been debated by economists, sociologists, political strategists, and other scholars ever since the first men and women realized the power that commerce wields over mankind. A major aspect of this debate has been what responsibility, if any at all, corporations owe to society; should companies promote social well-being, or should they only endeavor to earn as much money as possible within the confines of the law? Personally speaking, I believe that while it would be a boon to society if companies were to utilize their wealth for the public good, the only real obligation they possess is that to their shareholders.

In order to flesh out properly this argument, we must first clearly define what a corporation is. The most basic definition of a corporation is a group of people, company, or organization that has been authorized as a single entity. There are numerous distinct corporate designations, but the basic premise of all of them is the pooling together of resources with the purpose of mitigating individual liability for losses. Herein it can be seen that the very foundation of the existence of corporations is to maximize the financial gains of the people that have invested in the company, not to promote the well-being of society.

In fact, to expect or force companies to contribute to the well-being of societies can in fact prove detrimental. For example, during the initial backlash against tobacco companies in the USA during the 1970's, legislation was passed that required tobacco companies to allocate a certain amount of their profits to cancer research and other research related to the harm caused by tobacco. In an unsurprising twist, the organizations set up to conduct this research were staffed with scientists that were more interested in their salaries than exposing the ills of smoking, and thus the tobacco companies were able to spread misinformation on the addictiveness and carcinogenic nature of their products until mounting independent research exposed the truth decades later. Thus, even if one believes that companies should contribute to the common good, imposing such an obligation is no guarantee that companies will actually comply.

Of course, there are companies that are set up to be non-profit organizations. Organizations such as these may sell products and services for the express purpose of using revenues to aid underprivileged regions or promote other social benefits. However, while they are technically companies in the legal sense, they do not fit the definition implied by the statement, which it can be inferred is intended to mean for-profit institutions. Furthermore, there is increasing evidence that for-profit enterprises can provide greater benefits to a society than non-profit ones, simply by virtue of the nature of having the ability to grow and expand due to increasing revenues. For example, some African nations have set up organizations that allow limited hunting of endangered animals, donating many of the profits back to the community and using the rest to fund conservation. This is not to say that companies have a responsibility to the public; it is only that their capacity to help is greater.

In sum, I believe that companies, by their very nature, function only as money-generating institutions; requiring them to contribute to society will only lead to half-hearted, or even malicious, efforts. Therefore, while they have great potential to help society if it is the wishes of the owners and operators, companies do not have any inherent responsibility to do so.

114. Claim: Researchers should not limit their investigations to only those areas in which they expect to discover something that has an immediate, practical application.
Reason: It is impossible to predict the outcome of a line of research with any certainty. (Claim-Reason)

The speaker states that because it is impossible to know definitively what the results of research will be, researchers should not limit their investigations to areas in which discoveries with immediate practical applications can be made. While I agree with the claim to some extent, I completely disagree with the reasoning involved.

When it comes to making predictions about potential results of an experiment, the current level of knowledge that scientists have amassed about the laws of physics and the other ways in which the universe functions allows researchers to have a relatively high degree of confidence in the results of an experiment. For example, when we test a new aircraft design, our understanding of thrust, lift, aerodynamics, and other basic laws of flight points to a fairly clear set of possible results. Either the proposed design will function as intended, or unexpected system failures or overlooked design flaws will cause the craft to crash. At the very minimum, one of these two results is certain.

Of course, in more theoretical areas of science, such as particle physics or genetic engineering, it is far more difficult to make clear predictions of research results due to our relative lack of knowledge about the intricacies of these sciences. For instance, when the Large Hadron Collider, a particle accelerator developed by CERN, was close to completion, there was much excitement in the physics community because no one was quite sure what would happen after it was switched on. Some of the more paranoid even thought that it would rip a hole in space and time. Similarly, when it comes to genetic manipulation there are many unknowns regarding the particular functions and interactions of the human genome, making it difficult to predict what effect any changes in human DNA may have on a person's body and health, especially on the person's progeny later.

As for the claim itself, I think that researchers should look into more abstract areas of investigation, because in the rare cases where something truly unexpected does happen, it usually leads to some groundbreaking inventions or new insights into the way the universe functions. However, for the most part, research needs a clear goal to attain or a clear problem to solve to get any useful results. This becomes especially important when we consider the exorbitant costs associated with scientific research. Science is a business like any other, and people that invest in research expect a return on their investment at some point. Therefore, most research must produce practical results that can be used to profit, preferably immediately; otherwise, that field will eventually lose funding and with it, any future progress.

Thus, it can be concluded that the reason used to support the claim is not sound, as our understanding of the universe gives a fairly reliable model with which to predict the results of experiments. Additionally, the claim itself is fairly valid, with the caveat that achieving practical results is a necessary step in order to secure funding for future research.

115. Some people believe that our ever-increasing use of technology significantly reduces our opportunities for human interaction. Other people believe that technology provides us with new and better ways to communicate and connect with one another. (Address both views)

The current world we inhabit is one in which technology and the internet dominate almost every aspect of our lives. This includes the realm of social interaction, which many argue our reliance on technology has limited. Personally, though, I believe that modern technology has contributed to more human communication than it has taken away.

One of the most common complaints one hears from older generations is that because of smartphones and social media apps young people nowadays do not have as many face-to-face conversations anymore. While this is true to some extent, it does not mean that people communicate with each other less. The very fact that most young people, and middle-aged people for that matter, spend such a large amount of time on their smartphones browsing social media is evidence that they communicate with one another more often than in the past.

Consider the way in which people had to communicate before the advent of computers, smartphones and the internet: most people either had to make appointments to meet each other, scheduling around their work, school, or other commitments, or had to use their landline telephones at home. They could also write letters if they wanted more personal, albeit drawn-out, interaction. It could be argued that these interactions were more meaningful than the constant state of connectedness people have today, but there is no way to quantify such a statement in light of the fact that people's ideas about their relationships are subjective.

Also, new technologies have given us newer and more efficient ways to communicate with one another compared to the past. Take emojis for example. These simple facial expressions or pictures have been widely adopted in text-based conversations –i.e. most conversations – and they have added a versatile method of response, expression, and non-verbal communication. Some could argue that it oversimplifies language, but it could also be argued that the ability to interpret an entire sentence's worth of meaning from only three small faces or pictures is itself proof of a complex mode of communication.

Another benefit of powerful modern smartphones is that they contain the processing power to run translation software. Whereas in the past, a person travelling to a foreign country would either need to learn the language or need to hire a translator, nowadays all one needs is a smartphone and one can carry out basic conversations with the locals. Even if they are not traveling, such software allows people all around the world to interact online, and especially among people that play online games, international friends are common thanks to integrated translation technologies.

In conclusion, I feel that it is almost impossible to argue that technology has reduced our opportunities for human interaction. Instead, thanks to easy access to the internet and devices that can run social media apps, people are able to communicate more often, in different ways, and with persons in a wider range than ever before.

116. Claim: Knowing about the past cannot help people to make important decisions today.
Reason: The world today is significantly more complex than it was even in the relatively recent past. (Claim-Reason)

The speaker claims that since the modern world is far more complex than it was in the past, knowing about history cannot contribute to making important decisions today. Certainly, this is true in terms of scientific theorems and technological designs; however, some important lessons from history can be applied in other areas, making history not completely useless for modern-day situations.

Technology has advanced so far and so fast in the past century that few, if any, devices from before the Industrial Revolution have any practical value to modern design or engineering. Nowhere is this more apparent than in the realm of digital technologies such as computers and smartphones, whose internal circuitry and computer processors were almost beyond imagination before the turn of the century.

Even in other areas of science, much of our basic understanding of how the world around us functions has changed so radically in the modern era that the preconceived notions that our predecessors held are laughable. For example, it was not until the late 1800's that germ theory became mainstream and washing one's hands, a commonsense practice today, began to reduce deaths due to infection. The primitive, or flat-out incorrect, ideas that people possessed about science in the past, therefore, have no practical value today beyond that of a yardstick with which to see how far humanity has come.

Yet when it comes to social and political issues, a knowledge of history is absolutely vital for proper decision-making. This is due to the fact that unlike technology, human social interactions have not changed significantly over time. All people still operate according to the hierarchy of needs as outlined by psychologist Abraham Maslow. Thus, when making decisions on how to best manage a country, leaders must still consider the same concepts of food, safety, and social harmony, as have kings and rulers for countless generations.

In fact, it could be argued that society as a whole has become less complex, at least in terms of the various social interactions. Hundreds of years ago, when most nations were still dominated by monarchies and hierarchical aristocratic systems, this meant that people of differing levels in society had to follow strict unspoken rules when dealing with one another, and leaders had to balance the needs and demands of their lords and the volatile lower classes. Policies enacted during this period are important to study in both their successes and failures, since they may offer insights as to how modern societies can avoid similar problems and reap similar benefits.

In brief, history is not completely useless for making modern decisions, at least not for the reason that the modern world is more complex. To be sure, technologies are far more sophisticated, but in almost all other respects the world is no more complex than it was in the past.

117. Claim: Knowing about the past cannot help people to make important decisions today.
Reason: We are not able to make connections between current events and past events until we have some distance from both. (Claim-Reason)

The speaker asserts that knowledge of past events is unhelpful for making important decisions today because we are able to connect the past to current events only after we have distance from both. I am unable to agree with this statement based on the reasoning, as it oversimplifies the basic intelligence of people.

To begin with, the given reason basically states that people are incapable of drawing parallels between events that are occurring in the present and those that took place in the past. While this can be true in some situations in which a lack of information about what is currently happening can make it difficult to make any assessments, a person possessing the relevant knowledge of the past can easily use past experiences to make important decisions. In boxing, for instance, after many hours of studying the punching combinations and movement patterns of their opponents, fighters will look for slight movements during their match in order to decide how, when, and where to strike in real-time. Without such knowledge, even the most competent fighters would have a difficult time successfully winning a bout due to human beings' limited reaction time. Thus, the claim is not valid, as knowing the past can have an immediately beneficial effect on the present when one's understanding of and ability to apply the lesson are honed through practice.

In a situation with more far-reaching consequences, such as international politics, there are likewise clear tales that leaders utilize or ignore when making policy decisions. For example, in the past ten years, more and more US soldiers have returned from mostly fruitless fighting in the Middle East to a home that is unconcerned for their welfare. Already, advocacy groups have been drawing comparisons between the current situation and that in the years following the Vietnam War, such as the disenfranchised and often psychologically scarred veterans having difficulty reintegrating into society, as society itself looks to blame the government's over-spending on the conflict as one of the major contributors to the nation's current problems. It takes only a high school history class's worth of knowledge and a habit of watching the news to make these connections, so it is disingenuous to try to argue that we can only understand the similarities after looking back from the distant future. Based on such connections, advocacy groups can formulate effective strategies to influence public opinion and in turn policy, seeking the best compensation for the soldiers involved. Therefore, the claim is not credible for it is demonstrably feasible to utilize the past to make important decisions today.

There are certainly some situations in which one can only connect current events to those of the past after both have taken place. This occurs most often when people deal with machine failures, where in the heat of the moment, people are more concerned with their safety than with trying to understand exactly why the failure took place. Some of the more dramatic examples of this can be seen in disasters in metal foundries. Dealing with extremely high-temperature metal is a delicate process, and when something goes wrong, people tend to run for their lives to escape the inevitable fiery blasts that occur after a mistake is made or some machinery fails. It is only after the fires are put out and an investigation team reviews security camera footage and the wreckage that they can ascertain the cause of the disaster – any comparisons to past disasters are utterly irrelevant in the moment, when one is running for dear life from a wave of molten metal. Therefore, in situations of immediate mortal threat to the people involved, it can be fair to claim that past experiences are not much help for problems in the present, with the caveat that this is a transitory phenomenon – the aftermath can allow for many proactive measures to be applied on the basis of the lessons learned from the disaster.

In sum, it is an unfair argument to try to claim that history has no use for modern decisions based on the speaker's reasoning. Humans are fully capable of connecting past events to the present moment because that is one of the basic functions of memory and it is only when severe stress triggers our fight-or-flight reflexes that this function is inhibited.

118. Educational institutions should actively encourage their students to choose fields of study that will prepare them for lucrative careers. (Discuss positive and negative consequences of the policy)

The singular purpose of education is to prepare students for their future careers. To this end, it is in the best interest of students if their schools make the effort to encourage them to pursue fields of study that will guarantee high-paying jobs. To do anything less would be a disservice to the incredible investment made by students and their parents when choosing an institution to study at.

It is important to remember that in the highly competitive economic environment in which we live today there is little leeway for mistakes when students choose a field of study and, by proxy, a future career. Since students are usually not as knowledgeable as their adult counterparts in the education administration, it is not always a good idea to allow them to choose whatever field they wish to study. Take liberal arts majors as an example; some of them lead to the lowest paying careers after graduation since few real jobs are available to degree-holders in these areas other than teaching the same subjects which they have studied. There are certainly large sums of money to be made in these fields for those savvy enough to apply their knowledge and skills in the right way, but such skillsets are not often taught in school, but rather learned through experience.

There is no doubt that most students will be initially unhappy with adults advising them to give up what they believe to be their dream jobs in favor of other means of employment, but this preliminary dissatisfaction will often give way to greater overall contentedness once they find that the career path suggested to them will provide a salary which supports a lavish lifestyle. In addition, what most people presume is their passion, as with many aspiring musicians and other artists, is often downgraded to a hobby or minor interest when faced with the titanic amount of practice needed to hone their ability, as well as the compromises they must make in order to turn such skills into a profitable means of employment.

One likely negative consequence of implementing the policy is that educational institutions may give the wrong advice: what was initially deemed the fields that promised gainful employment may prove the opposite when students graduate. This has been known to happen before. For instance, in the USA during the early 2000's the law field gained enormous interest as globalization picked up more steam, and as a result there was a projected need for new corporate lawyers and a boom in the legal field in general as the standard of living increased. Thus, academic institutions advertised heavily to encourage students to get legal degrees, not only was the profession highly respected, but it was also very lucrative. Predictably, this boosted law major admissions substantially, but the result was that it became difficult to find a job in the legal field due to the overabundance of law graduates. However, this boom-bust cycle in education and employment opportunities has been heavily researched in recent years, and many colleges and universities now use up-to-date job market analysis to recommend majors to students. In this way, schools can still be reasonably relied upon to persuade students to choose majors that prepare them for profitable jobs.

In summary, while it may not be exactly what students want, it is in their best interest to be advised by educational institutions to find a major that would be ideal for finding a high-paying job. The financial stability brought about by a better career would, in time, compensate them for the short-term sacrifice of giving up a hobby-oriented major.

119. Educational institutions should actively encourage their students to choose fields of study in which jobs are plentiful. (Address challenges to your position)

The singular purpose of education is to prepare students for their future careers. To this end, it is in the best interest of students if their schools make the effort to encourage them to pursue fields of study that will guarantee many jobs. To do anything less would be a disservice to the incredible investment made by students and their parents when choosing an institution to study at.

It is important to remember that in the highly competitive economic environment in which we live today there is little leeway for mistakes when students choose a field of study and, by proxy, a future career. Since students are usually not as knowledgeable as their adult counterparts in the education administration, it is not always a good idea to allow them to choose whatever field they wish to study. Take liberal arts majors as an example; some of them lead to the lowest paying careers after graduation since few real jobs are available to degree-holders in these areas other than teaching the same subjects which they have studied. There are certainly large sums of money to be made in these fields for those savvy enough to apply their knowledge and skills in the right way, but such skillsets are not often taught in school, but rather learned through experience.

There is no doubt that most students will be initially unhappy with adults advising them to give up what they believe to be their dream jobs in favor of other means of employment, but this preliminary dissatisfaction will often give way to greater overall contentedness once they find that the career path suggested to them will provide a salary which supports a decent lifestyle. In addition, what most people presume is their passion, as with many aspiring musicians and other artists, is often downgraded to a hobby or minor interest when faced with the titanic amount of practice needed to hone their ability, as well as the compromises they must make in order to turn such skills into a profitable means of employment.

The most compelling reason that may be used to challenge my position is that educational institutions may give the wrong advice: what was initially deemed the fields that promised an abundance of jobs may prove the opposite when students graduate. This has been known to happen before. For instance, in the USA during the early 2000's the law field gained enormous interest as globalization picked up more steam, and as a result there was a projected need for new corporate lawyers and a boom in the legal field in general as the standard of living increased. Thus, academic institutions advertised heavily to encourage students to get legal degrees: not only was the profession highly respected, but it was also very lucrative. Predictably, this boosted law major admissions substantially, but the result was that it became difficult to find a job in the legal field due to the overabundance of law graduates. However, this boom-bust cycle in education and employment opportunities has been heavily researched in recent years, and many colleges and universities now use up-to-date job market analysis to recommend majors to students. In this way, schools can still be reasonably relied upon to persuade students to choose majors leading to plenty of jobs.

In summary, while it may not be exactly what students want, it is in their best interest to be advised by educational institutions to find a major that would be ideal for finding a job. The financial stability brought about by a better career would, in time, compensate them for the short-term sacrifice of giving up a hobby-oriented major.

120. Educational institutions have a responsibility to dissuade students from pursuing fields of study in which they are unlikely to succeed. (Discuss how the statement could or could not be true)

In the endeavor to provide a nation with citizens that are both highly skilled and well educated, I believe it is most definitely the obligation of educational institutions to discourage students from studying fields in which they are unlikely to succeed. While it is a popular belief that, as individuals, students should have the right to choose whatever path in life they wish to follow, the far-reaching consequences cannot be ignored of having too many people in a country without proper employment, a situation compounded by the significant financial burden that education places upon students and their families.

First of all, consider the current situation in the USA, where throughout the 1990's and early 2000's there was an explosion in the number of university attendees due to the relaxation of regulations on student loans. This, combined with the perception that a college degree would allow students to obtain higher positions and salaries after graduation, meant that many students decided to choose majors in difficult fields, such as engineering, finance, and law. However, these majors require a specific mindset and much dedication, which many students were unable to live up to, resulting in quite high dropout rates. These dropouts then found themselves in a position where they had already invested a considerable amount of time and money into a fruitless education and were at a disadvantage when entering the workplace since they had no other viable skills. This problem continues even today, leading to a significant proportion of the US population fit only for service jobs, and thus remaining in a position of financial limbo that disallows their contributing to the economy through spending or investment. Colleges and Universities have the ostensible purpose of preparing people for professional careers, and if they are to continue to be viewed as such, they should put more effort into ensuring their students pursue majors in which they can succeed. This has already been accomplished to some extent through placement exams for certain levels of mathematics and sciences, but more stringency should be applied in order to eliminate cram students or those who prepare only for the tests.

Pursuing less than appropriate majors has another potentially disastrous consequence in the form of bad debt. As previously mentioned, the relatively lax lending laws in the USA in regard to student loans mean that many students have tens of thousands of dollars in student debt. Add this fact to the aforementioned difficulty in finding gainful employment and one can understand the current debt bubble that exists in the USA. It has been regarded by economists as a situation that is potentially as severe as the 2008 economic crisis, especially since most student loans are given out at the same time and will thus likely default all at once. Had these students received the proper guidance while choosing a major, then this situation could have been avoided. For instance, every college has a "drop-add" period during the first week or two of each semester. In this period if students are closely monitored for performance or levels of stress, then those who seem incapable of grasping the concepts of the courses or unsuitable to the workload could be advised to move to majors in which they would perform better.

The statement might not hold true when it comes to students' right to choose their career path. Ultimately, they choose to enter college as a voluntary action to improve their own future. They devote their time and their money to their education for their own reasons. To this end, the school functions much like any other service provider in our society, and in this sense the institution has no right, beyond a slight suggestion, to attempt to change students' mind on which subject they wish to study. Yet, even in the context of a service provider, there are instances where the party delivering the service should attempt to discourage a customer from choosing a potentially detrimental product. Just as a waiter at a restaurant, if aware that a diner has a food allergy, would be expected to recommend that the customer not choose a dish which contains allergens, so schools should attempt to dissuade students from choosing areas of study that, based on test scores or past performance, would likely end in failure.

In sum, I think that schools and other educational institutions have an inherent responsibility to guide students away from career paths that do not suit them. In my mind, the national benefits such a responsibility would garner, along with the disasters it would aid in avoiding, trump the individual freedom of the students.

121. **Some people believe that competition for high grades motivates students to excel in the classroom. Others believe that such competition seriously limits the quality of real learning. (Address both views)**

As the number of students entering the education system has increased exponentially since the turn of the century, and continues to rise at a staggering rate, the value of competition for high marks has diminished significantly. Where once the desire to be head of the class was both a productive and obtainable goal, the sheer number of students in any given class, combined with the standardization of course materials, eliminates any meaningful differences between students that strive to achieve. Additionally, the labor market needs that the grade-based system was designed to meet no longer exist. Therefore, while there was once some semblance of an argument for having students compete against one another for high grades, I find myself agreeing with the statement that such a system serves only to inhibit true learning – regardless of the level of schooling.

If one is to walk into the classroom of any developed nation at the moment, one of the first things that becomes apparent is the number of students in the classroom. In most European and American schools, the average class size is about thirty students, whereas in parts of East Asia, class sizes reach upwards of seventy students per class. Take into account the total number of students in a single school and then extrapolate for all the students in the county, province and nation, and it becomes obvious that the academic performance of a single student, or even a group of students is not very impressive. This becomes clearer still considering the increasingly test-based education system, where a standard curriculum must be taught in preparation for level-determining exams. Since a human being can only effectively study a limited amount of material each day, whenever one finds a group of high-performing students in a single class, the notion of competing for the highest grade is more counterproductive than not, as the minute differences in scores do not accurately represent differences in the retained knowledge between students. Indeed, the students become so focused on getting the top score that they forget the reason why they need to learn the class material in the first place.

This brings us to the next point, that the purpose of the education system as it currently exists is not conducive to real education. Schools are in the form that we generally think of them, classrooms have rows of seats, and ringing bells signal beginning and ending of class time and lunch time. All of this was designed during the Industrial Revolution to create a society that provided a minimum level of education that would prepare people for work in factories. One sees the parallels in the orderliness, the scheduling, and even the authoritarian hierarchy of teacher and student, quite different from the equally rigid, but far more intimate and personal apprentice system of the pre-industrial eras. Simply put, technology and society have developed past the necessity of the current school system design. Competing for grades is analogous to the factory line in that it trains students to compete to see who can perform the most menial tasks in the most efficient way possible. It does not encourage critical thinking; it rewards only those that can exactly meet the criteria on the curriculum, nothing more, nothing less. Thus, when students from this system enter the modern workforce, they are ill-equipped to meet the needs of a tech-based society that requires innovators.

Some may argue that competition for high grades promotes students' performance in the classroom. After all, competition is a major driving force of success in many fields. Look at how the technological arms race has driven nations to develop ever more advanced devices and systems for use in our daily lives. If the same importance of having high grades can be instilled in students, then a drive to excel in one's classes would naturally result. However, it has proven tricky to do this, as young adults seem to be biologically inclined to rebel against the accepted norm. In a certain phase of human development, young people yearn to prove the established truths wrong and rebel. Thus, attempting to convince all young people in school to compete for higher grades, is something that has proven elusive to educators. Therefore, the system of competing for good grades has not produced many high-performing students but has led students to question why they must get a better arbitrary number or letter than their classmates.

All in all, competing for high grades is a method of preparing students for a life in the factory, not for a life of learning and development. It may have been effective in its time and may even aid some people in getting some education, but it does not contribute to knowledge and skills required in contemporary society, and the system is, therefore, obsolete.

122. Claim: Major policy decisions should always be left to politicians and other government experts.

Reason: Politicians and other government experts are more informed and thus have better judgment and perspective than do members of the general public. (Claim-Reason)

The speaker claims that politicians and other government experts should be the only people to make major policy decisions, based on the notion that they are more informed and have better judgement and perspective than the general public. I unequivocally agree with this line of thinking, as politics and civics management are increasingly complex, and the consequences for poor decision-making can be devastating.

As societies become more democratic, it is understandable that average citizens may wish to assert more of their own opinion on how the country should be run. What they often fail to consider is the disparity between the way their local area functions and that of the nation as a whole. When experts make a major policy decision, every step from formulation to implementation must undergo rigorous analysis from legal, financial, scientific, and other perspectives. Teams of experts spend weeks or months poring over stacks upon stacks of drafts, revisions, proposals, and references. Having the general public take part in this process would only serve to convolute it even further, as time is wasted educating everyone ignorant of any of the aforementioned fields.

The years of experience of certain members of government also play a vital role in decision-making, especially in the context of international relations. Having inexperienced, non-government citizens voice their opinions can even be a threat to national security. The refugee crisis in Europe is a good example of this issue. Due to civil wars and general instability in parts of Africa and the Middle East, millions of people have sought asylum in European countries. Since societies in Europe had been shifting towards more social justice and diversity-oriented views, the people of Great Britain, Germany, and other nations demanded that their leaders open their border to provide a safe haven for refugees. This went against the better judgement of those in the security and public management administrations, as such a large influx of people with dubious backgrounds and means of self-sufficiency posed a risk to local budgets and safety. Sure enough, there are consistent reports of increased crime and extremism in the cities of these countries that listened to the demands of the citizens instead of their experts.

Another example of the failings of the public when it comes to making important government decisions can be seen in the USA's involvement in the Vietnam War during the 1960's and 1970's. While the morality of the conflict itself and the methods used will be debated by ethicists in perpetuum, there is not much debate now over the reason for USA's "loss" of the war: mainly a loss of will to continue fighting on the part of the American people. By all modern accounts, the North Vietnamese were on the brink of total destruction near the end of the war and American soldiers and their allies had conducted brutal bombing campaigns and anti-insurgent operations. However, it was the hippie movement and the public's overall dissatisfaction with the handling of troop training and behavior in Vietnam that led the USA to pull out. At the time, the military experts were confident that with just a few more months the war would be decisively won, but the general public would have none of it. Had more knowledgeable minds prevailed, the USA could have avoided losing the war that started its general decline in the following decades.

In sum, I totally agree with both the claim and the reason it is based on. The public may not always like the decisions of qualified experts in government, but as long as those officials are indeed experts, their advice and decisions on major policies should be adhered to.

123. Some people believe that universities should require every student to take a variety of courses outside the student's field of study. Others believe that universities should not force students to take any courses other than those that will help prepare them for jobs in their chosen fields. (Address both views)

In pursuing a university education, students should, aside from their major-related courses, be required to attend a diverse range of other classes, including history, economics, and other courses. Not only do such classes provide the student with a wide range of knowledge to draw on when he or she enters a chosen profession, but they also contribute to the creation of a more informed society.

If one analyzes the greatest innovators, regardless of field or era, one finds that they all, without exception, strive to educate themselves in a variety of areas of expertise. This polymath-like behavior is regarded by these great minds as one of the key factors in aiding them when they attempt to develop creative ideas. One of the better-known examples was given by the late Steve Jobs, who, in his famous Stanford commencement speech credited the unique font style that made his early Macintosh computers so popular to the calligraphy classes he attended. A similar message was conveyed during an interview by the great animator Chuck Jones, creator of beloved characters such as Bugs Bunny and Daffy Duck as well as some of the most well-known animated shorts in history. He stated that inspiration could come from anywhere, and that creative people should open their minds to more than one discipline, including literature, art, and other aspects of the world when brainstorming.

The benefits of such courses are enjoyed not only by the individual, but also by a society and nation. Having a citizenry that possesses a broad understanding of a variety of subjects is vital for a nation to develop efficiently. For one thing, people that stay informed about various topics are more likely to be receptive to new technology and ideas, thus allowing technological advances and social policies to diffuse throughout society more effectively. For another thing, in societies that have representative governments, students, i.e. future voters, that study a variety of topics are able to make better decisions. A perfect example of how a lack of this negatively impacts society can be seen in the USA, where the education regarding medicine and health has deteriorated to the point where some parents are unwilling to vaccinate their children for unscientific reasons, leading to outbreaks of previously eradicated illnesses such as the measles.

There is, however, an argument to be made against forcing students to take courses beyond what is necessary for their degree. First and foremost are the financial and time costs associated with extra college courses. With ever-increasing tuition rates per credit-hour, the added financial strain would make a college education for many lower-income students prohibitively expensive. It could also be argued that our students are already distracted enough as it is with social media and other forms of entertainment that take away from much needed study time for mastering their respective fields. Yet these concerns are responsibilities for the individual students to manage, and universities have a more pressing obligation to benefit society than to meet the particular financial needs of every student.

To conclude, I believe that a mandate requiring students to take a number of classes without a direct relationship with their major is ultimately an advantageous decision for both the students' future careers and the development of society as a whole.

124. It is more harmful to compromise one's own beliefs than to adhere to them. (Discuss how the statement could or could not be true)

The truth in the issue stated above revolves around the word "compromise". If the speaker had used the word "change" instead, then the door would have been opened for refutation, but the statement using the word "compromise" can generally be supported in its martyr-like glory by geniuses of the decades in acquiescence with the whispering of the individual soul. Through the life of Martin Luther, the musings of Shakespeare and the philosophy of Socrates the importance of self-belief and maintaining the integrity of that belief is manifest.

Martin Luther, a controversial priest and theologian, was so dedicated to his "heretic" beliefs posted in *Ninety-five Theses* and his renouncing of the concept that sins could be forgiven via money, that when Pope Leo X and the Holy Roman Emperor demanded a retraction of his writings he refused and was excommunicated, a fate worse than death as it involves not just mortal salvation. Luther understood that rescinding his writings and compromising his beliefs might provide immediate physical comfort, but the torture his conscience and soul would have endured would be worse than any death or punishment doled out by men. Luther's foil is another priest, Arthur Dimmesdale, from Hawthorne's *The Scarlet Letter*. Dimmesdale first compromises his beliefs and role as a minister by having an affair with Hester Prynne, and then after the affair he allows Hester to accept sole responsibility and shame for the misdeed, betraying his belief in justice and honesty. Though Dimmesdale is portrayed in a kind manner, it is he, not Hester, who feels the depths of hell raging within and swallowing up his existence and ability to progress. Though Luther received greater public punishment and pain than Dimmesdale, it was Dimmesdale who truly suffered.

Shakespeare was also aware of the importance of steadfastness in belief and action. In *Hamlet* Shakespeare's character Polonius directs his son Laertes saying, "This above all: to thine own self be true." Polonius's parting words were a reminder that no matter where Laertes would go or with whom he would come in contact his responsibility was to keep his integrity and beliefs intact; without this sense of self and anchor of truth and morality Polonius knew his son would be easily swept into disrepute. Yet, it is not only the self which benefits from a constant and unwavering nature; as Polonius continues his speech he tells Laertes that, "And it must follow, as the night the day, Thou canst not then be false to any man." If Laertes remains true to his beliefs his lack of compromise will not only benefit his life and soul, but his strength of character will be imparted to all in his presence, and the world will benefit.

One of the earliest documented discussions on the purpose of integrity is found in the writings of Plato and attributed to his mentor Socrates. Socrates believed that self-knowledge was the great goal of society; this was a dramatic shift for his time as looking at the outside world was seen as a higher form of thinking than studying the condition of humankind. He also believed that a self-aware person would reach the peak of his or her potential for becoming a "philosopher-king", while someone unaware and compromising in his or her beliefs will remain ignorant and incapable of greatness. Socrates believes so strongly in constancy based on knowledge that for him, people willing to compromise their beliefs are not even real people. Like Plato's forms, these people are only shadows of what a real person could be.

However, the statement might not hold true when one's beliefs are proven to be erroneous, or even harmful to the people around one; then, it may be best to compromise those beliefs. The late actor Sean Connery was a beloved film icon and was considered the image of the ideal man for decades after his debut as James Bond in the eponymous spy movies. However, his reputation was irreparably tarnished in an interview conducted later in his career, wherein he espoused the notion of hitting a woman during an argument. People accused him of being in favor of domestic abuse, and he even reiterated his position years later in a subsequent interview. There were rumors that that initial interview cost him millions of dollars in lost film roles due to that opinion. Had he moved on with the times and understood how abhorrent his opinion was, he could have avoided the ostracization he suffered as a result.

While one's beliefs may be compromised in a few cases, without constancy in belief and character people are doomed to mediocrity. It takes well placed beliefs and strong character to withstand the burgeoning tide of doubt, but those who emerge on the other side are forged with the strength of transcendence.

125. **Claim: Colleges and universities should specify all required courses and eliminate elective courses in order to provide clear guidance for students.**
    Reason: College students — like people in general — prefer to follow directions rather than make their own decisions. (Claim-Reason)

The speaker claims that if colleges and universities spell out compulsory courses and remove elective courses direction would be clearer, based on the notion that college students and other people would rather follow directions than make their own decisions. The reason, though scary, bears some weight. The claim is misleading and completely inappropriate.

On first reflection I found appalling the notion that people would prefer to follow direction rather than make their own decisions. This goes against everything the activist in me would like to believe and fight for. Decisions can be difficult, but the sacrifice is worth the empowerment that comes with choosing one's own path. This is what the idealist in me wants to believe, but when I reflect on life as a whole, I find the assertion right. In most aspects of life, it is easier and simpler to follow directions. I enjoy cooking, but I lack the time and interest to make up every recipe. I find that most dishes even taste better when I follow the directions provided by someone else. When I go to the gym the same idea applies. I want certain results, but have not put in the time to see which exercises will yield those fruits. Instead, I look to trainers and programs to assist me in my goals. I concede that I do make many choices, but even for these choices I find it easier when I am limited and know clearly what I desire.

Though the speaker's reason has merit, the claim is not a logical or thorough remedy. The speaker feels that it is the choices of courses that college students are avoiding, but I find that more often it is the responsibility that is difficult. I can choose between wearing a green shirt or an orange shirt, but if you add the responsibility of choosing the color for an entire team of people the stress is compounded. It is the responsibility, not the choice, that most people tend to avoid. The reason parenting is so challenging is that now parents are ultimately responsible for a whole person. There are no tailor-made directions, and though there are support groups each person's experience is unique.

Yet, just because the responsibility can be difficult or stressful to cope with does not mean it should be taken away. Colleges and universities are supposed to expand horizons and teach students not only what to learn, but also how to go about learning. This includes figuring out one's portfolio of required and elective courses after one reads the institution's guidelines and consults with one's advisor. Within this formula comes the need for failure and also the opportunity to be responsible. The more students are taught, the more responsible they become to themselves and society. The adage that "with great power comes great responsibility" definitely applies, and if the responsibility were taken away the power would be as well, allowing a visionless society without real innovation or purpose to prevail.

The speaker's reason given here exposes a basic fear which drives most individuals, including college students, the fear of responsibility. The claim of letting this fear take over colleges and universities, let alone life, shows how bleak a world could become. While there are many everyday decisions made easier through directions and depending upon others, such as choices of college courses, a life without a sense of purpose or the courage to make choices and accept the responsibility that comes with this may become just a show and a passage of time instead of a genuine life and a rite-of-passage.

126. No field of study can advance significantly unless it incorporates knowledge and experience from outside that field. (Discuss how the statement could or could not be true)

This statement claims that outside influences are necessary for significant progress in any field of study. I mostly disagree with this notion, as it relies on an oversimplified idea of how research works and ignores the true nature of progress.

The notion that important advancement in a field requires the incorporation of outside knowledge partly stems from modern pop-culture's vague regurgitation of scientific principles for mass-consumption in media. In films, a team of researchers will embark upon a montage of scientific inquiry, only to encounter a problem which cannot be solved until the team happens upon a layman or piece of knowledge from another field which sparks a Eureka moment. With the overuse of montages in the media, most people's understanding of training, research, and progress in general is skewed from reality. It is unfortunate that this occurs, because it tends to undermine the real achievements of most scientists that have made breakthroughs by hard work and perseverance in their own field alone.

Even in genuine eureka moments, such as Archimedes' legendary original, the inspiration is often related to the field being studied. A quick refresher on the Archimedes story: our scientist in question was tasked with ascertaining whether a particular crown was made out of the total amount of gold allocated for its construction. In trying to find a suitable method to compare a pure gold crown to the one of uncertain composition, Archimedes had already considered using differences in volume as the means of measurement. It was only after noticing the displacement of water in his bathtub that he supposedly found the proper method. Here it can be seen that there was a clear connection between Archimedes' research and inspiration for his breakthrough.

To be fair to critics, there are some cases in which ostensibly unrelated fields converge to create major progress. For example, modern surgery would be completely impossible without the combination of anesthetics developed through chemistry, sterile tools resulting from materials science, and various other fields. Even outside of technology, the field of economics as we know it today is a culmination of decades of research in sociology, psychology, statistics, and more. However, it is exceedingly difficult to combine fields consciously to force progress; as shown by the two examples just presented, the progress that is achieved usually results from an organic interinfluencing of various fields over long periods of time.

While I concede that unrelated fields can be combined to achieve great progress, advances in most fields are the result of intense study within the related area of research.

127. True success can be measured primarily in terms of the goals one sets for oneself. (Discuss how the statement could or could not be true)

The statement asserts that true success can be measured by the context of one's personal goals. I believe that this is, for the most part, true – as long as the goals challenge one's abilities beyond a reasonable level and the methods used are ethical.

If we are to judge true success by the goals one sets for oneself, we must understand the actual capabilities that one possesses. For example, if a person comes from a poor family in an undeveloped country torn apart by war, then reaching adulthood could be considered a success for that person. Any goals people have and achieve beyond that would be praise-worthy by virtue of the hardships they have had to endure along the way. On the other hand, for individuals born into a wealthy family that resides in a fully developed country, the expectations for their achievements are much higher because of the greater number of resources at their disposal. If, as an extreme example, the children of Microsoft founder and multibillionaire Bill Gates had "going to college" as one of their goals, it would seem quite pretentious of them to feel a sense of achievement from meeting such a goal.

Success is itself defined as the accomplishment of some aim that people set. Therefore, as long as they continue to place incrementally more difficult demands upon themselves, they can look back upon their progress and growth feeling a well-deserved sense of gratification. People may judge a person's success by comparing the person's achievements to those of others, but as previously touched upon, the unfortunate fact of the world is that not everyone is born into equal means. For some people, going to college is an unattainable goal, whereas for others it is a basic requirement for entering adulthood. Therefore, the relevant argument in favor of measuring true success based on others' achievements only works among people of equal demographics.

One final, but no less significant, factor in measuring true success is the way in which individuals achieve their goals. As an extreme example, conqueror Timur wanted to unite his people and build an empire. He accomplished his goals, but did so by committing horrendous acts of murder that were abhorrent even in the relatively brutal context of his era. Therefore, few people genuinely praise him or use him as a role model for success, as there is no practical or humane way to emulate him.

To conclude, true success should be measured in terms of the meeting of reasonable goals that one sets for oneself. The differences in resources, upbringing, and other factors make it next to impossible to measure success by comparing one's achievements to those of others, and Machiavellian "ends justifying the means" success is simply immoral.

128. **The general welfare of a nation's people is a better indication of that nation's greatness than are the achievements of its rulers, artists, or scientists. (Address challenges to your position)**

Throughout history, those nations that we look back upon as prime civilizations have always been admired for the singular achievements of their scientists, artists, and leaders. Yet these achievements were not necessarily what made the nations themselves great. Rather, it was the well-being of their citizens that determined whether the country flourished and was held in high esteem by its neighbors.

To begin with, it should be noted that genius can come from almost anywhere. Even the least developed nations have had their own great minds arising from their populations, but this does not make the nation great. For example, the great civil rights leader Mahatma Gandhi is an icon of political thought and protest, yet India could not be considered a great nation during his lifetime. In Gandhi's time, India was still a colony of Britain, and the oppressive regime there had stifled the economic development of almost the whole country. Poverty and famine were rampant, and no matter how impactful Gandhi's words and actions may have been on the future of India, the nation itself during Gandhi's time was not considered great. Now, however, things have changed drastically, in terms of technological and economic development India's people have flourished, and the nation is now considered one of the most powerful on the world stage.

Another example can be seen in the self-proclaimed great nation of Nazi Germany. A large portion of scientific discoveries from the 1940's and 1950's was made by or with the help of German and Austrian scientists fleeing the Nazi regime. If the nation had truly been as great as it alleged itself to be, then there would not have been so many great minds that left it. At the time, persecution of a variety of categories was common; political, religious, social, and virtually all other aspects of life that may have posed a threat to the regime were ruthlessly culled by the Gestapo secret police. The country was still unsustainable from an industrial standpoint; the entire Sudetenland annexation was planned in order to seize the natural resources and utilize the labor force of nearby nations to feed the German economy. As a result, the revolutionary discoveries of Nazi Germany's scientists were almost completely overlooked in most cases since their achievements did little to improve the nation's overall well-being.

The most convincing reason that could be used to poke holes in my argument is that the general welfare of a great nation is often inextricably intertwined with the accomplishments of its rulers, artists, and scientists. In other words, the general well-being of a great nation is almost impossible without competent rulers and difficult to achieve without notable artists or scientists. This means that the achievements of such eminent people demonstrate as clearly as the general well-being of the nation's people that the nation is great. A historical example can be seen in Tang Dynasty China, the era which is generally accepted as one of the nation's greatest premodern periods of cultural and scientific development. The people in China at the time were extremely well-cared for as compared to previous eras, and some of the most iconic Chinese poets, such as Li Bai and Du Fu, became ensconced in the annals of cultural greatness. To this day, the people of China still look back to the Tang Dynasty as a period to be emulated in regard to its artistic accomplishments as well as the welfare of the people: accessible education, cultural enrichment, available food, and other resources; the list goes on.

While achievements of a nation's rulers, artists, or scientists indicate its success in some cases, one could pick a great leader, scientist, or artist from almost any nation at any point in history; that fact alone says little about the prosperity or success of those nations. Instead, the benefits which the general populace enjoy are touted as indicators of a powerful and successful nation.

129. The best test of an argument is the argument's ability to convince someone with an opposing viewpoint. (Discuss how the statement could or could not be true)

Argumentation is a highly nuanced art which spans a plethora of fields. Over the course of human history, some have concluded that the best way to ensure the strength of an argument is to sharpen it against the minds of others, and through the success of convincing those who disagree, determine whether the argument has merit. The notion of an argument's persuasiveness as the best test of an argument certainly has value, but there are a number of problems with relying on this method as a rule.

To begin with, simply because one can convince a skeptical party of an argument does nothing to support its objective validity. This is due to the fact that a person's ability to be persuaded depends largely on the person's knowledge of all factors pertaining to the argument in question. It may be the case that the person in disagreement is ignorant of some key fact which would verify his or her skepticism and render the argument erroneous. Such was the case during the 1800's in the USA, where countless "snake oil" salesmen were able to hock phony tonics and elixirs on townsfolk who lacked the education of basic scientific principles to spot the ruse. The fact that they were convinced of the salesmen's quackery certainly displayed the swindler's persuasiveness, but in no way verified the truth of the supposed cure's efficacy.

However, it could be claimed, from a purely rhetorical standpoint, that an argument which succeeds in convincing a nonbeliever to agree with it is a successful one. This is because the goal of rhetoric is to persuade, not necessarily to seek objective truth. Therefore, in any instance in which a debate results in a change of opinion, the argument used has proven itself to be a valid one and has served its intended purpose. This is evident in many of the white lies which parents tell their children in order to convince them of the need to perform certain tasks in lieu of the lengthy explanations of the real reasoning due to the inability of their children to grasp adults' concepts. Nonetheless, this is a dangerous line of thinking that is intellectually bankrupt when used among adults, as it pollutes the logic used in society. If the only true test of an argument is accepted as the ability to persuade others, then objective reasoning is eventually discarded, and it becomes impossible to progress due to so much misinformation.

A far better method of testing an argument involves how it stands up to facts and logical contradictions. This does not require someone to disagree with the argument, but needs someone who is willing to be honestly critical. This is already a widespread method in academic communities; it is known as the peer-review process. Through this method, the argument is scrutinized based on how it holds up to analysis of its underlying facts, and the applicability of the argument to a variety of different situations. Merely convincing those who disagree with the argument is not nearly enough, and only after it has been dissected and scoured for inconsistencies is it deemed to be worthy of publication. Through this trial, which in an ideal situation is repeated over time, arguments are synthesized into their best possible forms.

In the end, merely relying on an argument's ability to convince a person who disagrees with it is not a viable method to determine its validity. It may be a good start, but it is insufficient when one wishes to develop a truly resilient thesis. To do so requires an analysis of the argument's foundational logic and facts, not just once, but repeatedly, until there is no room left, at least in the present moment, for error. In this way, one can be sure that one's argument has reached its pinnacle of persuasive power.

130. The effectiveness of a country's leaders is best measured by examining the well-being of that country's citizens. (Discuss how the statement could or could not be true)

The speaker argues that the best way to evaluate leaders' effectiveness is to observe the well-being of their country's citizens. While it is hard to disagree outright with this notion, the statement is too vague and absolutist in its stance and calls for some investigation and clarification.

In order to attach the "effective" label to leaders, we need to determine what powers they have to influence legislation and society as a whole, especially whether the well-being of the citizenry will be the metric by which such "effectiveness" is measured. For example, if a country's leader is not afforded any meaningful powers, or has power but no means to apply it, then it would be almost impossible to prove that the current status of the public, whether positive or negative, is the fault of the leader. On the other hand, if the leader is in possession of a consolidated power structure, there would be more connections between their decisions or mandates and the effects of such on the populace with which we determine their efficacy.

From a historical perspective, it is far easier to assess past national leaders in this way, as governments in the past tended to lean toward a centralized system with monarchs as their heads. Hence why there are names for kings such as Alexander the Great, or Ivan the Terrible. Yet even with the benefit of hindsight, such titles do not necessarily stem from the quality of life enjoyed by the people: few historical records describe the relative change in daily life before and after Alexander the Great ascended the throne; his triumphs were primarily military in nature.

This begs an important question: is leaders' effectiveness only judged by the well-being of people during their term as a leader, or by the long-lasting effects of their rule? This is an oft-debated concept in American politics, where incoming leaders blame all current problems on the incumbent and attempt to reap the glory for all of the beneficial policies enacted by the incumbent. This complicates the statement's assertion then, since a current leader may appear to be completely ineffective in the present moment, but may at the same time enact policies that will allow their nation's people to prosper for years to come.

In conclusion, taking the statement at face value would be a bit hasty, as it does not consider the amount of power a leader may hold, nor does it consider the effects a leader's policies may have in the future. With such caveats, it is reasonable to use the well-being of a country's citizens as a metric for determining the effectiveness of their leader.

131. Nations should pass laws to preserve any remaining wilderness areas in their natural state. (Address challenges to your position)

One of the more pressing environmental issues currently facing the world is the loss of forests and other wilderness areas to development. Therefore, I believe it is necessary for governments to take drastic measures and pass legislation to protect whatever wildlands that remain. It is my firm belief that such policies are the only way to effectively halt the destruction of habitats and return some semblance of homeostasis to the environment.

An important part of this argument that must be considered is the current rate of habitat loss that is occurring even at this very moment and the harm it poses to human life. Most of the breathable oxygen on our planet is generated by rainforests such as the Amazon. Yet, every year nearly 80 million acres of the Amazon is burned to make way for development. It is therefore no surprise that the air quality of Brazil's major cities has declined over time. Passing laws to conserve the Amazon and other rainforests would not only serve to protect the many endangered species that call these habitats home but would also aid in improving the air quality of nearby cities. Naturally, it would prove to be an inconvenience to farmers and other developers hoping to turn rainforest land into valuable real-estate, but the long-term benefits of conservation far outweigh the short-term greed.

If it is monetary gain that drives much of the destruction of natural habitats, then instituting laws which promote conservation for the purposes of eco-tourism would be a win-win for both sides. Many wilderness areas are places of astounding beauty, such as the icy northern reaches of Alaska and the arid desert regions of the Midwest USA, which also boast unique indigenous cultures. Certainly, if these regions were legally protected, then they would prove to be valuable sources of revenue for the local people, who can sell their native crafts, and the tax coffers by proxy. There are already similar programs in place, the famous Yellowstone National Parks being the most famous. Every year, thousands of people pay for hunting licenses, tour trips, and other tourist activities to the parks, which in turn finances their continued conservation. This not only incentivizes their continued upkeep but also makes it difficult for developers to match the financial gains that they could offer in lieu of the annual tourist revenue. Thus, legislation to conserve wilderness habitats not only preserves the wealth of natural beauty these places offer, but also contributes real wealth to the government through tourism.

Of course, many industrialists argue that it is a waste to leave the untapped resources of the wilderness undeveloped. A contemporary example is the desire of large oil companies to drill in the Arctic regions of North America. The oil companies argue that the regions are mostly uninhabited and thus their drilling would pose little threat to ecosystems. However, their arguments are misleading, as the Arctic regions are an important part of seasonal migration for caribou and other forms of wildlife, the destruction of which would cause a negative chain reaction throughout several distant ecosystems. Additionally, the amount of oil that would be extracted from these regions would be an insignificant percentage of the nation's oil consumption. Laws protecting these regions would ensure that the ecosystems which rely on the animals that migrate through the Arctic would remain intact and prevent the often-irreparable damage that follows industrial development.

In conclusion, I think that policies that preserve forests and other wilderness areas in their natural states are both necessary and beneficial. Not only do they protect ecosystems from annihilation, but the natural havens which are preserved through these laws can still benefit humanity health-wise, and even economically in some cases.

132. In any field — business, politics, education, government — those in power should be required to step down after five years. (Discuss positive and negative consequences of the policy)

While it may be tempting to allow a seemingly faultless leader to continue to rule, a change in administration is absolutely necessary after a term of five years, regardless of the field. In this way, success is all but guaranteed, as obsolete ideas can be replaced with new ones, reducing the probability of stagnation and failure.

There are plenty of instances in which a long-serving singular ruler, though initially competent and even highly regarded, has brought ruin upon those they had hoped to benefit. Frederick the Great of Prussia was and still is hailed as one of the few 'enlightened despots', a wise and intelligent leader that brought Prussia out of the Seven Year war during the mid-1700's. He made various contributions that allowed the arts and sciences of his nation to flourish during his reign, but ultimately his militaristic and nationalistic ideals promoted the expansionist mindset, which he applied for the entire 46 years of his reign and led to the destruction and partitioning of Prussia in the 19th century. His continued annexation of neighboring territories throughout his many years in power gave rise to much animosity of other powers, such that his death marked a power vacuum which was readily exploited. Had Frederick served a shorter period of rule, perhaps his militaristic inclinations would not have left such a sour taste in the mouth of Prussia's rivals, and they would not have been so eager to see his empire fall.

The dangers of endless leadership are not owned by politics alone but may also be seen in the realm of business. Steve Jobs is famous for his founding of Apple, the tech giant that has been a revolutionary force in consumer electronics for decades. However, Jobs' extended leadership between 1976 and 1985 was fraught with controversy, and his poor business decisions, along with his often-violent mood swings, forced the company to strip him of his executive powers in the late eighties. The board had felt that Jobs had, after experiencing so many years of unfettered creative control, become too arrogant in his position and feared that he would rather see the company ruined than give up his own personal vision for the products Apple created. It was only after he resigned that Apple was able to achieve the success, however lukewarm it might have been, in the nineties, which set the stage for his return and subsequent fresh ideas to turn the company into the international juggernaut we know today.

However, there is no guarantee that new leadership will most assuredly lead to success. The need for new leadership can be seen in the current education system in the USA, where the federal administration has seen little real change in decades. Sure, there have been new department heads, but the majority of them tout the same line of policies such as standardized testing and budget cuts. This has led to a severe stagnation of education quality in US public schools, contributing to a disparity between subsidized education and private schooling that was not as much of an issue in previous years. There is a growing sentiment that the fall in international education rankings, which has been steadily becoming more dramatic, is a direct consequence of hiring the same kind of educational administrators over and over, despite the fact that they replace former leaders.

In conclusion, in order to ensure the long-term success of any organization, whether it be a nation, company or other collective, a regular change in leadership is vital. Even though this may not be the most reliable path to prosperity, doing so allows new ideas to be implemented and tested, while stagnation is avoided.

133. Some people claim that the goal of politics should be the pursuit of an ideal. Others argue that the goal should be finding common ground and reaching reasonable consensus. (Address both views)

The world of politics is unique in its breadth and diversity. Issues that may arise in political areas can span from moral issues of what many consider to be of spiritual importance on one extreme to more commonplace and almost mundane administrative tasks of government on the other extreme. The goal of a politician may vary from occasion to occasion. In cases of strict moral issues, a politician must persist in the pursuit of an ideal. However, in instances of more commonplace administrative tasks, the goal should be to find compromise and consensus to accelerate the political process.

Political issues of a strict moral nature demand the dedication of those involved to pursue a solution they believe is right. Politics and government are one instrument of social change, and it is imperative to a well-balanced society that those entrusted as public servants are willing to pursue a difficult and complex issue to secure a right solution when the alternative is, in a moral sense, wrong. Consider, for example, William Wilberforce, a member of British Parliament in the late eighteenth century. At the time, the slave trade between Africa and other British colonies was at its peak. For religious reasons, Wilberforce believed the practice of buying and selling human beings as slaves was wrong. In his opinion, many other politicians had compromised their beliefs to cater to the desires of businessmen who profited from the slave trade. Wilberforce led a political movement to end the slave trade that nearly cost him his career. He was, in the end, successful, and his efforts ended a practice that he believed to be wrong.

Other issues, such as the practice of slavery in America, abortion, or the practice of same-sex marriage, are moral issues that have entered the political arena. In these cases, politicians have a moral obligation to pursue what they believe is best, as the political resolution is often interpreted to reflect the moral views of the society they represent.

Not all political matters are concerned with moral issues, however. Many political issues involve much more common concerns that are not cast in terms of right or wrong but are constructed in terms of determining the utilitarian "greatest good for the greatest number of people." Some examples of this type of issue are decisions on zoning, voting districts, budgeting, and other administrative tasks that are determined by a political body. In these cases, no solution is necessarily superior to another in a moral sense. Rather, the best solution is the one that will help the most people politically or socially, or the one that will increase efficiency in administration. On these issues, the political machine should not be viewed as a vehicle of social change, but as an incubator for brainstorming to find the best solution to a problem. The goal of a brainstorming session is to combine the best components of different people's ideas to find the best possible hybrid of ideas. This combination of different ideas is, in essence, a process of compromise. Then, on issues of only administrative or utilitarian importance, the goal of politics, or of a politician, should be to compromise to find not only a suitable solution, but the best solution to meet the diversity of needs and interests of the people.

In sum, the goal of politics must depend on the situation and on the issue at hand. Those employed as public servants have a responsibility to recognize which issues are moral issues and which are not, and then to handle each issue appropriately. Moral issues should be pursued with ideals in mind. Issues not of a moral nature should be pursued with an attitude of compromise.

134. The best way to solve environmental problems caused by consumer-generated waste is for towns and cities to impose strict limits on the amount of trash they will accept from each household. (Address challenges to your position)

While limiting the amount of trash that towns and cities accept from each household can contribute to easing environmental problems that stem from consumer waste, I do not think it is necessarily the best way, because there are some potential issues with this method and other more effective methods exist.

To begin with, the idea of placing limits on the amount of garbage towns and cities will accept from households is an intriguing one. On the one hand, it does propose to deal with waste directly and split the labor among the citizenry. But on the other hand, there are numerous potential disadvantages to this idea. For one thing, simply refusing to take more than the allotted amount of trash from a household does not mean that people will buy less. In fact, depending on the culture of the country, people may simply decide to dump illegally the trash that is not taken; this is already known to be done by some construction companies and people in rural areas. Thus, there is a chance that this method could contribute to even greater pollution as a result of improper waste disposal.

Even if all goes according to plan and people comply with the new limits, it does not deal with the issue of the toxicity of the waste itself. True, the rate at which waste enters the environment would be reduced, but the waste would still be increasing. The type of waste is also an important factor to consider. Metals, plastics, and other materials may be highly toxic and non-biodegradable, and as the amount of waste in a landfill increases, the concentration of these hazardous materials renders them even more potent. Thus, this plan by itself would likely do little to mitigate the problems caused by consumer waste.

A far better plan would be to place the burden of cleanup on the manufacturers of the products. Not only is there the moral aspect of them having knowledge of the dangers their products pose to the environment, but also they fully control the materials and fabrication of their products, so the onus is on them to clean up the mess they ostensibly create. This was the case for certain products such as glass and plastic bottles in the USA until the 1980's. Prior to that time, there were laws that required companies to buy back any bottles or cans that people brought to the factories. As a result, far less waste was caused by these products at the time. An implementation of similar policies for far more kinds of products, combined with the proposed plan of limiting waste, could be much more effective.

While the idea of limiting the amount of waste taken from each household is good-intentioned, it is not the best way to combat pollution caused by consumer products. It could certainly help the situation; however, a more robust plan that places more responsibility on the companies that produce these items, combined with the limited-trash pickup, would be a far superior option.

135. We learn our most valuable lessons in life from struggling with our limitations rather than from enjoying our successes. (Address challenges to your position)

It is said that one's life is an endless compilation of lessons that one learns over time. Some would argue that the most useful of these lessons come from enjoying one's success, whereas others trace the source of the most valuable lessons back to struggling with one's limitations. While success can certainly be an important experience that everyone should have at some point, I do not feel that the most significant lessons are learned by relishing one's accomplishments. Rather, I would assert that it is only through suffering and working through the hurdles of life that a person can glean truly useful knowledge.

To begin with, we can analyze an age-old aphorism: "Necessity is the mother of invention," or as it is more commonly quoted: "Desperation breeds innovation." This oft-quoted phrase encapsulates a widely accepted truth that people need to struggle in order to improve. In the same way that our bodies need the pull of gravity in order to maintain muscular strength and bone density, our minds need problems to solve in order to remain active. In fact, it could be argued that only by testing our limits can we improve at all, since learning itself is the process of acquiring previously unknown information.

On a similar note, the common notion of "hitting rock bottom" is used to refer to people who have addictions or other behaviors that are harmful to their lives, and the cathartic struggle they must go through. In this process, individuals must fully face their limitations by losing everything important to them, and only then are they able to rebuild themselves into something better. While this may be extreme for many people, the core concept of the process is the same: only by tackling one's walls to success head-on can true growth and success be achieved. In this respect, it can be understood why almost every successful person has stories of the struggles that have led to his or her success: both Bill Gates and Steve Jobs went through periods of near poverty before hitting upon their ideas for their companies; one of the wealthiest men in the world, Jeff Bezos, spent years operating Amazon out of a pitifully small one-room office before it transformed into the international juggernaut it is today. These individuals and others learned far more from their failures prior to ever reaching success.

Yet, there is something to be said about the educational value of success. In achieving one's goals, one learns the value in taking time off and dealing with the increasing amount of responsibility that one is given once one's accomplishments are recognized. For many people who are used to struggling to reach their goals, they must learn to relax or risk cutting themselves off from the people closest to them. For instance, almost every CEO works at least sixty hours or more a week. Such workaholic ethics can easily cause relationships with one's friends and family to deteriorate, which is why many successful people learn to take seasonal vacations. Furthermore, in obtaining leadership positions, one learns the important lesson that one's actions have significant effects upon others, and that care must be taken when one makes decisions. However, none of these lessons can be learned without first going through a significant number of trials and tribulations to get to leadership positions.

In conclusion, I strongly believe that it is only after individuals have struggled with their limitations that they can gain truly valuable life lessons. Resting on one's laurels may offer some minor bits of knowledge from time to time. However, just as a diamond requires intense pressure to form, so one must deal with the pressure in overcoming one's individual boundaries that imparts wisdom.

136. Claim: While boredom is often expressed with a sense of self-satisfaction, it should really be a source of embarrassment.
Reason: Boredom arises from a lack of imagination and self-motivation. (Claim-Reason)

The speaker asserts that boredom is something that people should be embarrassed about, on the grounds that boredom stems from poor imagination or having no self-motivation. While I can see some merit to this point, I cannot agree that the assertion is always true.

In most cases, boredom results from people's lack of their preferred entertainment. For example, teenagers may like to play video games, but after completing all games in their possession, they may feel bored now that they no longer have a challenging virtual world to conquer. It is reasonable in this case to assert that teenagers lack self-motivation or imagination, as there are several other forms of entertainment they could occupy their time with. They could socialize with friends, watch television, or engage in self-improvement activities. The same can be said for adults, who have relatively little time to be bored. Working adults who find themselves feeling bored either are slacking off at work or are not properly encouraging themselves towards developing their talents. This is because being bored at work is a sign that there is no longer a challenge, and if people are not challenging themselves then they are simply going through the motions rather than growing their skillset. In this case, people should be ashamed of their boredom because they could have used their imagination and motivation to enrich their life or excel in their work.

Furthermore, the lack of imagination argument is certainly an issue in the modern era. With the advent of technologies that provide instant gratification, the need to exert efforts in order to be entertained is all but eliminated. Take, for example, the difference between traditional stage plays and modern television programs. In the past, people would need to interpret the complexities of stage performers' movements and spoken words, which were often in poetic form as in the plays of Shakespeare. Yet nowadays, special effects and closeup camera work leave nothing to the imagination, allowing the audience to consume the events in television programs with no effort at all. Thus, it is easy to see why individuals would get bored quickly, with modern technology that has supplanted their imagination. Again, people should feel guilty of their boredom for relying too much on such technology.

However, it is unfair to say that being bored is always the result of not motivating oneself or lacking imagination. For example, boredom is a common occurrence among more intelligent students who are forced to participate in classes where the material is far below their level. Why should they be embarrassed for being bored when they have no control over the curriculum being taught to them? In this case, the school or curriculum developers should be embarrassed for not accounting for the possibility that students may find their material trivial and unchallenging. Yet this is a narrow example, and it should be mentioned that once outside of school these high-performing students have every opportunity to advance their knowledge beyond the confines of the classroom.

All in all, the reason sufficiently supports the claim in general. Most people who feel bored nowadays simply do not take advantage of the various forms of entertainment that are available if they have the motivation to pursue them. Also, modern forms of entertainment have coddled the minds of people today, limiting the use of their imagination. Yet, there are still some settings where no manner of self-motivation or imagination can stave off boredom, so it is not fair to apply this reasoning indiscriminately.

137. Some people believe that the most important qualities of an effective teacher are understanding and empathy. Others believe that it is more important for teachers to be rigorous and demanding in their expectations for students. (Address both views)

Teaching is certainly one of the most notable professions people can undertake, since it requires them to dedicate their lives to the betterment of the next generation. As a science, the field of education must constantly analyze what methods are best for optimal learning in classrooms. Similarly, determining which qualities comprise the most effective teacher is also pivotal to teaching students in the best manner. However, there is a debate over whether understanding and empathy, or having rigorous and demanding expectations are the best qualities for a teacher to possess. In my opinion, the former is superior to the latter, but there are merits to both.

When it comes to how to deal with students, it is important to create an environment in which they can grow and thrive. The key to doing this is to be able to relate to their specific needs and adjust accordingly. Being able to empathize with and understand what is going on in students' minds is paramount to discerning how to resolve their individual issues so that they may learn more effectively. For example, if students are having trouble with bullies at school, it is vital that their teacher can discern this from the students' emotional state and monitor their classroom performance. A teacher who is unable to empathize with the students' suffering and understand how that affects their academic success will not be able to aid the students in question in achieving their learning potential.

Naturally, there are some benefits to having high expectations of students. When students know there are tight deadlines and difficult coursework, self-motivation becomes a must, and through such rigor valuable time-management skills and work ethic are learned. This is often the case in STEM fields in college, where only the best students may progress through the echelons of ever-more difficult subject matter and graduate with professional degrees. After all, mediocrity breeds further mediocrity, an undesirable trait in STEM professionals. To this end, teachers who burden students with rigorous expectations breed only the best candidates for future careers.

However, teachers who have empathy and understanding will enable the largest number of students to succeed compared to those that have rigorous standards for their students. For instance, teachers that try to know their students will develop lesson plans and tests which challenge their students' knowledge but still allow for incremental improvement. In contrast, having strict expectations will certainly separate the wheat from the chaff in terms of skilled students, but as a result so many will fall through the cracks due to being unable to meet the stringent requirements. Therefore, understanding the abilities of their students is critical to creating an effective learning environment for the largest number of students, which is ultimately the goal of the education system.

In summary, I feel that a balance of having high standards for students with a necessary level of empathy and understanding is best for effective teachers. While I prefer an empathetic teacher to a strict one, I recognize the need for both traits in order to develop the most successful students. Not only is a teacher with such traits able to address unique issues of individual students, but also he or she can motivate them to work harder on their own and educate the largest possible number of students throughout his or her career.

138. Claim: Though often considered an objective pursuit, learning about the historical past requires creativity.
Reason: Because we can never know the past directly, we must reconstruct it by imaginatively interpreting historical accounts, documents, and artifacts. (Claim-Reason)

Delving into the past to uncover the truth of history requires individuals to put aside their personal biases and present a factual picture of the past. Yet, some have argued that creativity is required to reconstruct and interpret events since we cannot experience the past directly. This is an opinion which I cannot agree with, as several ethical concerns are involved in inserting one's own creative flourishes into historical recounting. Additionally, I disagree with the notion that historical accounts, documents and artifacts are wholly unreliable in forming an objective picture of the past.

To begin with, when recounting the past people already have an unhealthy tendency to inject their own personal bias into their retelling. Whether it is an opinion about a person they dislike, a recommendation about a place in which they had a previously negative experience, or the like, bias has a way of creeping into our recollections of the past. Historians must strive to avoid this habit; otherwise, our view of the past will be skewed. Professionals in the field of historical research must already deal with bias of the authors of the documents they use in their research. For instance, any war historian can explain the difficulty of distinguishing truth from fiction when reading opposing accounts, as it has always been common practice to paint one's opponents as being viler and crueler than they may have been. Only by collecting as much evidence as possible and combining it into a whole can we piece together an accurate view of the past. Creativity in this instance would only serve to further muddle the truth of the events.

It is true that there is often difficulty in gleaning facts from historical accounts. Uses of language, techniques of historical recording, and the ignorance of the authors can provide a far too vague image of the past. But this is not in and of itself a reason to embellish the past with one's own ideas. In fact, the existence of historical research itself is predicated on the notion that a dedicated historian must master various skills, such as ancient languages and cultural understanding, in order to interpret the words of our ancestors. In this way, these accounts of the past and historical documents become far more reliable than they would have been if they were only read literally or without the context of their era. Thus, I do not think that any creative additions are necessary in the historical field, unless we are talking about historical fiction. Indeed, most historians would likely be very much against using imagination to fill in the gaps of history, unless there exists a suitable amount of evidence to support the claim. Doing anything else is just telling fairytales.

On that note, there is some value in speculating on the past. When artifacts, documents, or historical accounts are in short supply, it can be helpful to make some educated guesses on past events. For example, in the famous case of the disappearance of the Roanoke Colony in North America, historians had little evidence and virtually no historical accounts of what happened to the settlers, aside from some journals pointing towards a rough crop season and a cryptic message carved on the message pole in the center of the town. With only these facts to go on, historians speculated that the settlers migrated to live with nearby natives, with whom they had traded before, in order to escape a famine. For decades, this was only a hypothesis until in modern times DNA testing was used on native descendants in the region and it was found that they had European DNA that matched the settlers', thereby confirming historians' suspicions. Thus, in this case, some imaginative guesswork can be useful in learning about historical events.

All in all, I cannot condone the use of imagination as a filler for missing information in historical research. Granted, in some cases where adequate numbers of clues can point towards a certain conclusion an educated guess can be presented as a possibility. However, overall, presenting one's own opinions as historical facts is unethical and misuses the artifacts, documents and historical accounts that are given. Furthermore, the documents we possess from the past are more reliable than the argument gives them credit for, and historians simply need the skills to decipher them properly.

139. Claim: No act is done purely for the benefit of others.
Reason: All actions — even those that seem to be done for other people — are based on self-interest. (Claim-Reason)

The image of good Samaritans, people who help others in need out of the goodness of their hearts, is iconic in western nations. It is often espoused that good people ought to do good deeds without any thought for themselves. However, I agree with the claim that no act is done purely for the benefit of others. I believe that humans are selfish by nature and that those who present themselves as helping others unconditionally are guilty of being purposefully deceptive.

From the moment we are born we cry out in supplication; we demand warmth, food, and safety from our mothers. It has been found that onward into infanthood, babies can lie to get what they want and cry when no problem is present simply to receive the attention they desire. This demonstrates that humans are, to some extent, hardwired to be selfish. This is not necessarily good or bad, but simply a survival mechanism. To this extent, I would argue that no matter how kind a person may act, there is always a motivating factor beyond wanting to help people, even if it is subconscious. Individuals may enjoy the good feeling their brain rewards them with when they perceive their actions to be helpful, or perhaps it is the look on their beneficiaries' faces that warms their heart. Either way, it is not the fact that helping others is objectively good that sustains such people, but the chemical reward system in their brains that, like imbibing narcotics, ushers them onward to find the next noble cause to apply their next fix.

Similarly, the social conditioning we undergo in our youth plays a large part in shaping our actions towards others. Taught repeatedly that helping others is good, people feel that there is a social stigma to not helping others. To this end, beneficial acts towards others become a part of the social contract, a requirement that must be met in order to fit in with society as a model citizen. Take the act of opening a door for another person. Doing so is perceived as polite and kind, and we often do it reflexively. The social perception of individuals who do not hold open the door for others is that they are rude or inconsiderate. Thus, it behooves one to take part in kind actions in order to maintain a positive image in society, again, more a subconscious action than one actively pursued.

It is true that some actions are not based on self-interest. Some charity leaders espouse the kindness of their organization and the need for traditional family values as a form of pure goodness. Indeed, charity people contribute their time and even money to helping those in need. Yet, these people reap benefits such as material rewards or other type of recognition at the same time. Therefore, actions not motivated by selfish purposes do not necessarily mean that they are done merely for the benefit of others. In fact, those who assert that they are bereft of self-serving thoughts should be most feared. These people actively attempt to promote themselves as good in the eyes of others but are later revealed to be as vile as or viler than the rest of humanity. These "kind" and "benevolent" leaders are often caught in some depraved act and embezzle the donations they were given by the community to further their cause and help others bent on selfish decadence. Therefore, it is often the people who try to appear more gracious than others that turn out to be the worst examples of human beings.

In conclusion, while I do not think doing good is a bad thing, I think it is misleading to present charitable actions as stemming from unselfishness. Humans have a natural tendency to look out for their own best interest; it is simply evolutionary survival. Nonetheless, our societies require us to maintain a modicum of politeness in order to keep civilization intact. That said, I am always wary of those who seem too good to be true, for like all things, they often are.

140. To understand the most important characteristics of a society, one must study its major cities. (Discuss how the statement could or could not be true)

This statement claims that one should analyze the major cities of a country if one is to understand the most significant traits of its society. It is certainly true that the major cities of a nation provide insights into various cultural aspects, especially concerning contemporary music and art. However, I disagree with the claim as a blanket statement, as cities are themselves individual microcosms that are not necessarily similar to one another, much less representative of society as a whole.

To begin with, we can look at the counter-culture revolution in the USA during the 1960's. This period is ensconced as a significant contributor to modern music, art, literature, and social ideologies. The focal points of the movement were of course in major cities such as New York and San Francisco, places where young people of the era flocked in order to be a part of the new wave of ideas. Yet if one were to look at these cities during this time and assume that the cultural aspects that were dominant there were indicative of the nation's society as a whole, one would be greatly mistaken. Much of the USA, especially the rural areas, during the 1960's was very conservative and stood in stark contrast to the values and ideas that gained popularity in the cities.

Another example of how major cities fail to provide enough details about a society as a whole is the fact that not all countries are fully urbanized, and thus the major cities in such a nation would not represent a large enough proportion of the population to be informative. This is especially true in certain African nations in which various tribal groups live in relative isolation from one another. Said groups have their own unique cultures and lifestyles; therefore, the dynamics of the cities in these countries, whether social, political, economic, or otherwise, are not faithful representations of the nations as a whole.

One way in which the statement might hold true involves the situation where a country has been populated by a single ethnic group for a significant portion of its history. For instance, in Scandinavian countries, such as Sweden or Norway, the ethnic demographic has been homogeneous for hundreds of years. As a result, there is virtually no difference between the society of one city and that of another within these countries. If visitors were to travel to any major city in Sweden, they would experience nearly all of the important characteristics of that society, such as customs, religion, food, that the rest of the nation had to offer. However, even in this case, there are still numerous regional differences, especially in cities that lie near a neighboring nation's border. In these places, there is a unique mix of cultures whose interplay has a significant effect on the overall sociocultural picture of the country. It would, therefore, be unfair to assume one fully understands any society simply by analyzing one or two of its major cities.

While major cities can provide some useful data of certain demographics, and by no means should be ignored, they are not perfect examples to study if one attempts to gain an understanding of the essential characteristics of a society as a whole. When it comes to countries that have primarily rural-dwelling populations, this is especially true, but the same also goes for more developed countries.

141. Educational institutions have a responsibility to dissuade students from pursuing fields of study in which they are unlikely to succeed. (Address challenges to your position)

In the endeavor to provide a nation with citizens that are both highly skilled and well educated, I believe it is most definitely the obligation of educational institutions to discourage students from studying fields in which they are unlikely to succeed. While it is a popular belief that, as individuals, students should have the right to choose whatever path in life they wish to follow, the far-reaching consequences cannot be ignored of having too many people in a country without proper employment, a situation compounded by the significant financial burden that education places upon students and their families.

First of all, consider the current situation in the USA, where throughout the 1990's and early 2000's there was an explosion in the number of university attendees due to the relaxation of regulations on student loans. This, combined with the perception that a college degree would allow students to obtain higher positions and salaries after graduation, meant that many students decided to choose majors in difficult fields, such as engineering, finance, and law. However, these majors require a specific mindset and much dedication, which many students were unable to live up to, resulting in quite high dropout rates. These dropouts then found themselves in a position where they had already invested a considerable amount of time and money into a fruitless education and were at a disadvantage when entering the workplace since they had no other viable skills. This problem continues even today, leading to a significant proportion of the US population fit only for service jobs, and thus remaining in a position of financial limbo that disallows their contributing to the economy through spending or investment. Colleges and Universities have the ostensible purpose of preparing people for professional careers, and if they are to continue to be viewed as such, they should put more effort into ensuring their students pursue majors in which they can succeed. This has already been accomplished to some extent through placement exams for certain levels of mathematics and sciences, but more stringency should be applied in order to eliminate cram students or those who prepare only for the tests.

Pursuing less than appropriate majors has another potentially disastrous consequence in the form of bad debt. As previously mentioned, the relatively lax lending laws in the USA in regard to student loans mean that many students have tens of thousands of dollars in student debt. Add this fact to the aforementioned difficulty in finding gainful employment and one can understand the current debt bubble that exists in the USA. It has been regarded by economists as a situation that is potentially as severe as the 2008 economic crisis, especially since most student loans are given out at the same time and will thus likely default all at once. Had these students received the proper guidance from academic advisors or professors while choosing a major, then this situation could have been avoided. For instance, every college has a "drop-add" period during the first week or two of each semester. In this period if students are closely monitored for performance or levels of stress, then those who seem incapable of grasping the concepts of the courses or unsuitable to the workload could be advised to move to majors in which they would perform better.

The most compelling reason that may be used to challenge my position is that students have the right to choose their career path. Ultimately, they choose to enter college as a voluntary action to improve their own future. They devote their time and their money to their education for their own reasons. To this end, the school functions much like any other service provider in our society, and in this sense the institution has no right, beyond a slight suggestion, to attempt to change students' mind on which subject they wish to study. Yet, even in the context of a service provider, there are instances where the party delivering the service should attempt to discourage a customer from choosing a potentially detrimental product. Just as a waiter at a restaurant, if aware that a diner has a food allergy, would be expected to recommend that the customer not choose a dish which contains allergens, so schools should attempt to dissuade students from choosing areas of study that, based on test scores or past performance, would likely end in failure.

In sum, I think that schools and other educational institutions have an inherent responsibility to guide students away from career paths that do not suit them. The national benefits such a responsibility would garner, along with the disasters it would aid in avoiding, trump the individual freedom of the students.

142. Scandals are useful because they focus our attention on problems in ways that no speaker or reformer ever could. (Address challenges to your position)

In the early 1900s, the Triangle Shirt Factory in New York City erupted into flame. Hundreds of female factory workers died as they attempted to escape this crowded, unsafe factory. Fire escapes were either inaccessible or too structurally weak to bear the weight of so many; as the inferno raged women resorted to jumping from the windows. In the aftermath of this highly publicized tragedy, legislation demanding that companies be responsible for working conditions gained new momentum, soon passing.

Scandals, although embarrassing and often dangerous, nevertheless have the unique ability to galvanize an entire nation. The muckraking journalists transformed the triangle-shirt factory fire from a tragedy into an attack on the greed and corruption of the factory owners who chose the bottom line over the safety of their employees. History and current events provide numerous supporting examples of this pattern.

One example from recent history involves the scandals that shook the White House throughout the 1990s. Of these, perhaps the most memorable was Bill Clinton's illicit affair with various interns. The political fallout, highly satirized, proved catastrophic for the Democratic Party, which would not regain control in Washington for another ten years.

Further analysis of this event, however, reveals how this affair, more than defaming the reputation of an individual and his party, galvanized an entire nation into an awareness of its own cultural hypocrisy. Taken from this angle, the political backlash against Clinton, culminating in impeachment, not only focused the nation on the moral repugnance of this man but also reminded the nation that it had strayed from its foundational moral principles. Using this scandal as fuel, the Christian right expanded its influence as consequence of the shock this scandal generated. Flashing forward six years, the 2004 presidential election results reflected the natural consummation of this disgust and the high-water mark for moral conservatism.

Besides sordid sexual scandals, however, other revelations of political indecency have radically altered how a nation perceives itself. The 1970s in many ways embody the final disillusionment of the American people with government. First, the release of the Pentagon Papers led people to suspect that US involvement in Vietnam had been driven by less-than-pure motives. Thousands of pro-war voters were forced to challenge their own assumptions about the justice of the conflict they supported. If it was not the American government, then whom could they trust? Similarly, the Watergate scandal shattered the last remnants of idealism regarding the transcendent goodness of American governance.

Although all these scandals greatly disillusioned the public, they nevertheless positively impacted American politics. Party identities have dissolved as people began to understand the corruption inherent in that system; this experience, while making the American public more cynical, also made them wiser. Elections have been increasingly characterized by policy instead of inflammatory debate; voters, more aware of their responsibility to understand government, have demanded more from elected officials.

The most convincing reason that could be used to undermine my position is that some scandals are just muckraking, that is, they do not accurately represent what is happening, and are exposed for the sake of exposing. The political campaigns of the USA during presidential elections are an example of this. In most cases, opponents will attempt to expose any piece of information that casts their rival in a bad light. It could be the most minor of details: a stutter, a poorly given speech, or a parking ticket from many years ago. Many of these smear campaigns serve little purpose but to muddy the discourse so much that the public discourse is skewed from the policy platforms of the candidates to a vague notion of what they are like as people, which ultimately harms the election process. Nevertheless, there is a benefit to having so much information exposed to the public. It sends a message that there is virtually nothing that can be hidden, and thus encourages a more honest life from candidates. In this way, the eagerness with which scandals are exposed has reduced the level of corruption in United States politics, since it is difficult to hide anything about oneself nowadays.

History, in short, is replete with examples of scandals galvanizing the public to act in ways that no demagogue could. For all their negative consequences, the least of which is loss of faith in institutions, scandals awaken people to the dangers of their own complacency. And ultimately, this awakening positively shapes how people view themselves and the world around them.

143. Claim: Governments must ensure that their major cities receive the financial support they need in order to thrive.
Reason: It is primarily in cities that a nation's cultural traditions are preserved and generated. (Claim-Reason)

The melting pot of urban areas is unique in its mixture of cultures and traditions. While they can be the breeding ground for new traditions, they are definitely not the place where preservation is most likely to occur. Therefore, it is not major cities that should receive the financial support they need.

Cities are saturated with diverse cultures, languages, and ideals. Unlike agrarian areas people cannot normally survive off the land or without constant interaction in the world around them. As men and some women are forced to take jobs in the public sector, they begin to make sacrifices and to change. In a city there are no communal days off; there is a lack of traditional places of worship and the children in the city are constantly being influenced by the media, their friends and the language revolving around them. These conditions are not suitable for maintenance of a culture, but only for change. In the play *Fiddler on the Roof*, the father Tevye is thrust into cultural calamity when Russian officers begin living in his Jewish settlement. The influence of these "outsiders" is often scary for the town, but the real impact for Tevye comes in the marriages of his three daughters: the oldest daughter chooses her own husband, the second marries a scholar and leaves her family and the third does not even ask her father's permission when she marries a Russian man, cutting her off from her family and faith. No! Mixing cultures and people does not lend itself to preserving tradition.

Cities may not preserve tradition, but they can be hot beds of cultural generation. When groups of people meet and interact in cities new traditions and cultures are formed. New York City, one of the infamous melting pots of the world, has its own sub-culture, complete with accents, traditions, foods, and stereotypes. In the popular sitcom *Seinfeld*, the main characters take a humorous look at the singular culture of a New Yorker. The generating of tradition becomes apparent as Jerry, Elaine, George, and Kramer form their own modern family: eating at the same café, discussing life's taboo topics, and navigating their own idiosyncrasies with the help of their friends. The stereotypical lack of empathy and display of all the unique characters inhabiting New York create an entertaining display. Cities can also bond groups of the same culture in modern ways. Cities are often stratified by ethnicity, forming a mini version of the country of origin. The people might not even come from the same region, but this new society thrusts them together and they learn to depend on each other for camaraderie and often employment. Though they do not preserve tradition cities exemplify the unique ability of the human spirit to thrive in a new and shifting environment.

Urban centers do not necessarily need funding from their government in order to create or preserve cultural traditions. In cities, traditions intermingle and change over time, and this cultural cohabitation is often celebrated by city dwellers. Traditions are preserved through the aspects that survive in city culture, and most attempts of preserving traditional culture in its entirety have failed due to the sheer number of different cultures vying for the spotlight. If it is preservation of culture that the government is seeking, then its money should be given to small towns and villages. It is in these sequestered environments that the greatest chance for preservation lies. Just outside of Coimbatore, India is the village of Chavadi. The women of Chavadi grind rice on a stone, beat their own laundry, collect water with buckets and wear wool hats in the morning to avoid getting a cold. This clandestine existence reinforces the cultural values, language and ritual previously set in place and gives these women a pre-determined outline for their life and the life of their children. These types of villages provide a singular view into ancient cultures and are the fore-front of preservation.

Cultures shift and change with exposure. If the government wishes to preserve existing cultures, it needs to safeguard the areas of least exposure while allowing the city to generate new traditions of its own accord.

144. **Some people believe that government funding of the arts is necessary to ensure that the arts can flourish and be available to all people. Others believe that government funding of the arts threatens the integrity of the arts. (Address both views)**

Art, especially what is generally referred to as "high art" is not free. Great works, whether sculptures, paintings, or performances, all require a significant amount of funding to create. For this reason, I can understand why some people believe that government funding of the arts is vital for the proliferation and accessibility of the arts. Yet I think that government involvement inevitably damages the integrity of art and should therefore be kept to a minimum.

Let us start by looking at the benefits that government funding can bring to the arts. One example can be seen in government's financial support of ethnic arts. For instance, numerous grants are given to university art departments which foster the creation and preservation of traditional handicrafts. This has led to the styles and motifs of countless cultures, from native American tribal art to Scandinavian patterns, to diffuse into the mainstream cultural consciousness through their inspiration of fashion designers, product designers, and furniture craftsmen. Another example can be seen in the post-WWII USA, where numerous government grants were offered in order to encourage the creation of statues, stage plays, and other great works. Such funding was provided on the grounds that whatever was created would be made free for the public, and as a result, the American arts flourished. However, there was a dark side to this movement led by the government, as artistic expression, while encouraged, was not completely free. Art that was deemed obscene or in opposition to "American ideals" was met with censure, and what later became known as McCarthyism was a death knell for many artists whose work was deemed subversive.

This kind of government oversight is the ultimate enemy of the free expression which is necessary for art to progress and develop. Looking at the art from each dynasty of some Asian countries, one notices significant periods of time in which there was no variation between styles or motifs during the centuries-long reign of each dynasty. This is largely a result of either the extremely strict limitations placed upon artists by the government patrons of the time, or worse, the wholesale destruction of works as mandated by new rulers to make way for the works they wished to fund. Moreover, while we can view many pieces of ancient fine art now, these works were by no means accessible to their average contemporary citizens, as they were treasured possessions of the nobility alone.

It is also worthy to note that the financial support of art by a government inevitably leads to the weaponization of artistic works in the form of propaganda. One need not look any further than Nazi Germany to see the multitudes of paintings and films propagating messages of vile animosity towards minority groups such as the Jews, culminating in the tragic genocide we now know of as the Holocaust. On the flip side, artistic freedom and integrity was perhaps the deciding factor in ending the United States' war in Vietnam in the 1970's. Were it not for the deluge of songs, poems, paintings, and other such works, which all derided the war as unjust and destructive, who knows how many more lives would have been lost to the conflict!

In a nutshell, it is my firm belief that the financial contribution to the arts made by governments is appreciated but decidedly harmful, for it acts as a chain with which the government enslaves art for its own devices. Art can be created and made accessible without the aid of the government, and all the better for it, since free expression is what allows great art to be made.

145. Claim: In any field — business, politics, education, government — those in power should step down after five years.
   Reason: The surest path to success for any enterprise is revitalization through new leadership. (Claim-Reason)

While it may be tempting to allow a seemingly faultless leader to continue to rule, a change in administration is absolutely necessary after a term of five years, regardless of the field. In this way, success is all but guaranteed, as obsolete ideas can be replaced with new ones, reducing the probability of stagnation and failure.

There have been plenty of instances in which a long-serving singular ruler, though initially competent and even highly regarded, has brought ruin upon those they had hoped to benefit. Frederick the Great of Prussia was and still is hailed as one of the few 'enlightened despots', a wise and intelligent leader that brought Prussia out of the Seven Year war during the mid-1700's. He made various contributions that allowed the arts and sciences of his nation to flourish during his reign, but ultimately his militaristic and nationalistic ideals promoted the expansionist mindset, which he applied for the entire 46 years of his reign and led to the destruction and partitioning of Prussia in the 19th century. His continued annexation of neighboring territories throughout his many years in power gave rise to much animosity of other powers, such that his death marked a power vacuum which was readily exploited. Had Frederick served a shorter period of rule, perhaps his militaristic inclinations would not have left such a sour taste in the mouth of Prussia's rivals, and they would not have been so eager to see his empire fall.

The dangers of endless leadership are not owned by politics alone but may also be seen in the realm of business. Steve Jobs is famous for his founding of Apple, the tech giant that has been a revolutionary force in consumer electronics for decades. However, Jobs' extended leadership between 1976 and 1985 was fraught with controversy, and his poor business decisions, along with his often-violent mood swings, forced the company to strip him of his executive powers in the late eighties. The board had felt that Jobs had, after experiencing so many years of unfettered creative control, become too arrogant in his position and feared that he would rather see the company ruined than give up his own personal vision for the products Apple created. It was only after he resigned that Apple was able to achieve the success, however lukewarm it might have been, in the nineties, which set the stage for his return and subsequent fresh ideas to turn the company into the international juggernaut we know today.

However, there is no guarantee that new leadership will most assuredly lead to success. The need for new leadership can be seen in the current education system in the USA, where the federal administration has seen little real change in decades. Sure, there have been new department heads, but the majority of them tout the same line of policies such as standardized testing and budget cuts. This has led to a severe stagnation of education quality in US public schools, contributing to a disparity between subsidized education and private schooling that was not as much of an issue in previous years. There is a growing sentiment that the fall in international education rankings, which has been steadily becoming more dramatic, is a direct consequence of hiring the same kind of educational administrators over and over, despite the fact that they replace former leaders.

In conclusion, in order to ensure the long-term success of any organization, whether it be a nation, company or other collective, a regular change in leadership is vital. Even though this may not be the most reliable path to prosperity, doing so allows new ideas to be implemented and tested, while stagnation is avoided.

146. In any field of endeavor, it is impossible to make a significant contribution without first being strongly influenced by past achievements within that field. (Discuss how the statement could or could not be true)

Every year, new systems, ideas, and inventions are developed by human minds that ease the lives of people around the world. Because of the abundance of inventions that currently grace the globe, it is necessary that, as the author says, experts research what has already been developed before they disseminate an idea. While there are exceptions to the statement, it is generally true. A thorough research of past failures and successes prevents ignorant duplication of another's work, which means time that could be spent elsewhere. Also, such study of past work provides a knowledge base upon which to build the work further.

It is true that there are exceptions to the statement. One way in which it might not be valid involves the serendipitous stroke of genius that has been known to occur in certain points of history. For example, Heraclitus was a pre-Socratic philosopher who was the first in his era to assert that there were predictable patterns of weather and other natural events that were not the result of the whims of deities. This was groundbreaking and controversial in his time and he stood alone for a while as a pioneer in philosophy in regard to the physical and metaphysical world. Yet this example and others like it most often took place in ancient history when humanity was just beginning to develop civilization and record-keeping. Once humanity had established a reliable system of information storage and transport, ideas diffused and were built upon one another incessantly.

History contains some examples of ideas being cultivated in different places at different times, which has led to repetition of conclusions and unnecessary investment of time. For example, in the mid 1800's, two famous biologists, Charles Darwin and Alfred Russel Wallace, developed theories on evolution and natural selection. Charles Darwin had spent many years in the Galapagos Islands studying both the native finches as well as the marine iguanas. As he built his research, he began to see trends that led to the development of the theory of evolution as well as the theory of natural selection. Likewise, Alfred Russel Wallace spent numerous years in South America and Asia accumulating evidence for theories similar to Darwin's. Even though their research contained very similar ideas, Darwin received most of the credit, because his ideas were more substantiated by research and he published his theory first. Even though Wallace developed similar ideas without influence from Darwin, he will never be known as the originator. This situation exemplified by Darwin and Wallace is more avoidable in today's world where communication is instantaneous and widespread, but it illustrates the importance of remaining current in one's field in order to avoid near-duplication of another's work and the associated investment of time that could be spent on other research.

Furthermore, a study of past work is critical because it provides a solid knowledge base concerning the question at hand and gives the scholar or scientist the ability to build on what has come before. Wilbur and Orville Wright, who receive the credit for inventing and building the first successful airplane, are an excellent example of the need to build on prior research and learning. They studied previously developed theories on flying, such as the Bernoulli's principle and the mechanics of designing a light, yet sturdy, contraption. As a result, they were able to develop the first flying apparatus with any sustained flight time. Another example of this can be seen among the most decorated scientists of modern days: the Nobel Prize winners in Physics, Chemistry and Medicine. In recent decades, it has become the norm for multiple recipients to share the Nobel Prize in a field for working on the same problem, often collaboratively. This collaboration may be the ultimate method of studying the successful work of others; by teaming up with other scholars who are exploring similar ideas, a scholar will constantly be moving forward and building on the work of colleagues to arrive at a more substantial conclusion, and perhaps in less time. These examples illustrate how a study of past work can provide a knowledge base that is critical for generating new conclusions that rely on previous work.

In conclusion, many can claim to be inventors, scholars, and scientists, but in order to be the true originator of a concept, theory, or mechanism, a person must have knowledge of previous contributions to the relevant area of study. Not only will this research prevent embarrassing and time-wasting duplications, but it will also enable the inventor to identify the areas that still require exploration and provide a knowledge base upon which to further develop his or her work.

147. Nations should pass laws to preserve any remaining wilderness areas in their natural state, even if these areas could be developed for economic gain. (Discuss positive and negative consequences of the policy)

One of the more pressing environmental issues currently facing the world is the loss of forests and other wilderness areas to development. Therefore, I believe it is necessary for governments to take drastic measures and pass legislation to protect whatever wildlands that remain, even at the cost of losing out on the economic gains that could be garnered by development of such areas. It is my firm belief that such policies are the only way to effectively halt the destruction of habitats and return some semblance of homeostasis to the environment.

An important part of this argument that must be considered is the current rate of habitat loss that is occurring even at this very moment and the harm it poses to human life. Most of the breathable oxygen on our planet is generated by rainforests such as the Amazon. Yet, every year nearly 80 million acres of the Amazon is burned to make way for development. It is therefore no surprise that the air quality of Brazil's major cities has declined over time. Passing laws to conserve the Amazon and other rainforests would not only serve to protect the many endangered species that call these habitats home but would also aid in improving the air quality of nearby cities. Naturally, it would prove to be an inconvenience to farmers and other developers hoping to turn rainforest land into valuable real-estate, but the long-term benefits of conservation far outweigh the short-term greed.

If it is monetary gain that drives much of the destruction of natural habitats, then instituting laws which promote conservation for the purposes of eco-tourism would be a win-win for both sides. Many wilderness areas are places of astounding beauty, such as the icy northern reaches of Alaska and the arid desert regions of the Midwest USA, which also boast unique indigenous cultures. Certainly, if these regions were legally protected, then they would prove to be valuable sources of revenue for the local people, who can sell their native crafts, and the tax coffers by proxy. There are already similar programs in place, the famous Yellowstone National Parks being the most famous. Every year, thousands of people pay for hunting licenses, tour trips, and other tourist activities to the parks, which in turn finances their continued conservation. This not only incentivizes their continued upkeep but also makes it difficult for developers to match the financial gains that they could offer in lieu of the annual tourist revenue. Thus, legislation to conserve wilderness habitats not only preserves the wealth of natural beauty these places offer, but also contributes real wealth to the government through tourism.

Of course, many industrialists argue that it is a waste to leave the untapped resources of the wilderness undeveloped. A contemporary example is the desire of large oil companies to drill in the Arctic regions of North America. The oil companies argue that the regions are mostly uninhabited and thus their drilling would pose little threat to ecosystems. However, their arguments are misleading, as the Arctic regions are an important part of seasonal migration for caribou and other forms of wildlife, the destruction of which would cause a negative chain reaction throughout several distant ecosystems. Additionally, the amount of oil that would be extracted from these regions would be an insignificant percentage of the nation's oil consumption. Laws protecting these regions would ensure that the ecosystems which rely on the animals that migrate through the Arctic would remain intact and prevent the often-irreparable damage that follows industrial development.

In conclusion, I think that policies that preserve forests and other wilderness areas in their natural states are both necessary and beneficial. Not only do they protect ecosystems from annihilation, but the natural havens which are preserved through these laws can still benefit humanity health-wise, and even economically in some cases.

148. People's behavior is largely determined by forces not of their own making. (Discuss how the statement could or could not be true)

In determining the source of individuals' actions and personality traits, people debate whether the greater responsibility lies with outside forces or personal choices. While individuals' choice of action certainly plays a role in their behavior, I think that most of what shapes how a person acts is determined by other influences such as genetics and environment.

The theory of "nature vs. nurture" is a frequently discussed dichotomy in behavioral psychology. While it is still undetermined that which of the two is predominant, it is generally accepted by psychologists that both play an important role in behavioral development. We tend to think of ourselves as individuals with full control over all of our faculties, but the truth is that much of who we are is dictated by certain factors, such as genetic predispositions to certain emotions, as well as learned behaviors. For example, recent research has shown that addiction is more of a personality disorder than a result of the contents of a drug. This is not to say that drugs are not themselves addictive, but certain people are genetically prone to addictive behaviors. This is further explained by a look at groups of people who take addictive drugs; some are able to cease using these substances without any adverse psychological reactions aside from normal withdrawal symptoms, while others appear unable to cope with life psychologically without their drugs.

On the nurture side of the issue, it has long been accepted that a person's environment goes a long way toward influencing the actions of a person. The most evident example of this is culture. In different nations, different cultures compel people in certain ways, whether it be as simple as eating etiquette or as complex as interpersonal relationships: what is considered taboo and acceptable is outside the control of the individual. Of course, there are people that choose to go against the grain and play outside the rules of society, but aside from hermits living in isolation, no one is ever fully free from societal influence.

It is important to note that this does not excuse individuals for taking part in taboo or illegal behaviors, especially if they are aware of the nature of their actions. People who grow up in many parts of the world understand that actions such as theft and murder are wrong, even if a violent and criminal upbringing perverted their conscience. When these people steal, they know they are taking that which does not belong to them and that there are other options available. The same goes with murder, a person who kills another knows that a gun or knife or bludgeon used with deadly effect will have no result other than the snuffing out of another's life. There is always a conscious choice, a weighing of conscience or consequence that occurs with each act, not matter how impassioned a person may be. However, attributing all crime and bad behavior solely to individual choice ignores the complex socio-economic histories that created the problems that nations around the world are trying to resolve.

In sum, I consider the actions individuals undertake to be largely the result of behaviors they were either born with or learned from their environment. It is easy to say that someone did something simply because they chose to, but we should be willing to look at the underlying cause of that choice, such as education, upbringing, and genetic predispositions.

149. Governments should offer a free university education to any student who has been admitted to a university but who cannot afford the tuition. (Discuss positive and negative consequences of the policy)

It is often said that education is the key to success, and in the endeavor to bring opportunity to the citizens of a nation there has, therefore, been a large movement in support of subsidized education for all university students who are unable to afford the increasing costs of tuition. I, for one, do not support the policy of socialized university education in this form, for it brings far more damaging consequences than benefits.

At first glance, it does seem like a lofty ideal to provide government funding to university students who cannot afford the tuition. After all, children have no choice of the economic status of their parents, and many young people of high intellect and academic achievement are forced to forgo higher education due to the financial limitations of their families. It is hardly fair to doom such promising individuals to a life of unfulfilled potential for circumstances beyond their control. In fact, it can be beneficial to offer free tuition to students from poorer backgrounds. Studies have shown that such individuals are exceptionally hardworking, as they feel a psychological need to "earn" their place among the ranks of professionals they work with. Additionally, it would incentivize more young people who are financially challenged to pursue college education rather than fall into delinquent behavior as a result of feelings of disenfranchisement when faced with prohibitive tuition fees.

However, it should be remembered that universities, even so-called state universities, are businesses first and foremost. They operate with a view to financial incomes regardless of whether they are for-profit or not, and as such this policy leaves the tax dollars of a nation open for exploitation by these institutions. Once universities realize that the government subsidizes low-income students, what is stopping them from lowering their attendance standards to allow as many students as possible into their schools in order to make a quick profit? This has already been seen in the USA, where colleges took advantage of relaxed student loan regulations and began accepting more and more students every year. While these institutions can suffer significant financial damage if loans are not repaid, they would have nothing to lose by taking the money the government provided for low-income students. This would drive up government spending and would not necessarily benefit the country as a whole.

But why would it not benefit the country to have more educated people? Many argue that a country always benefits from having skilled professionals. The answer is simple: because the number of graduates is not evenly distributed across all majors, meaning that certain fields, particularly those promising high salaries, receive far more applicants than others. Not only are these majors often the most expensive to pursue, leading to the aforementioned drain of government funds, but the huge influx of students that would occur due to the subsidy would lead to an oversaturation in the job market for those fields. Such a situation has already happened in some Asian countries, where partially subsidized college education and the value placed on education have led to so many students gaining business and STEM field degrees that many graduates have a hard time finding jobs that pay a decent wage.

Another issue with having subsidized university education is that the quality of education may decrease drastically. As stated before, colleges would have little to lose by accepting more students in order to gain the government money that came with them. In addition, there would be little motivation for colleges to improve or maintain their staff and facilities. All they would need to do is to keep them at acceptable levels to continue to attract students. Looking again at the situation in some Asian countries, one can see the truth in this. Public university campuses there are often run down, with obsolete or non-functioning equipment and teachers that care little about the success of their students. On the other hand, some private universities are on par with Ivy League schools in the West in terms of education and facilities.

While it at first seems like a noble cause to provide government assistance to students that cannot afford to attend universities, a blanket policy would be far too vulnerable to exploitation, and ultimately lead to a destruction of job markets and overall decrease in the quality of education.

150. Claim: In any situation, the best way to persuade other people is to present them with facts and statistics rather than with emotional arguments.
Reason: Facts are objective, so they are more persuasive than subjective appeals. (Claim-Reason)

The art of persuasion involves myriad techniques. When one attempts to sway other people's opinions, it may at first appear to be common sense that deploying facts and statistics which supports one's position will certainly win over a skeptical opponent. However, even though facts are objective, this is not necessarily the case, as humans are not creatures of pure logic. In fact, emotions often supersede a person's better judgement. Therefore, emotional arguments are often just as effective at persuading others as facts and figures and can be even more effective in some cases.

In the not-too-distant past, there was a consensus of what an expert opinion was. Citing experts and the data they presented was a sure way to establish the legitimacy of one's argument. Unfortunately, times have changed, or at least they have in the USA. The concept of "fake news" and "corrupt media/academic establishment" has become pervasive to the extent that citing statistics or facts in an argument is no longer as effective as it once was. This is especially true when it comes to politically polarizing topics, wherein one side simply blames a quasi-conspiracy involving the opposing political party and the experts involved skew the facts with bias. In such an environment, facts and data are of little use. Instead, emotional appeals to relatable situations are the most effective since they can build a sense of common understanding and rapport that may incline the other person toward facts and figures. The objectivity of the facts and figures is irrelevant, as the people being persuaded are hooked by the emotional message and will follow the figures presented even if they are misleading or taken out of context.

It is also interesting to see the superiority of the emotional argument as it is applied on a daily basis, for example, in the arena of sales. Every student of business knows that sales is the core of all commerce and selling is being done almost constantly at an emotional level. The advertisements a person sees for a new car are loud and flashy, eliciting a feeling of excitement, attractiveness, and freedom. Clothing adverts appeal to a person's desire to look sexy, fashionable, and professional. These are all emotional arguments, though most often unspoken, and the current consumer culture we live in is evidence of their incredible power. In a more rhetorical setting, one need only look to the speeches of great leaders who have stirred their nations into action, for good or ill. Adolph Hitler gave speeches which incited turn-of-the-century Germans to join his Third Reich, and his nemesis, Winston Churchill responded in kind from his own podium with the famous "We Shall Fight on the Beaches" speech that gave Great Britain an indomitable resolve against the Axis powers; no facts or figures were necessary. Had Churchill spent his speech recounting the numbers of soldiers Britain was able to mobilize or the time frame of the defense strategy, it would not have made for such a rousing battle cry as when he affirmed his countrymen's determination to protect their homeland.

This is not to say that statistics and facts have no place in an argument. Quite the contrary, they can be enormously powerful in their own right. Look again at the example of sales. When it comes to selling goods at a consumer level, there is little need for facts, as many purchases are made based on a preexisting need, and the customer is simply influenced emotionally to buy a particular brand's product. But look at the higher echelons of selling, such as business-to-business sales, and you will find that facts and figures play a dominant role. This is because a company's bottom line, its profits, is paramount. Therefore, any attempt to persuade a company to do something must be accompanied by exhaustive amounts of data to support the move in order to justify the expenditure. However, in these cases, emotion can be leveraged, too. There may still be some emotional components involved. For example, the decision makers may have a good relationship with the one doing the persuading, or have their own personal need satisfied.

While facts and statistics play an important role in convincing others to agree with a position, they pale in comparison to a well-crafted appeal to emotion. The efficacy of data as a rhetorical tool has greatly diminished in recent years, and it is important to remember that the day-to-day decision-making process of many people is based on an emotional framework rather than a rational one.

151. Some people believe that success in creative fields, such as painting, fiction writing, and filmmaking, primarily requires hard work and perseverance. Others believe that such success mainly requires innate talents that cannot be learned. (Address both views)

The intricacies involved in completing an artistic work have led many people to believe that creative success is the result of either innate abilities or resolute dedication to one's craft. While there may be some inborn talents at play when it comes to the foundation of an artistic project, I am not convinced that they are the sole contributors to success. Rather, I feel that hard work and perseverance play a far greater part in determining the quality and reception of an artist's work.

When visiting an art gallery, reading a book, watching a film, or consuming other forms of art, a person only sees the finished product of the creator's labor. The hours of painstaking planning, editing, starting over, reconsidering, and other trials and tribulations involved are not shown. Take film directors for instance; they must be able to understand the function and use of a high-performance camera, the dynamics of the movements and dialogue of the actors, the effect of scenery and sound, and a myriad of other variables in order to piece together a movie. The same goes for the humble painter, whose craft is honed over years of endlessly practicing various strokes, color combinations, and drafts of the forms of every imaginable object. Thus, it is easy to ignore the countless hours that have been put into the development of the craft and label the creator as an artistic genius or prodigy, however untrue that may be.

Granted, many individuals throughout history seemed to have been born with a natural gift for artistic endeavors. The great Renaissance sculptors and painters, composers such as Mozart, and many more have stunned consumers of art for generations with the genius of their works. Michelangelo is famously cited as having finished his La Pietà sculpture at only twenty-four years old, and Mozart was performing for royalty at age six. There can be no denying that these artists had an innate acuity for art. However, even the greatest natural artists had to hone their skills. In the example of Michelangelo and Mozart, both spent the entirety of their lives practicing their crafts. Therefore, to say that their success was solely the result of the talents they were born with is to make a simplistic argument.

Furthermore, a number of artists who are recognized for their talents in the present day were largely ignored in their own time. One of the most infamous cases is that of Vincent Van Gogh, who was a veritable failure during his life, to the point that he died in poverty and nearly insane. But after his death, a large collection of his works which he was determined to complete caught the attention of the art community, and now he is honored as one of the greatest artists of the Western world. Van Gogh was not born with a talent for painting; he dedicated his life to developing his craft. Though he was not rewarded for his perseverance in his own time, he is recognized later.

All in all, I do not agree that success in an artistic field is solely the result of an inborn knack for art. Instead, I strongly believe that it is the long-term dedication to the development of one's craft which forges a truly successful artist. Merely having a talent for art can only get a person so far, perhaps gaining status as a one-hit wonder, but only through hard work and perseverance can a masterpiece be created.

152. In business, education, and government, it is always appropriate to remain skeptical of new leaders until those leaders show that they are worthy of trust. (Address challenges to your position)

The claim states that remaining skeptical of new leaders until they have proven their worth is an appropriate mode of action in the worlds of business, education, and government. There is certainly merit to this claim because power can change a person and many people have sought power while having ulterior motives. However, I am not fully convinced that this behavior is always a proper course of action.

Leaders should always be given the benefit of the doubt. To deny them the respect that is due to their position of office simply because they are new is confrontational and not conducive to a collaborative environment. From a business point of view, a new manager or CEO requires his or her colleagues and subordinates to cooperate with his or her decisions in order to efficiently and effectively complete the task at hand. Similarly, in an educational institution, having professors or other staff members mistrust the principal or dean may lead to poor implementation of educational methods or policies which may harm both students and the institution itself. Most important is the trust which must be afforded a new leader of government. A nation relies on the direction of its leader, and if the governing members are skeptical of one another from the get-go, then the efficacy of executive and legislative powers becomes undermined.

However, I must concede that the claim is somewhat valid. New leaders bring with them a potentially unfamiliar or untested method of doing things, and until it is proven it should be scrutinized for its viability. In business, 2 out of 5 new CEOs fail in their first 18 months on the job, and they fall short for several reasons. Poor response to stress and success, and scandals are cited as some of the most common reasons; we can see why a healthy level of skepticism is retained when a new CEO is hired for a business. In the educational arena, there can also be need for holding some suspicion towards new leaders, as their ideas may have detrimental effects on a system that requires much balance and fine-tuning to meet the vast needs of students. For example, the most recent US Secretary of Education, Betsy Devos, has been widely considered to be a scourge on the public education system. Teachers mistrusted her from the beginning of her tenure in office, and rightly so as she dedicated her time to hobbling public education and offering boons to private institutions for the wealthy. Devos also stands as an example of the need to be distrustful of government officials until they have proven their worth. As an appointed official, had Devos been trusted and followed from the beginning, there is no telling how much damage she could have inflicted on the nation's education system. Yet, these are rather extreme examples, and the level of mistrust which is appropriate should be considered.

Moreover, it is one thing to hold some mistrust of new leaders within oneself and another thing to allow that mistrust to become outright ambivalence towards them. Look again at the US political system. The relationship between the two leading parties has become so polarized and full of animosity that any new leaders from the opposing side are actively attacked in every nonviolent way possible in an effort to defame and discredit them. As a result, the process of completing legislation that is beneficial for the general populace has been hobbled. Thus, it is important to keep the level of mistrust in check and not to let it warp one's better judgement when one aims to complete the ultimate goal.

To summarize, being mistrustful of new leaders is only natural, because they represent the new and unfamiliar, and should be watched for signs of weakness or failure. Yet, despite this, new leaders should be received with open minds; their colleagues and subordinates owe it to themselves and those they wish to benefit to at least try to accommodate the change in leadership. In this way, factional warfare and breakdowns in the efficacy of systems can be avoided.

153. Claim: Group assignments that students must work together to complete should replace a substantial amount of traditional lecture-based instruction in college and university courses.
Reason: It is vital for students to gain experience collaborating with peers to study a topic and to achieve a common goal. (Claim-Reason)

The claim and the reason upon which it is based are valid. Working together in a group is an extremely useful learning tool for students to become acclimated to collaborating with others to complete a task. To this end, I agree that group assignments should replace a certain portion of lecture-based instruction, at least at the college and university level.

Consider the state of the career world today: the need for cooperation is more acute than ever. Teams of professionals must apply their different skills towards completing various projects according to a timeline in an ever-changing environment. Thus, being able to effectively communicate and adapt to the needs of the situation is a critical skill to be acquired. Since the function of college and university courses is to prepare students for their place in a professional environment, it is appropriate for them to be trained in working together on projects with their peers. The traditional lecture format of instruction does little to aid in this endeavor, and realistically, is irrelevant to students' needs with the advent of ready access to online videos. Thus, spending more class time on group projects and the skills needed to effectively work with others should be prioritized.

Furthermore, the nature of working in a group has itself changed in recent times. While the workplace has shifted from the office to work-from-home environments due to the COVID-19 pandemic, the requirement that workers collaborate has not diminished in the slightest but the way in which they communicate and collaborate has. For instance, the use of online cloud collaboration software which allows multiple users to alter a shared document online has become more prevalent, but this is not a skill which is commonly taught in schools now. In such an environment, managing time according to a deadline is also important, but since workers are not clocking in at work and being watched by managers in the office, this is a group skill which must be acquired. Thus, college courses which implement a substantial amount of group work which requires students to remain in communication and collaboration with one another online according to a deadline would instill a cooperative skillset which would tremendously benefit them in their future careers. Conversely, a lecture format would do truly little to benefit students in this regard. Sitting in a room and listening to a professor pontificate on a subject is the furthest thing from collaboration and serves only to consume time which could be used to work with one's peers on a project.

However, there is an issue with replacing a significant portion of lecture-based instruction in college and university courses. For starters, it relies on the notion that students will take the initiative to set up group meetings and work together effectively. Indeed, a common complaint made by students who participate in group projects without the supervision of a professor is that one or two freeloaders always do little or nothing and still get credit. Also, lectures are slightly more efficient at conveying information about a subject than simply assigning group work. A professor can cover a topic and then answer questions at the end of class. In contrast, a group project requires all students to come together, discuss a topic, figure out who knows what and who is lacking certain information, then communicate this to the professor and wait for a response. It is therefore understandable that most college courses are still in lecture format, as the limited time each semester provides is simply not enough for a professor to do this with classes which may contain upwards of fifty students. Nonetheless, this is more of an issue related to class size and would therefore be less of a concern if universities were to hire more professors to teach more classes with fewer students in each one.

In sum, I strongly agree that the traditional lecture structure is not particularly conducive to the acquisition of collaborative skills which college and university students must have upon graduation. To this end, I support the replacement of lectures with group-work assignments which can lead to more effective learning of skills which can be applied to working in teams once students enter a professional setting.

4 Issue Topics Ordered by Frequency

The issue topics of the official pool may be grouped according to whether they have the same claim or keywords. Each row of the following table contains high-frequency keywords of the pool and the topics that share the keywords but have different instructions. Therefore, you should always pay attention to the instruction specific to each topic and the slightly different wording when you analyze the topic before you begin to write. It will be unfortunate if you write on a topic different from the one you are assigned just because you fail to pay attention to the specific keywords or claim of the topic! It will also be unfortunate if you fail to follow the particular instruction and instead write a vague response that seems to suit a very general topic.

Many topics are used more than once in the pool. The topic remains the same or almost the same, but it becomes a different prompt with a different instruction. Such prompts with a similar topic but a different instruction are put together in the following table so that you can study them as a group that is likely to be tested very frequently because the group accounts for a number of the topics of the pool. It is important to note that the order of a topic in the official pool may change in the future, and a few topics may be added or substituted every one or two years. Therefore, you need to search the keywords given below to locate similar topics in the latest version of the pool and analyze them as a group.

	Topic	Number of Topic*
1	The welfare of the general public is the best indicator of a great nation	16, 97, 104, 105, 110, 128; 70
2	variety of courses should be mandatory in universities	1, 34, 57, 86, 96, 123
3	lucrative career paths should be encouraged by schools	3, 82, 118, 119
4	Mandatory study-abroad in colleges and universities	67, 81, 84, 107
5	dissuading students from pursuing fields	141, 23, 120
6	suspension of funding for the arts	144, 65, 72
7	five-year limit on those in power	145, 95, 132
8	pass laws to preserve wilderness	147, 108, 131
9	a uniform pre-college national curriculum should be mandatory	2, 80, 100
10	choosing a major on the basis of availability of jobs	8, 20, 112
11	Teaching through praise	12, 17, 40
12	Similar ideas teach more than ones that contradict our own	37, 62, 102
13	Educators should incorporate student interests and suggestions into lesson planning	28, 74; 35
14	No more heroes for a society	32, 61, 69

15	No justification for intense efforts to save endangered species	51, 54; 19
16	The past cannot help with modern decision-making	60, 116, 117
17	cities generate and preserve cultural traditions	143, 101
18	people have no control over their own behavior	148, 83
19	governments should make university education free	149, 13
20	formal education limits minds and spirits	5, 55
21	understanding a society through its heroes and role models	10, 106
22	Basing teachers' salaries on their students' scores	18, 68
23	Things become more complex as we gain knowledge	21, 93
24	Withholding funding for unclear scientific research	24, 59
25	Learning quality is limited by competition for high grades	33, 121
26	Concepts should be taught before facts	36, 76
27	Government officials should use their own judgement instead of the will of the people	38, 99
28	Seeking realistic long-term goals over immediate fame and recognition	39, 58
29	Political consensus is more important than idealism	48, 133
30	Parents should volunteer at their children's schools	66, 79
31	Measuring a country's leaders by the well-being of its citizens	78, 130
32	Moral standards are important for public officials	88, 91
33	Only experts can give critical judgement	92, 94
34	Imagination vs. Knowledge	90, 109

*Number of Topic on the right of the table refers to the order of the topic in the official pool.